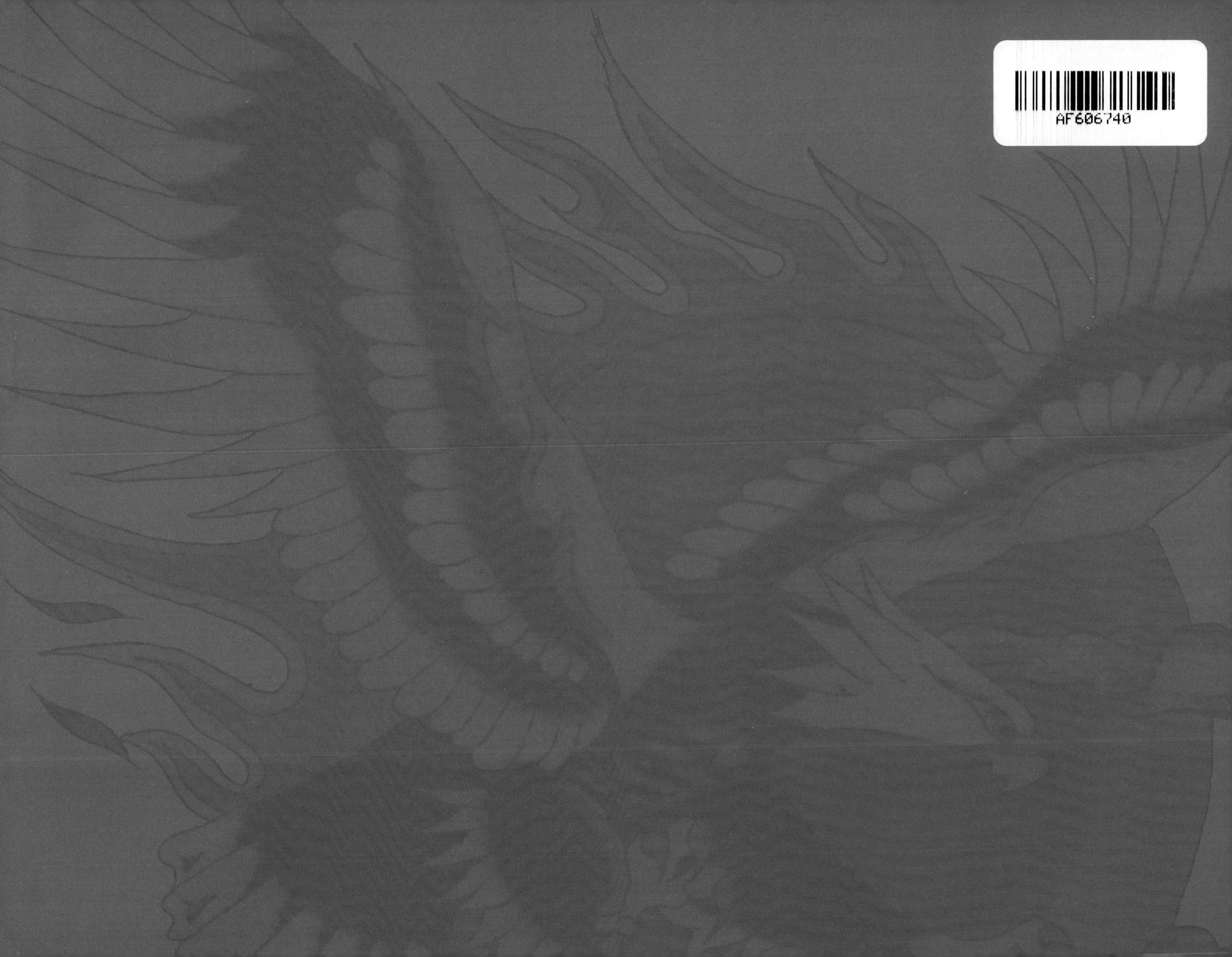

ORIGINAL TATTOO FLASH OF JOHN W. HARDEN

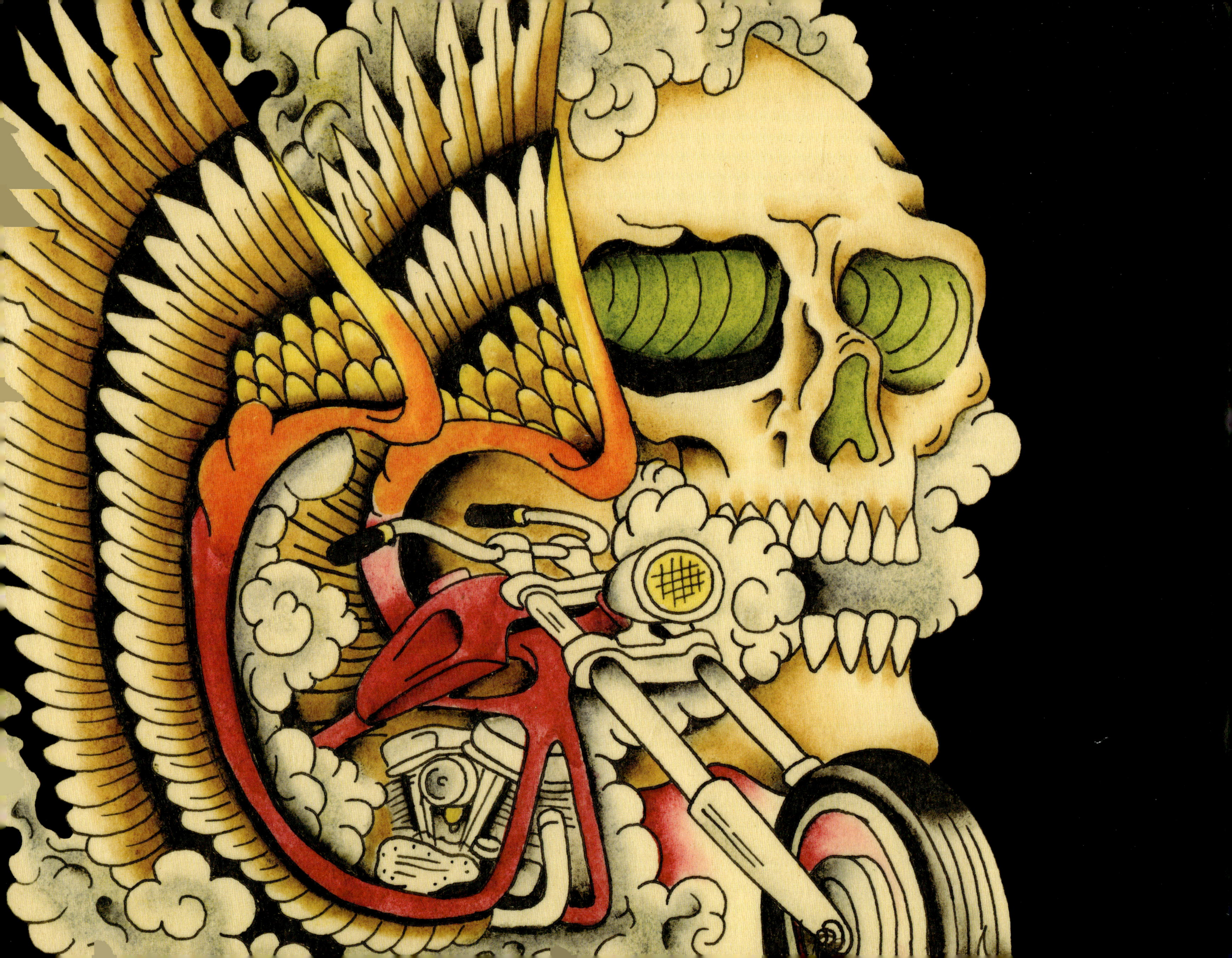

CHAD KNIGHT

ORIGINAL TATTOO FLASH OF JOHN W. HARDEN

OUTLAW INK MASTER

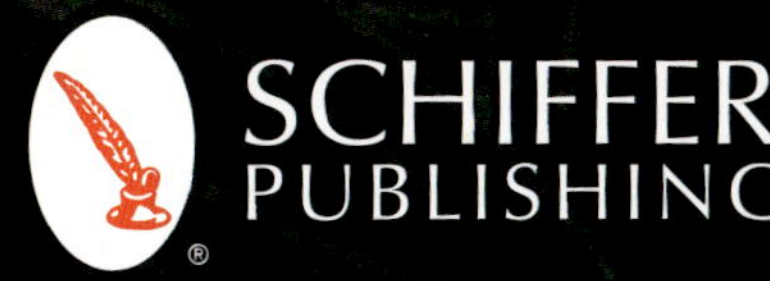

4880 Lower Valley Road • Atglen, PA 19310

Library of Congress Control Number: 2021948654

Edited by Ian Robertson
Designed by Justin Watkinson
Type set in Impact/Proxima Nova

ISBN: 978-0-7643-6398-6
Printed in Serbia

Published by Schiffer Publishing, Ltd.
4880 Lower Valley Road
Atglen, PA 19310
Phone: (610) 593-1777; Fax: (610) 593-2002
Email: Info@schifferbooks.com
Web: www.schifferbooks.com

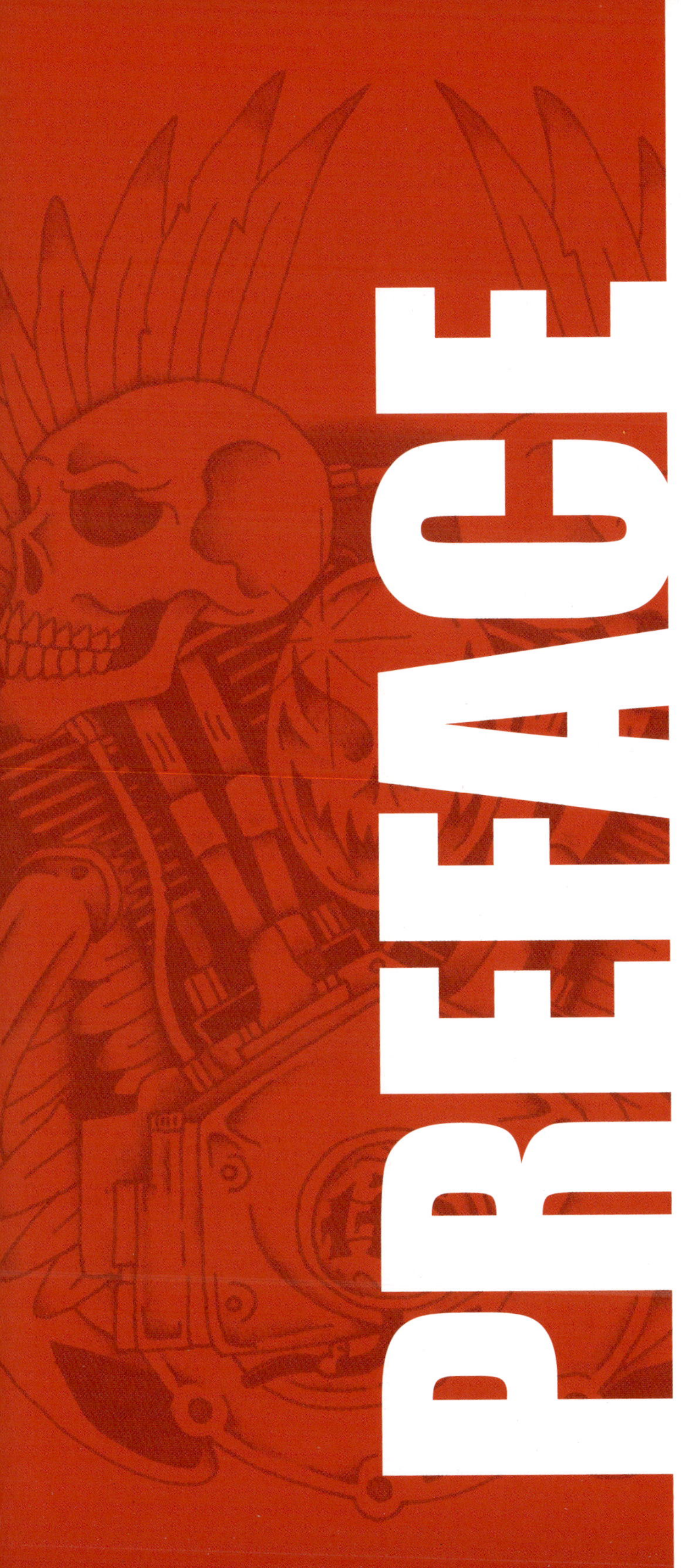

PREFACE

I first met John Harden in summer 1993, after moving back to Alabama. His shop was in a small town called Daleville, Alabama, right outside the gate to Ft. Rucker. John's shop was called Platinum Dragon Tattoo and was the only tattoo shop near that army base at that time. The first time I entered his shop, I was amazed at all of the hand-painted designs covering every inch of the walls. I tried to memorize as many as I could so that I could attempt to redraw them on my own. John entered the waiting area and asked me my age. I told him I was underaged, and he proceeded to kick me out of the shop. As I was in my car, about to drive away, he approached holding a small stack of flyers advertising his shop. He handed them to me and asked me to pass them out to friends that were eighteen or older, and told me to come back when I was of legal age to get my first tattoo.

During this time I would occasionally stop by his shop and try to ask questions pertaining to tattooing. I was looking for my "in" to the business, but John was secretive to any outsider and was no different to me at that time. I began visiting other shops all around the South Alabama and Florida Panhandle, looking for any bits of information I could find. While getting a small tattoo in a newer local shop, I expressed my interest to the artist of wanting to become a tattooer. He told me that I should talk to John Harden, because he needed help around the shop and also built machines, made ink, and owned a complete supply business. After we finished the tattoo, he said he would call John and put in a good word for me. He told me to go there the next day, and so I did.

Upon arriving the next day, John hesitantly greeted me and allowed me into his backroom. He immediately put me to work, teaching me as I went, filling orders from his supply business. From 1995 until 1997 I helped him out and learned many things necessary to be a fully self-sufficient tattooer. I learned to make everything from needles, needle jigs, tubes, and tattoo machines to power supplies. John made me purchase all my supplies from him, and I continued to do so for years after I left working with him.

John was not the friendliest of characters. He was annoyed and angered easily. He often said, "People don't come to me for my personality; they come because I do nice tattoos." He was extremely guarded and secretive and put up a wall that was not easily penetrated. He was a member of the Outlaws Motorcycle Club and proudly wore his Outlaws MC club tattoo across his entire chest. To his friends he went by his nickname, "Sleep." He chain-smoked cigars and loved his weed. His hair was long, white, and scraggly, and his beard wild and unkept. He was the perfect image of an '80s-style outlaw biker and possessed the qualities and fortitude to survive during those times. You had to be tough to be a tattooer in those days, and John did not disappoint.

Underneath his outlaw biker facade, "Sleep" was a prolific artist. The hundreds of hand-painted flash panels he created were an accomplishment I was much too young to appreciate during my time with him. He kept a filing cabinet full of line drawings ready to be put to paint. "Sleep" had a very distinctive style of drawing and painting. The lines were simple and flowing, and the color bright but often sparse. This allowed for the art to be tattooed quickly and efficiently. Like many tattooers of his time, "Sleep" replicated common and popular designs but managed to apply his own unique style to the imagery. During his career he sold production flash of his designs that hung in many shops throughout the country, brandishing the stamp and moniker of "INK MASTER." His name is often stamped on the back of his originals, as well as the Ink Master moniker on the front, but the production sheets carry only the "Ink Master" stamp.

During some of my final visits with Sleep, I learned he had been diagnosed with intestinal cancer. He dwindled in size after having undergone treatment and the eventual removal of a large portion of his intestines. He still wore the same large clothes he had when he was well over 250 lbs. but was now small and skinny. He moved around a little slower, but his sharp wit and abrasive tongue never skipped a beat.

I talked sporadically on the phone over the next couple of years with Sleep. He mentioned to me that he worked in Philly once after I moved there, but I was too wrapped up in my own life to pay attention and cannot remember where it was or could have been. He also told me he wasn't doing too well, but I just brushed it off because to me he represented one of the toughest individuals I had ever met. I figured nothing could stop him and he would persevere.

I lost touch with John over the next few years. I attempted to call him but to no avail; his number was disconnected. I drove from Philadelphia to Alabama in 2007 to look for him myself. To my surprise, the building housing his shop was demolished and now sat as an empty lot. I was crushed and made it my mission to find him and ask all the questions I was too young and naive to ask many years prior. Upon returning to Philadelphia, I began my search to discover what had become of "Sleep," many years after I had last spoken with him. Searching almost daily for any bits of information online came to a dead end. I came into contact with a small tattoo supply business based out of South Florida advertising a line drawing book by John Harden. The company owner informed me that the book was made years prior as a benefit to help John with his financial situation while dealing with being sick. He informed me that John had passed. I believe this was around 2008. I knew that such a vast collection as John had would have to eventually resurface one day, so I vigilantly checked everyone online, including eBay, waiting patiently for anything tied to him to pop up for sale for the next ten years.

In 2017, the first fourteen sheets came up for auction on eBay. I immediately bid on them all. I ended up winning seven of the fourteen sheets. The thought of seeing them again in person was beyond nostalgic. I bid every auction that came up, and won many sheets, but lost many as well. Eventually one seller sent me a letter asking me to call him. I had won so many auctions from this seller that he saw I was serious about compiling this collection. Over the next year I learned of how this seller came upon this collection, and his encounters with John Harden. He offered me the entire collection, but at a much-higher cost than I could afford. I still attempted to win as many sheets as possible, and in the meantime the seller sent me all that was left of John's personal possessions: letters and important paperwork, including his birth certificate and legal name change documents. All of this came as a surprise to me, and I was more than appreciative to the seller for passing all of this on to me. John Harden was always sort of a mystery to me when he was alive, but he became even more of one many years after his passing. Once again I am left with more questions than answers about a man that I spent time with and who basically molded my understanding of the tattoo business.

There are various other collectors with small collections of John Harden's flash panels. Some I have come to know personally, and others I have never heard of or met. The ones exemplified in this book come from my personal collection, from my close personal friend and tattooer Fred Patterson, and from another enthusiastic collector named Phil Hartman. Among us is the largest ensemble of John Harden's original paintings. I will be forever grateful to Phil for collaborating with me to amass this many sheets for this book. It was my wish to be able to bring recognition to John Harden and his legacy, to truly show how prolific an artist he actually was. Behind his rough exterior was an artist that was a true master of his craft, rightfully earning his moniker of "ink master." I only wish that John could have had the opportunity to enjoy the recognition of his work during this period of rediscovery. It has been a long and arduous task to amass this collection, and in the process trying to reflect on the lessons I learned from a man I thought I knew but never really did. Let this collection be a door that has opened but will never truly shut. I hope that you will be able to enjoy the imagery as much as I have. It has been a privilege for me to be able to compile the works of this man I called a mentor and friend. I do this in honor of his legacy. May he live on through his work. In memory of Sleep.

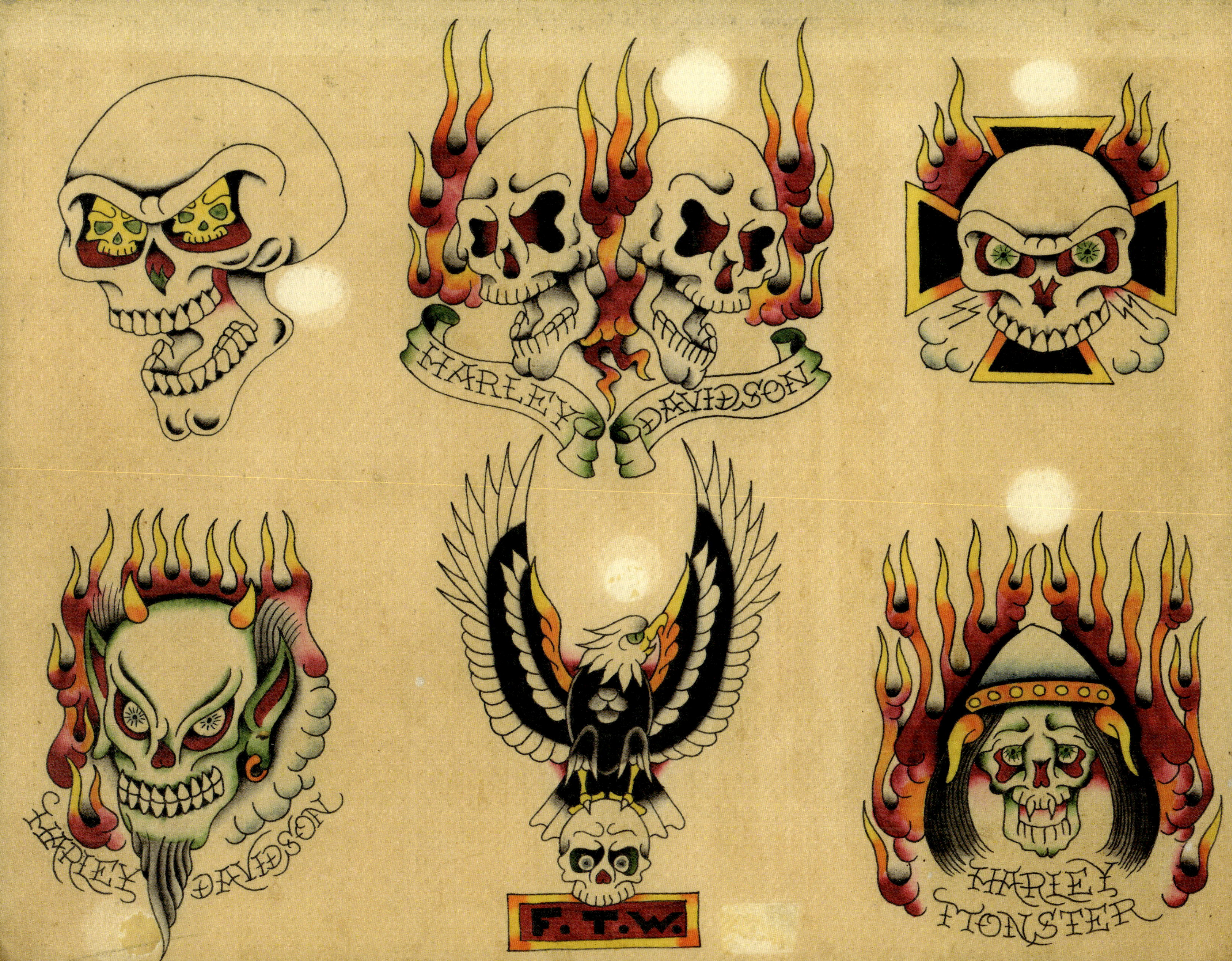

HARLEY DAVIDSON
HARLEY DAVIDSON
F.T.W.
HARLEY MONSTER

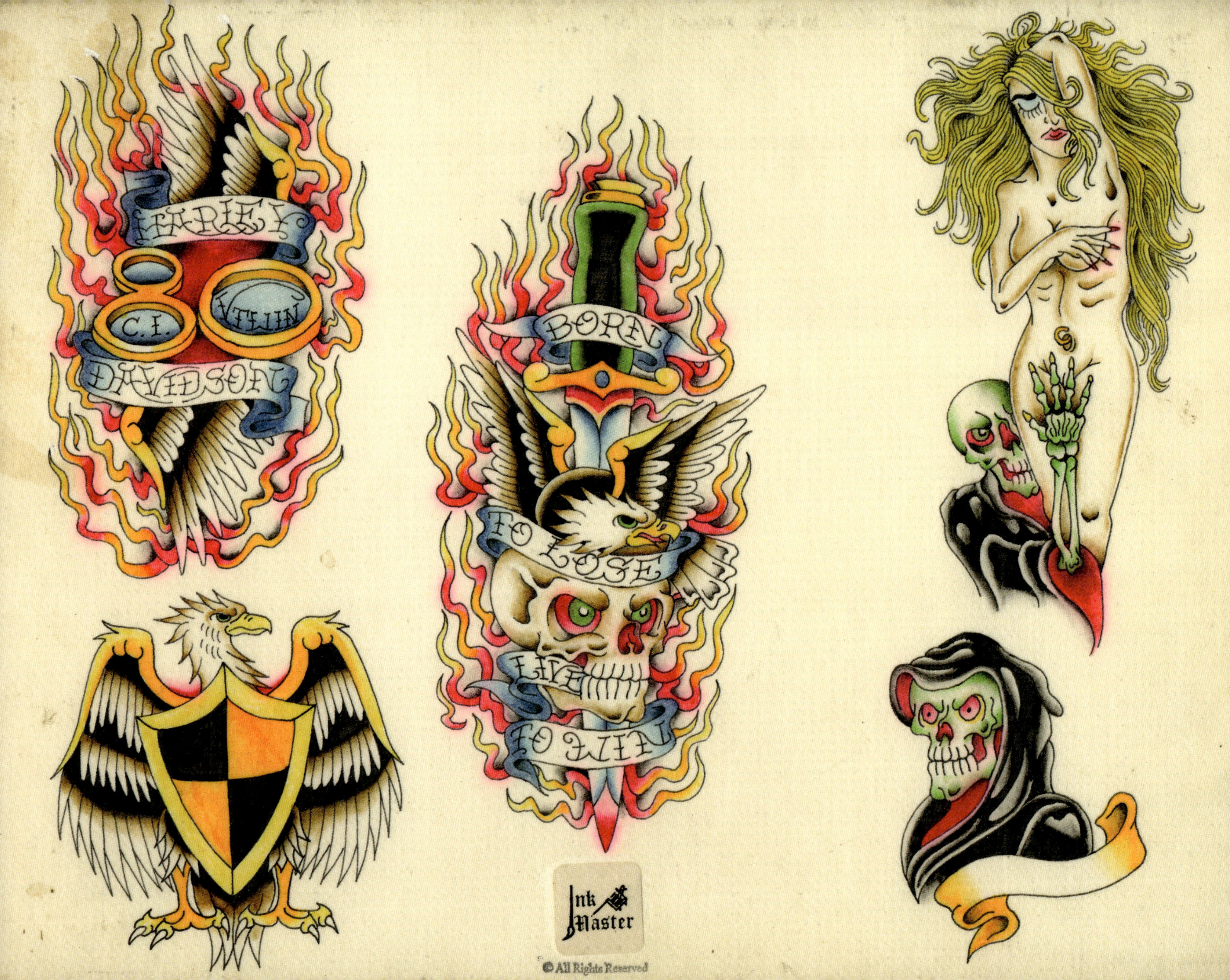
HARLEY
C.I.
DAVIDSON
BORN
TO LOSE
LIVE
TO WIN
Ink Master
© All Rights Reserved

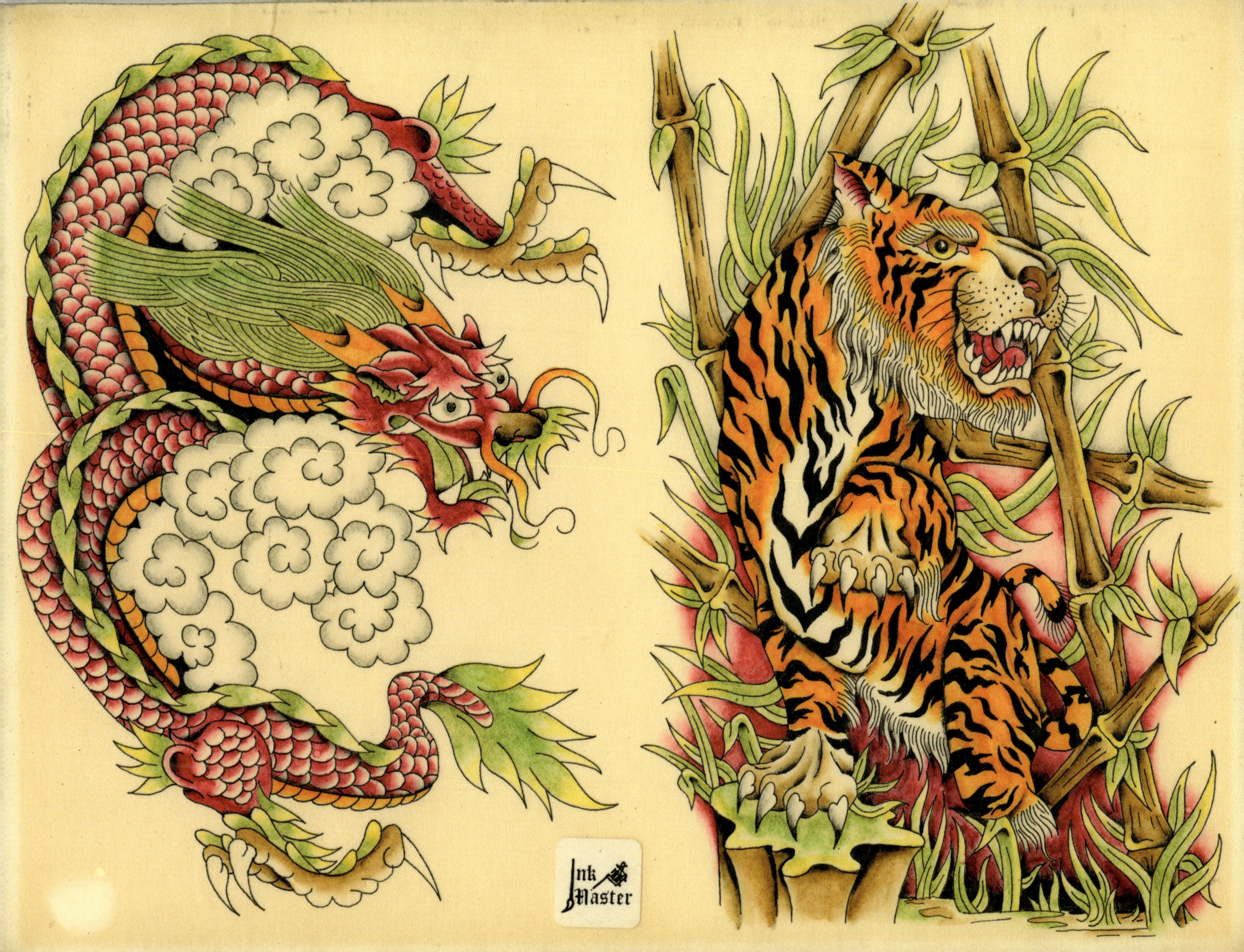
Ink
Master

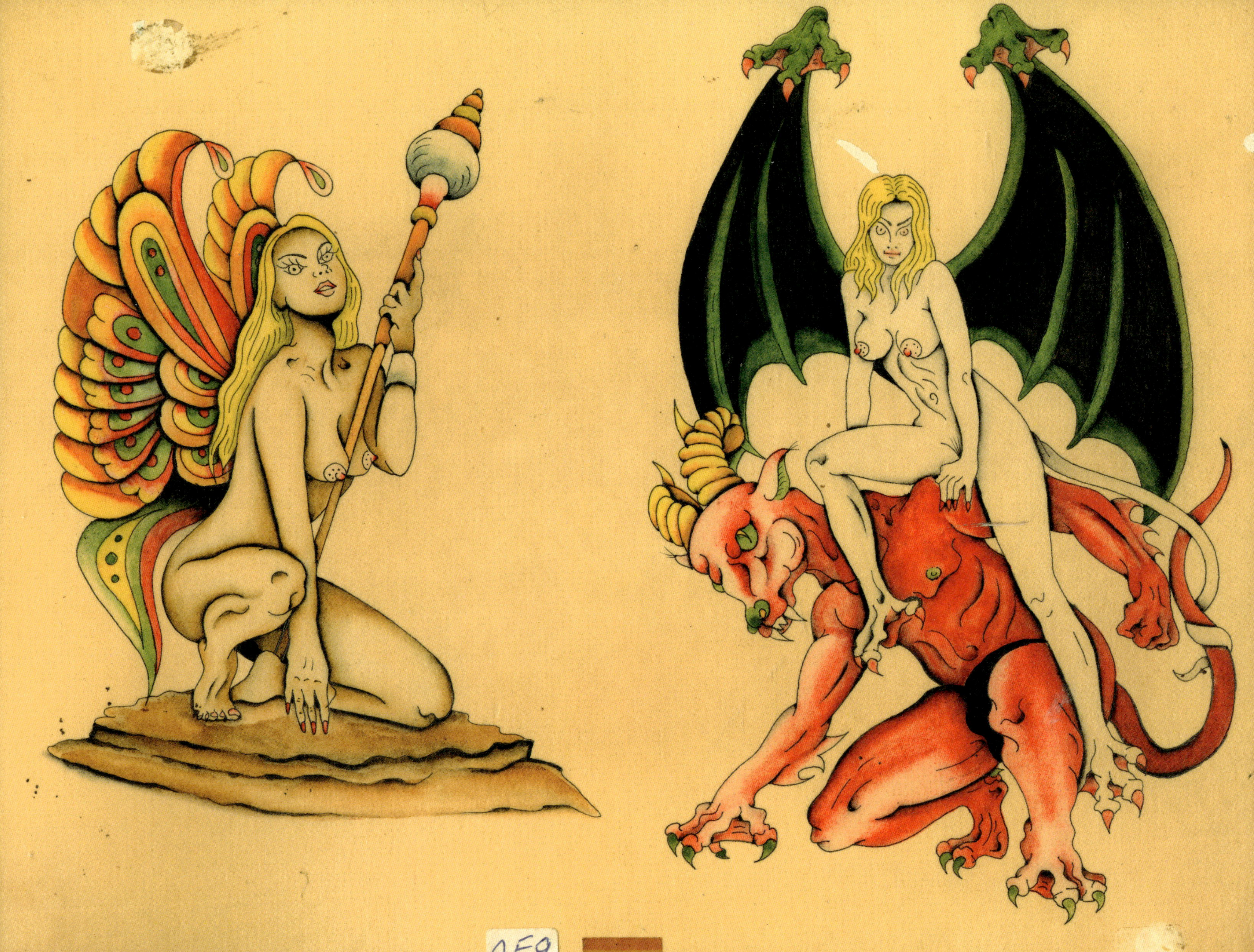
AF9

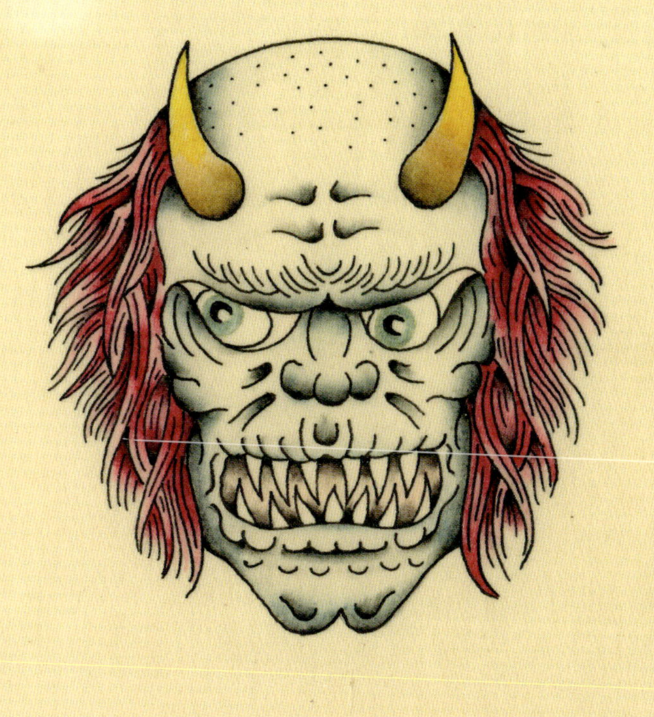
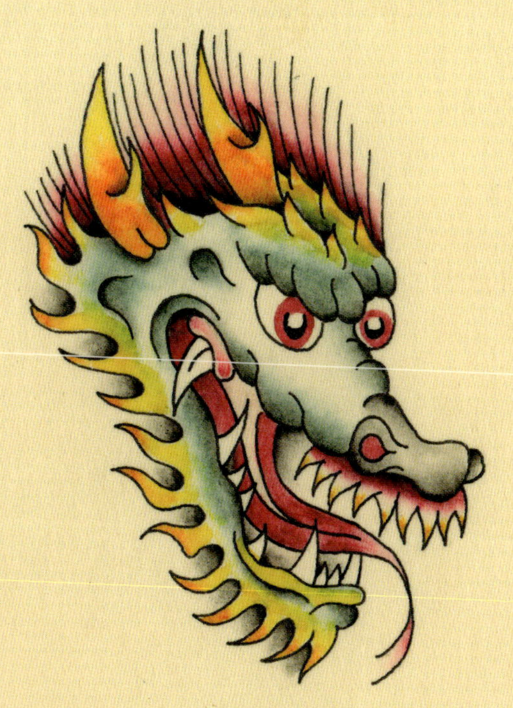
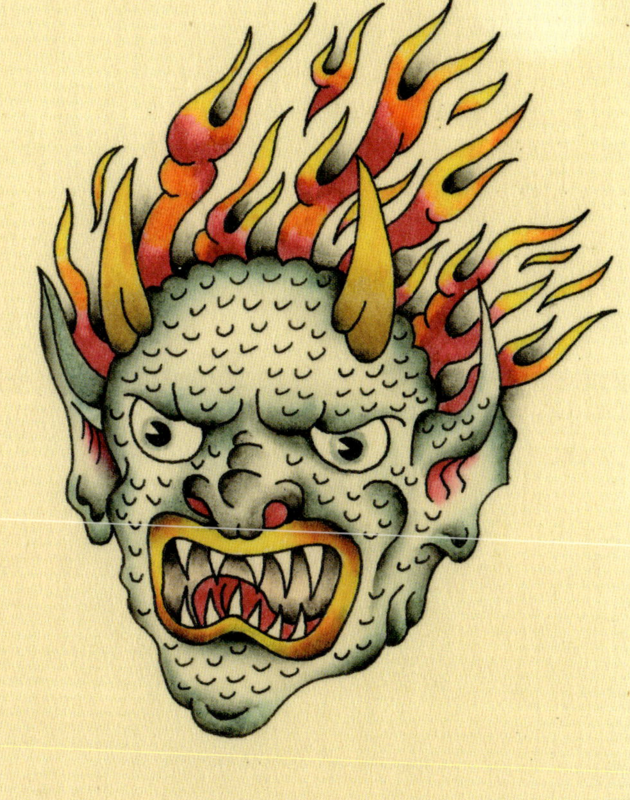
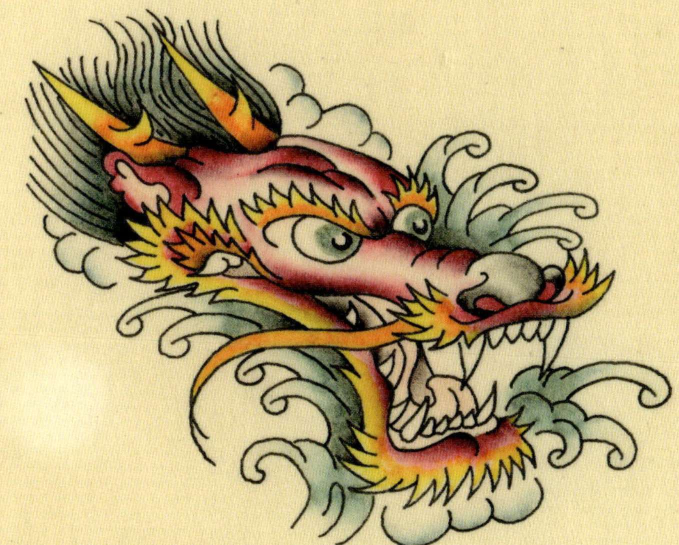
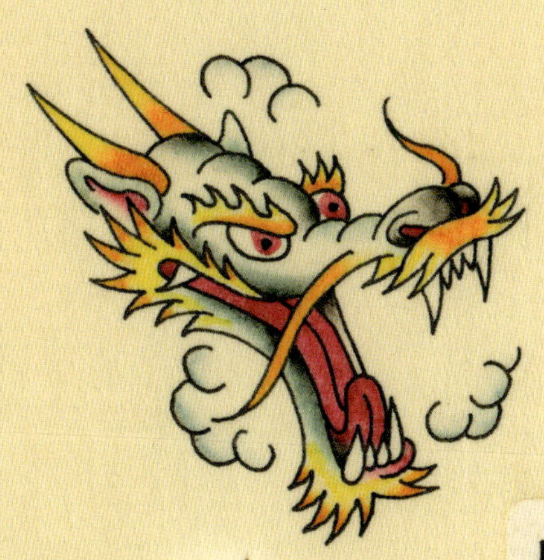

Ink
Master
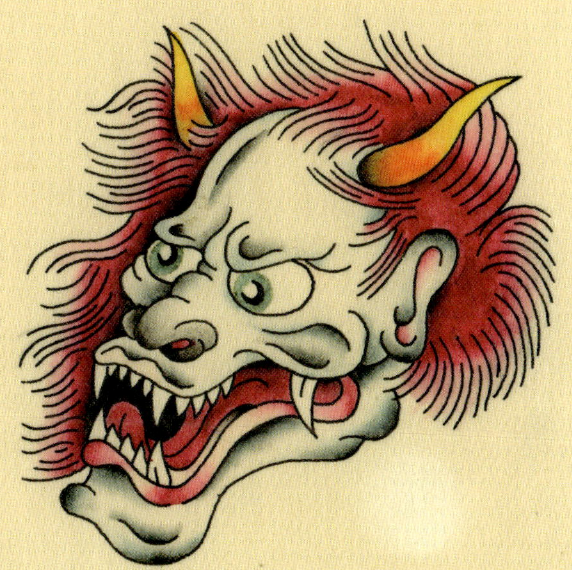

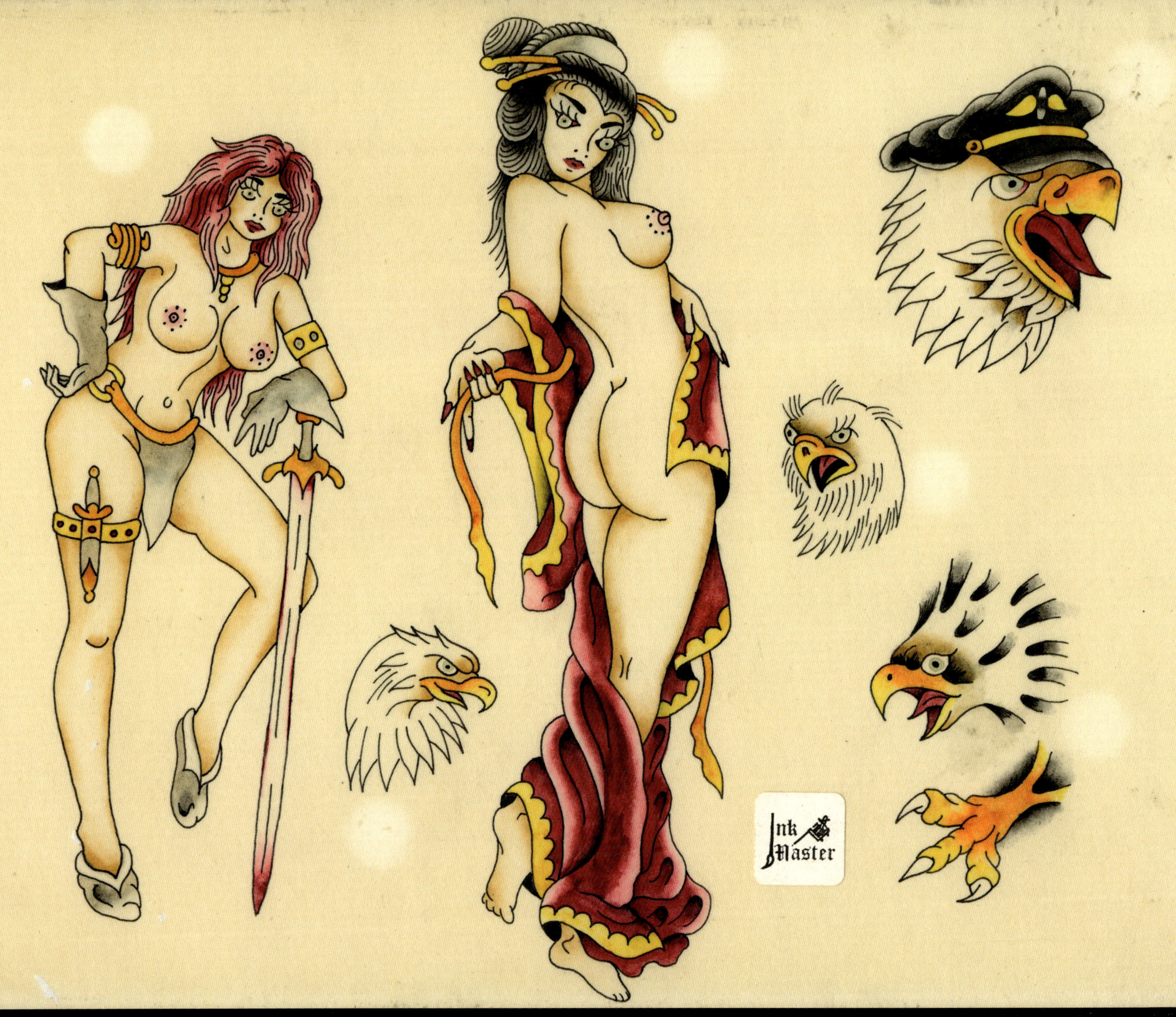
Ink Master

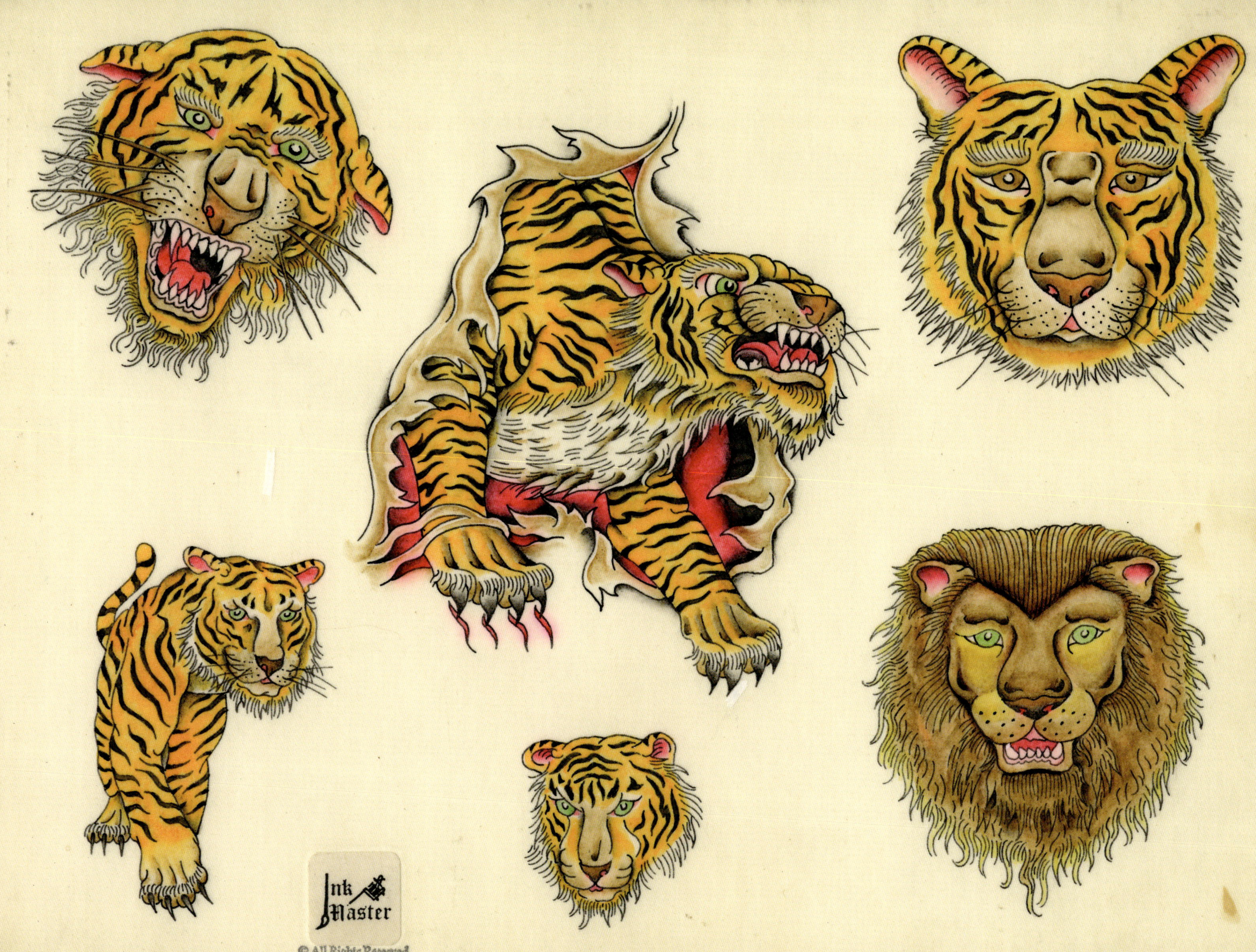
Ink Master
© All Rights Reserved

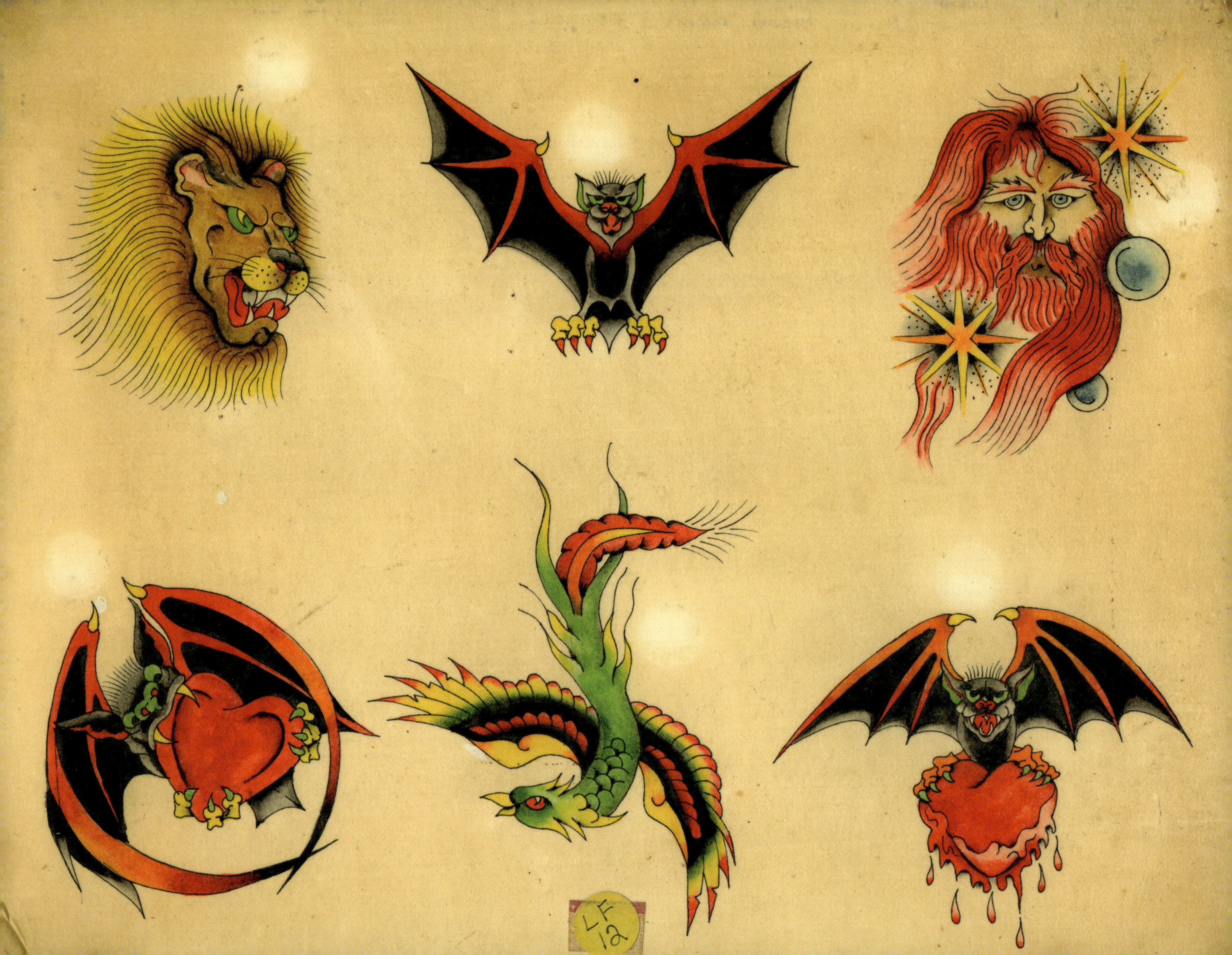
LF
12

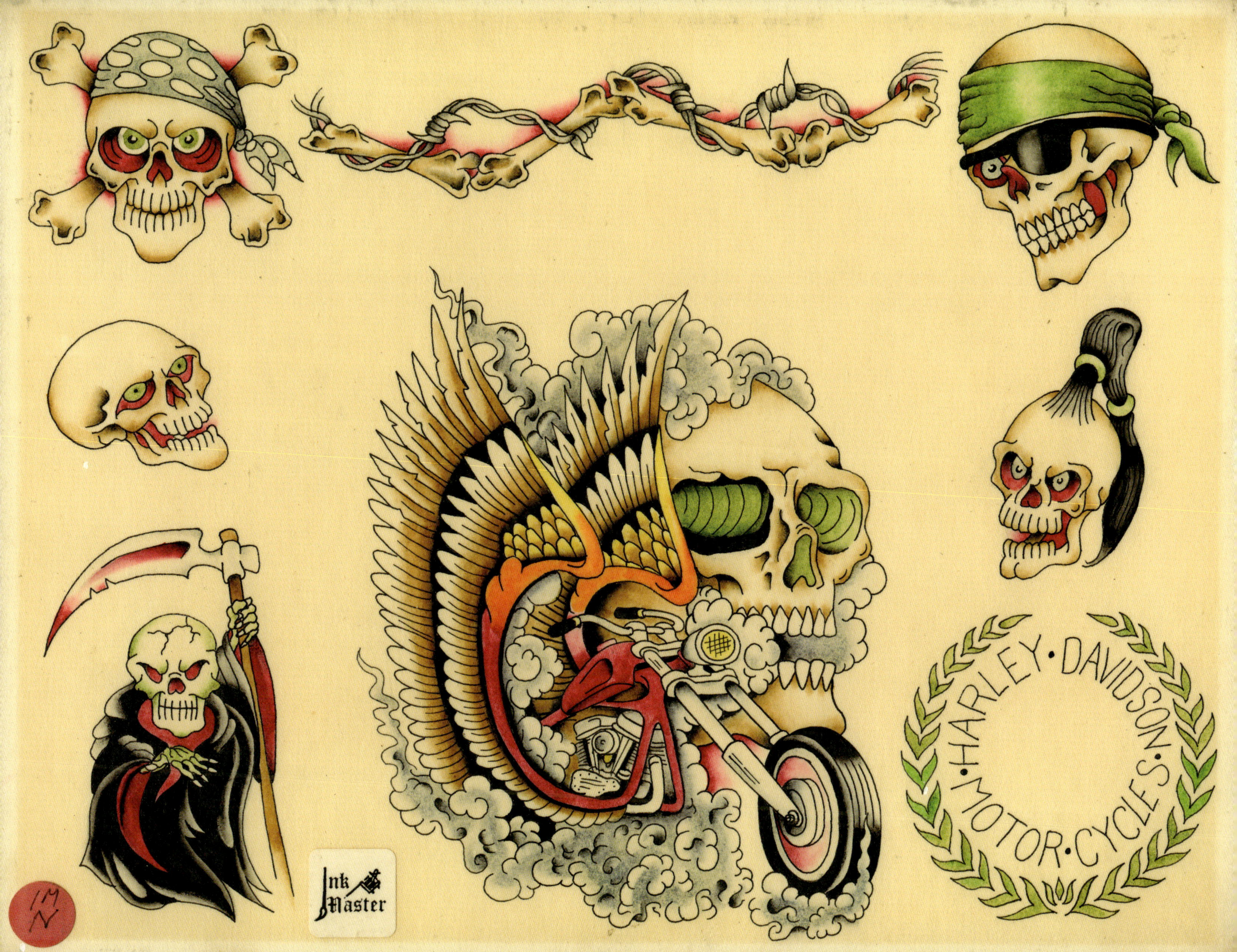
HARLEY · DAVIDSON
· MOTOR · CYCLES ·
Ink Master

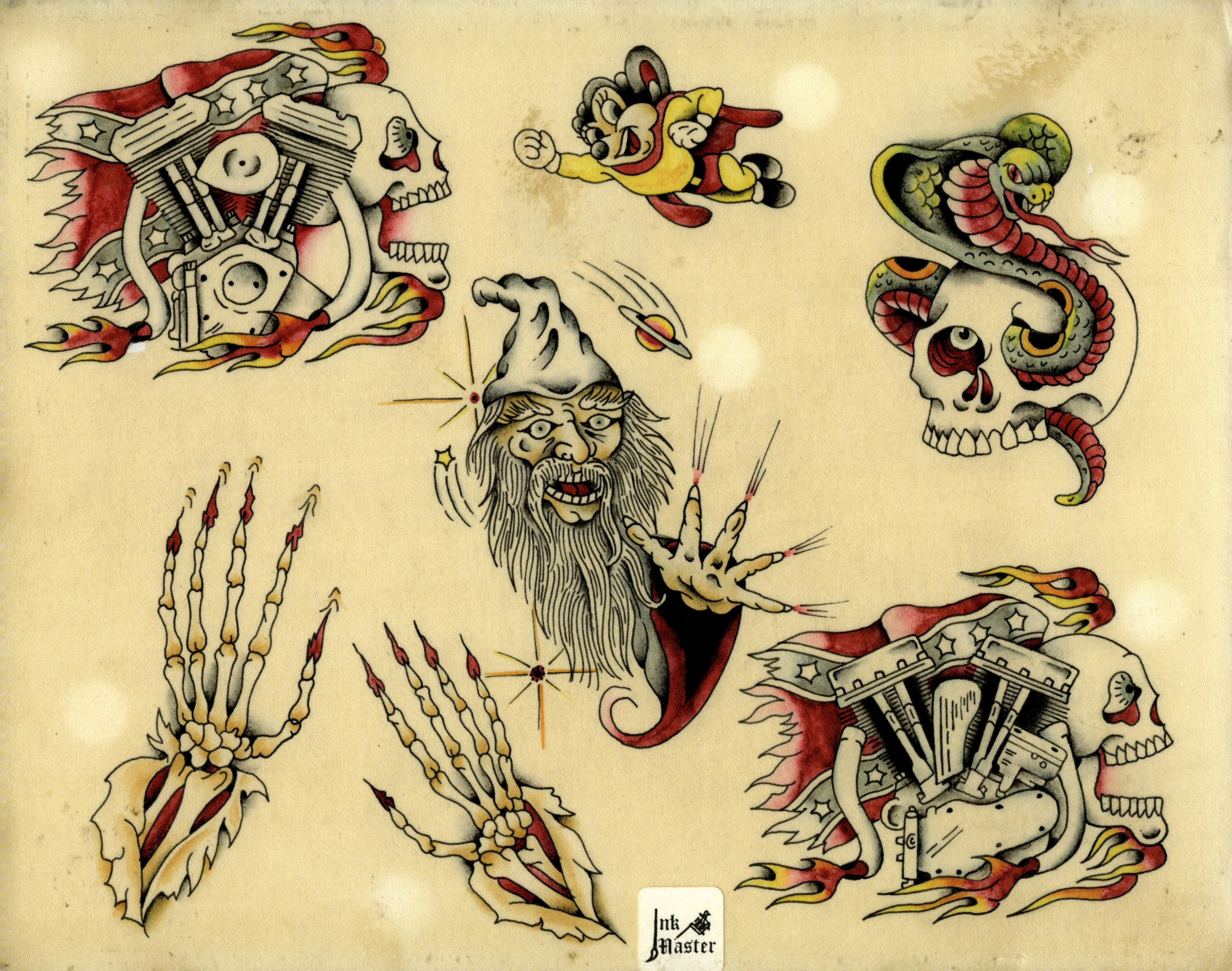
Ink Master

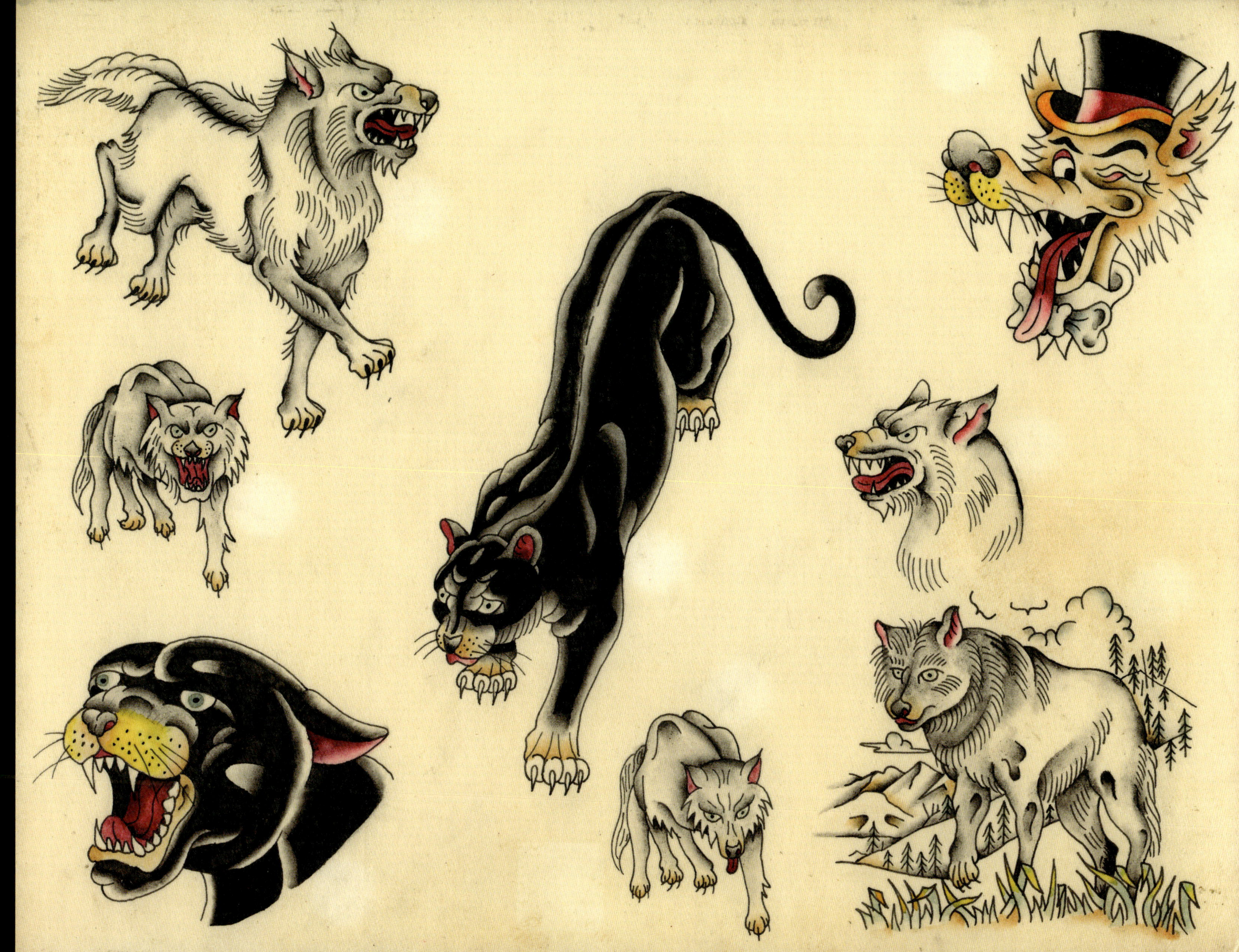

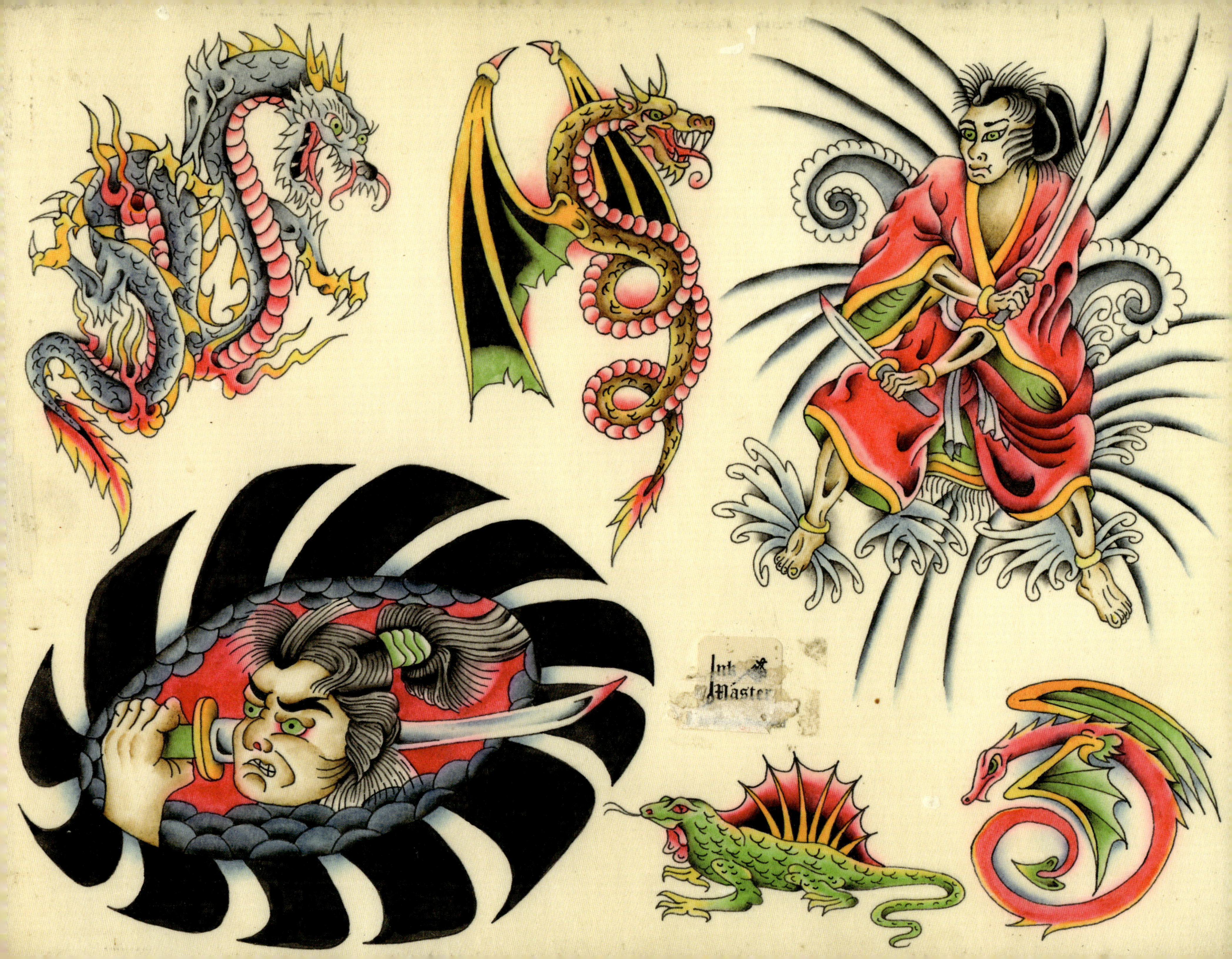

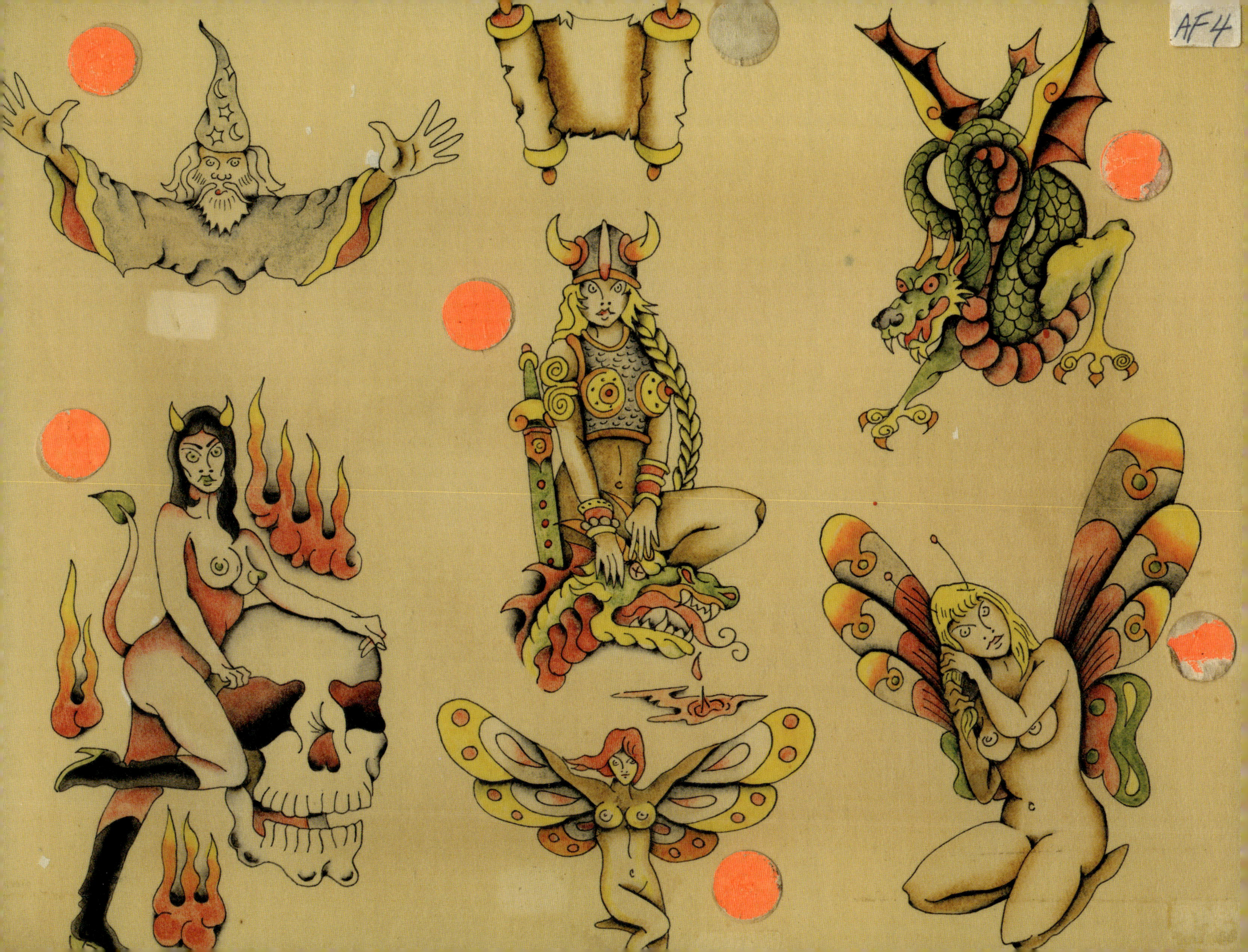
AF4

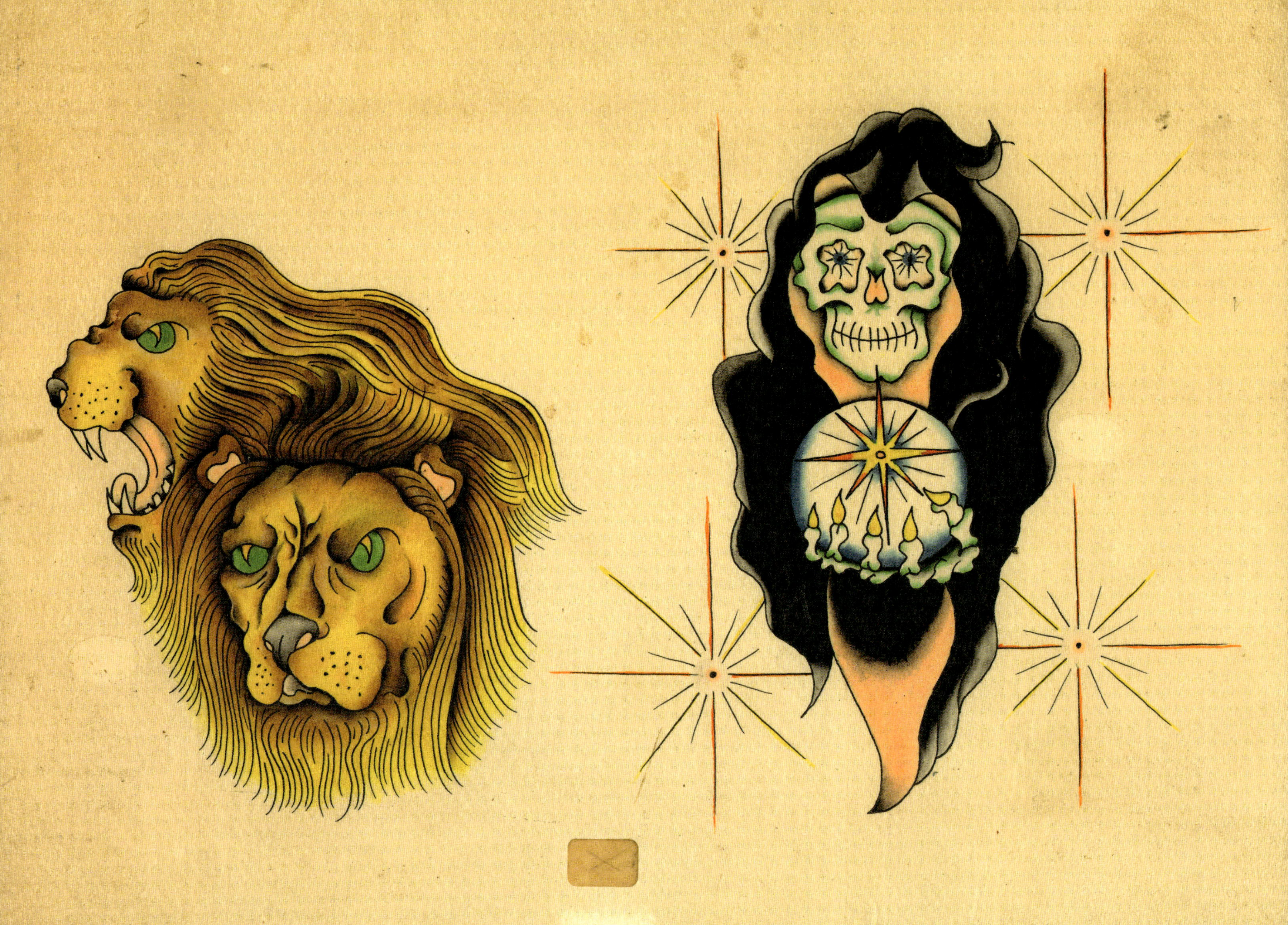

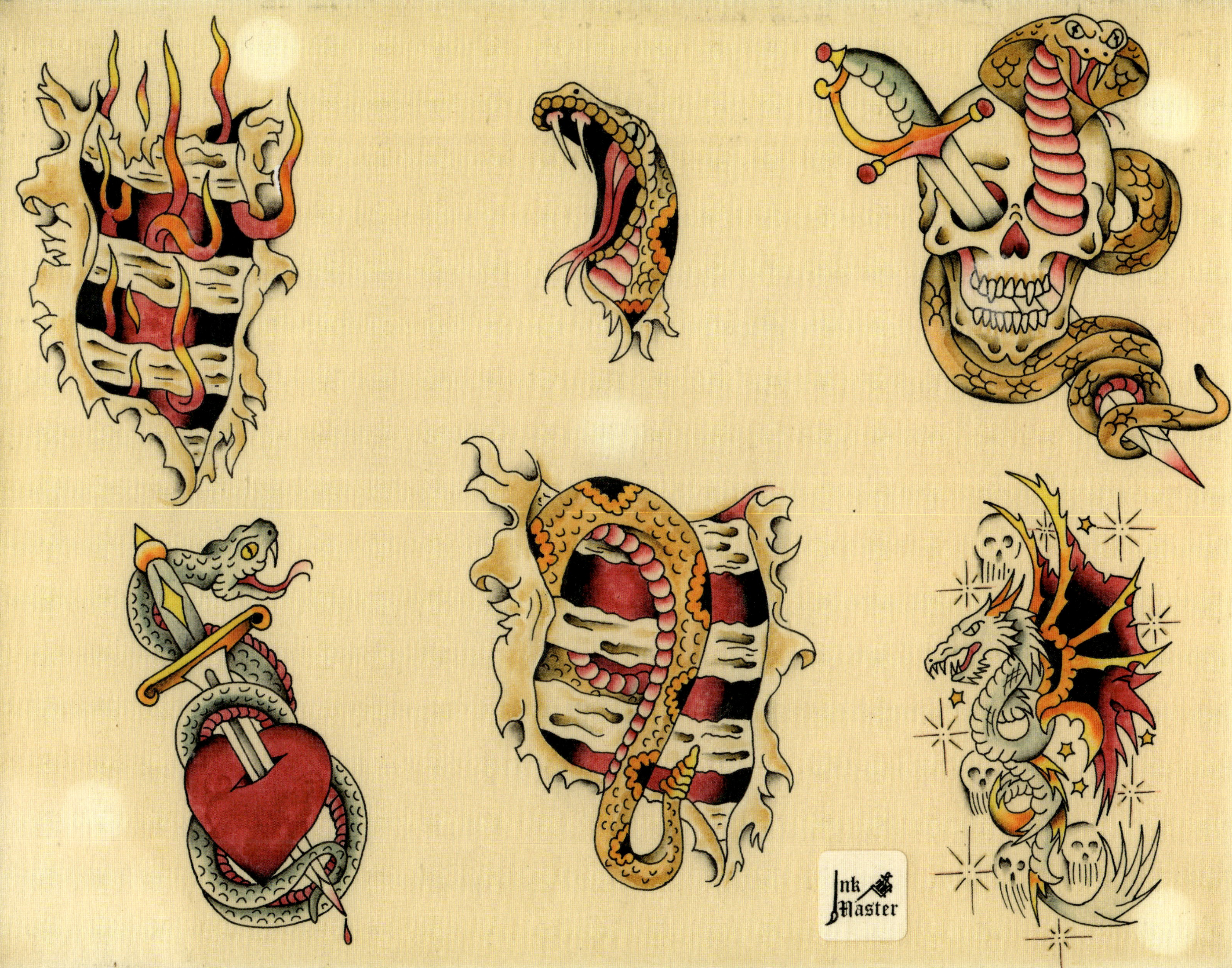
Ink
Master

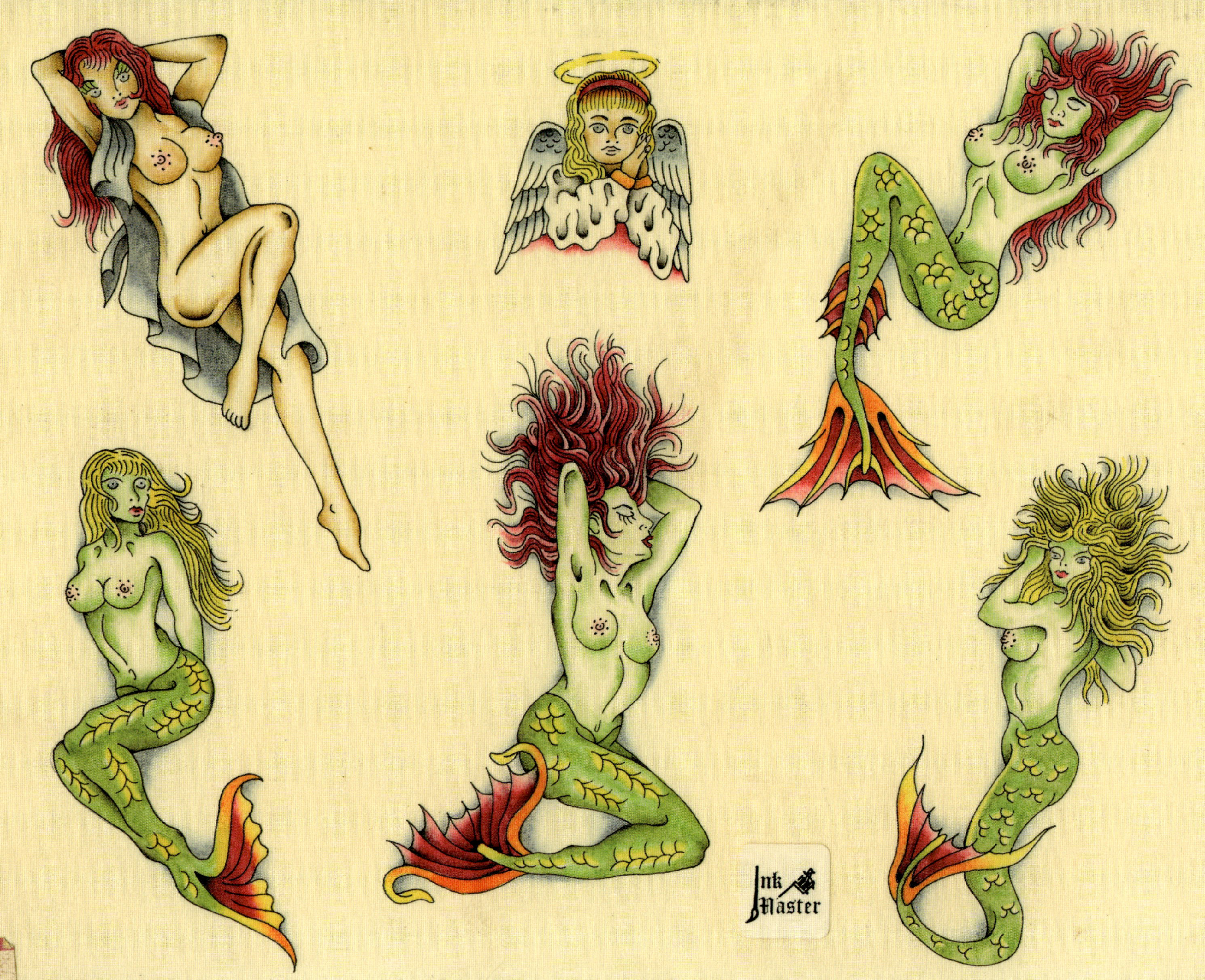
Ink Master

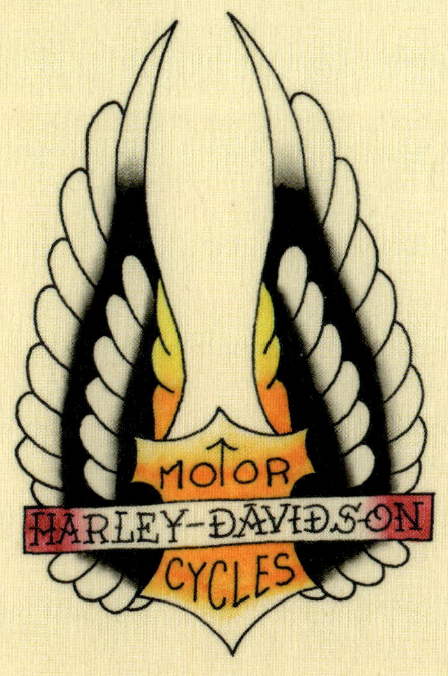
MOTOR
HARLEY-DAVIDSON
CYCLES

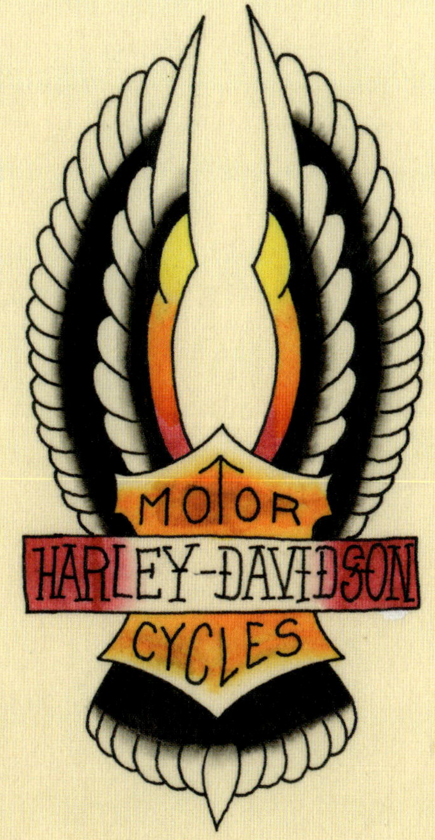
MOTOR
HARLEY-DAVIDSON
CYCLES

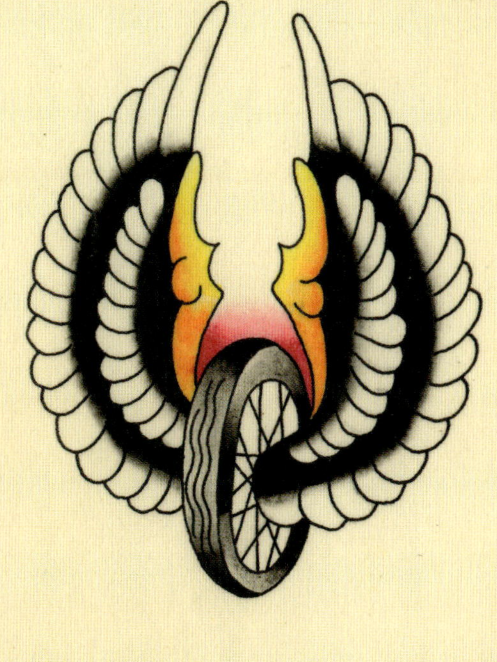

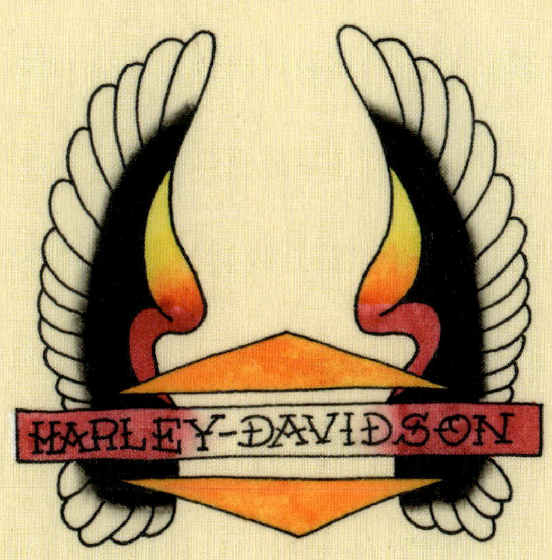
HARLEY-DAVIDSON

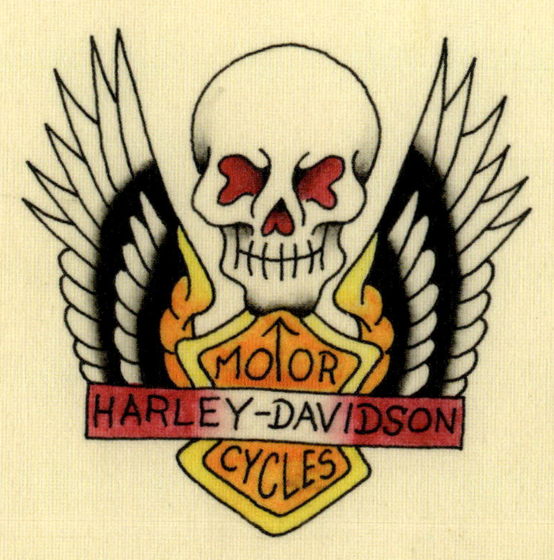
MOTOR
HARLEY-DAVIDSON
CYCLES

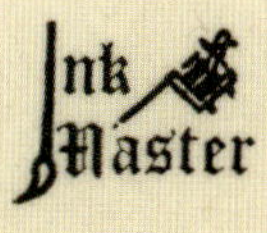
Ink
Master

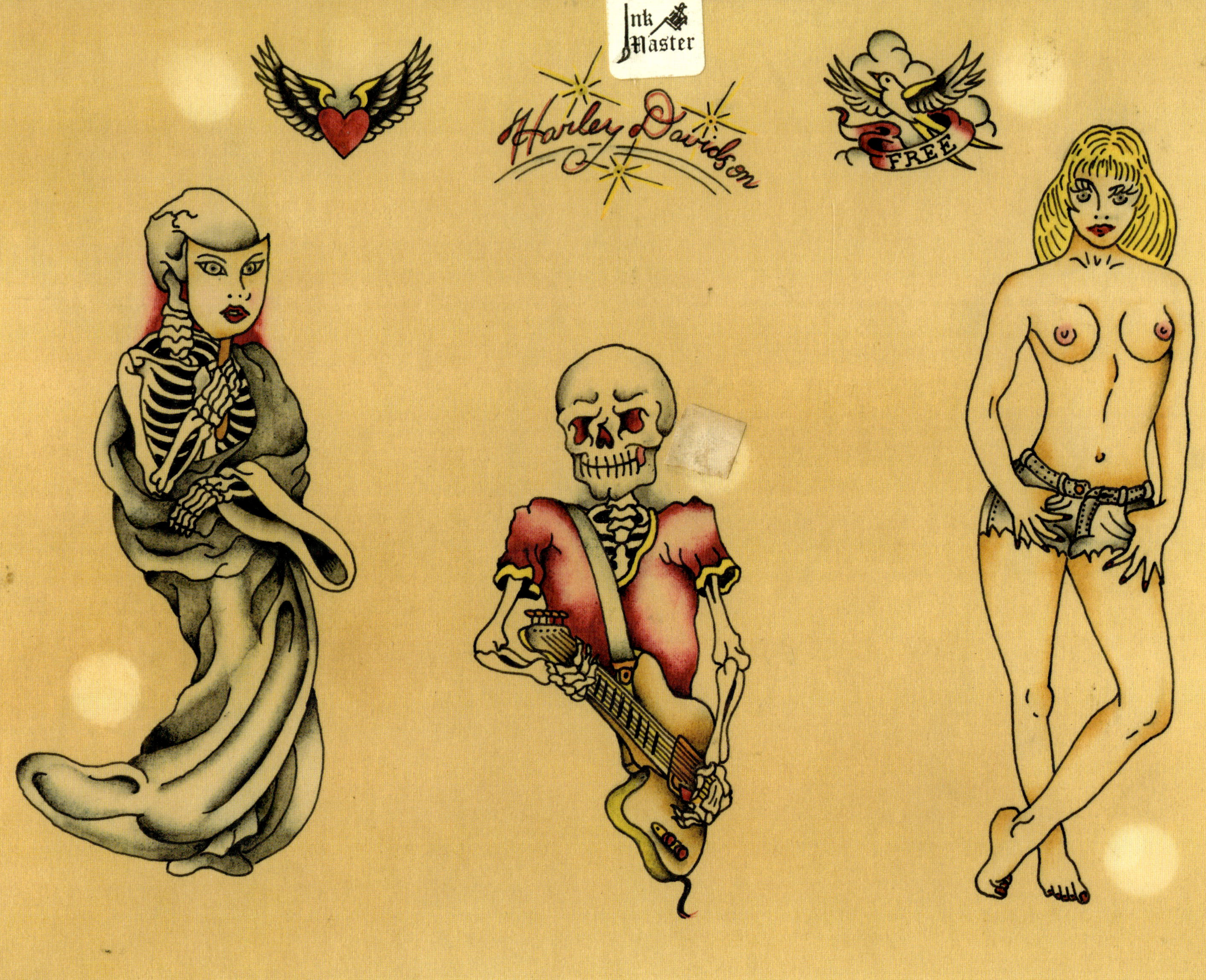
Ink Master
Harley Davidson
FREE

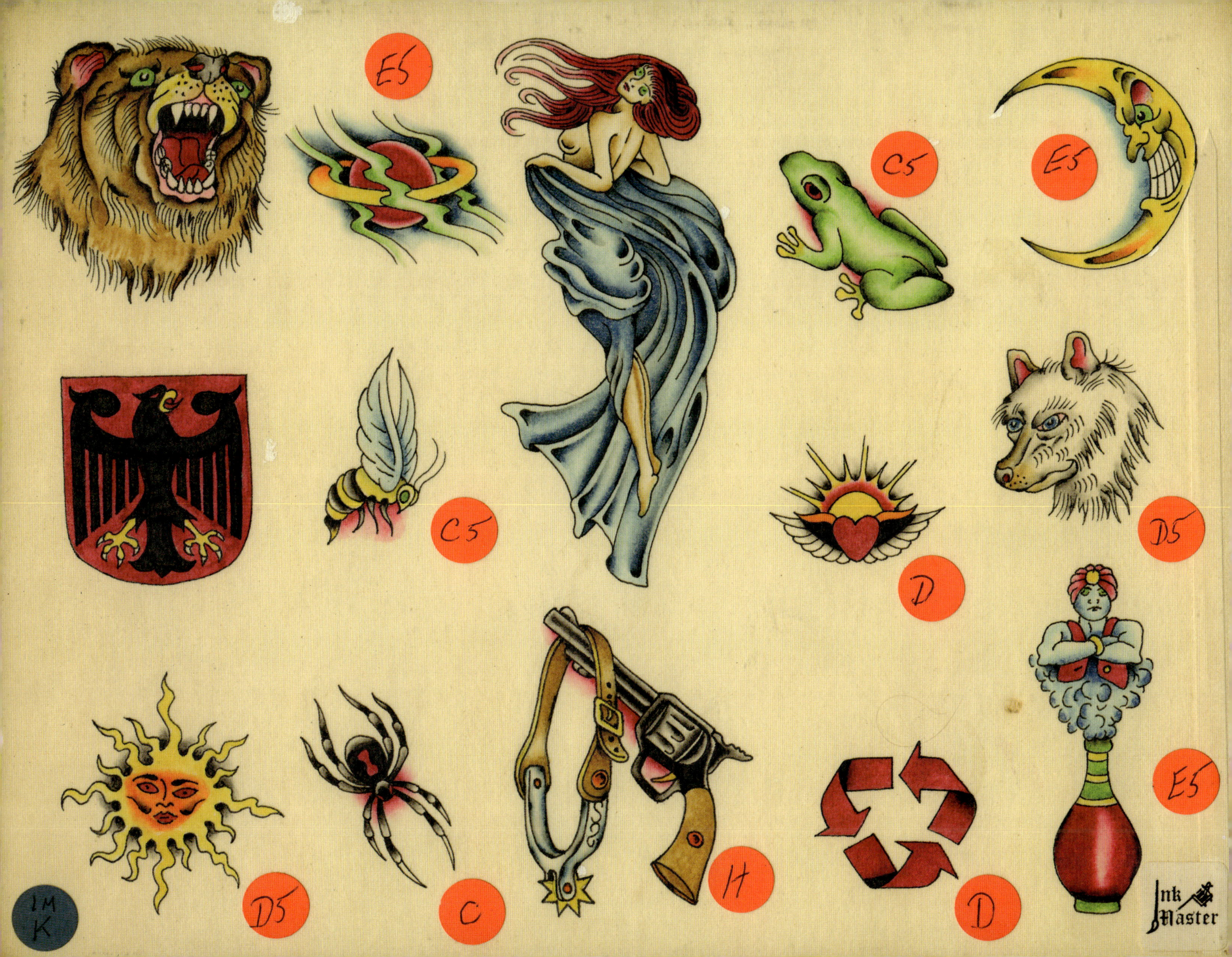
E5
C5
E5
C5
D5
D
E5
D5
C
H
D
IMK
Ink Master

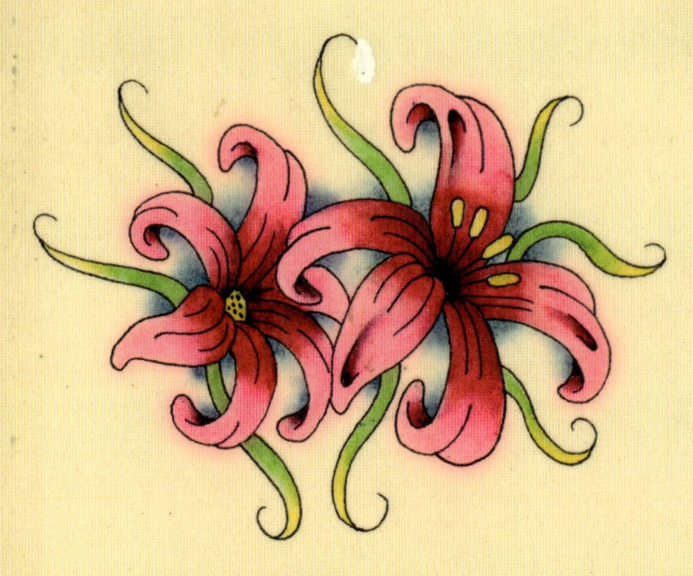
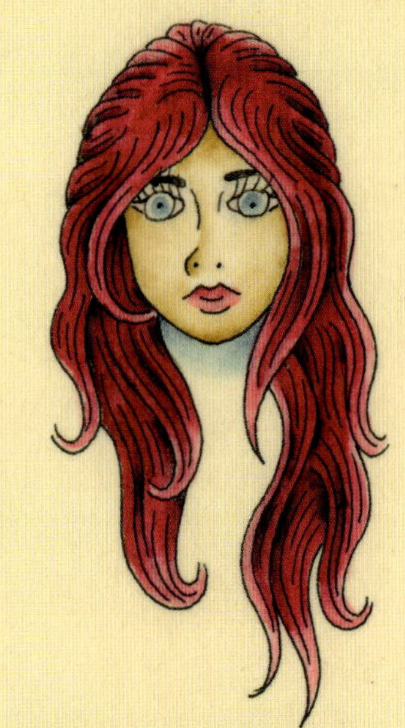
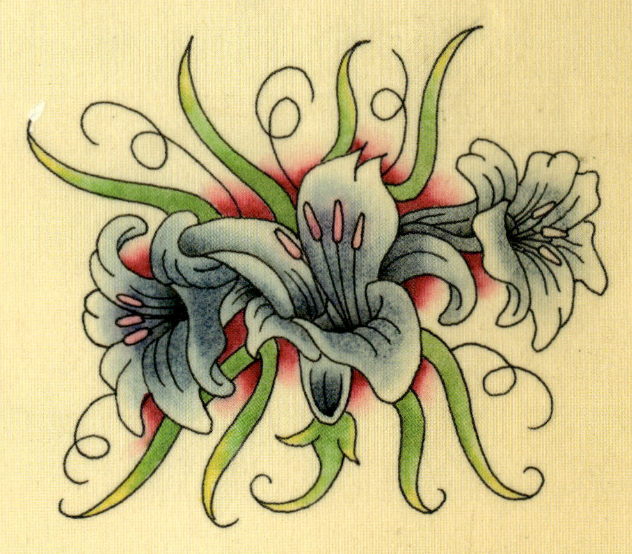
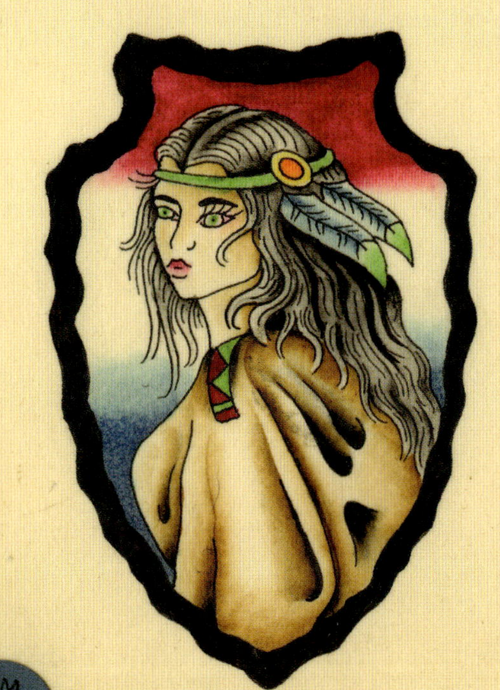
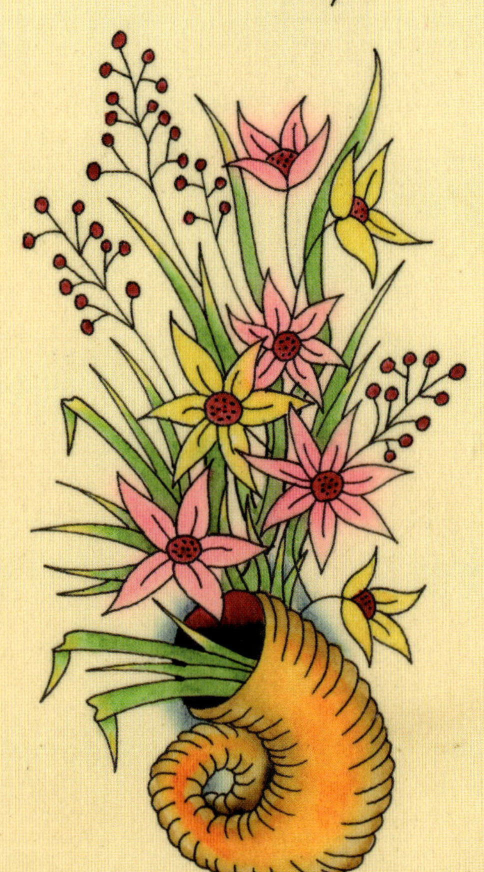
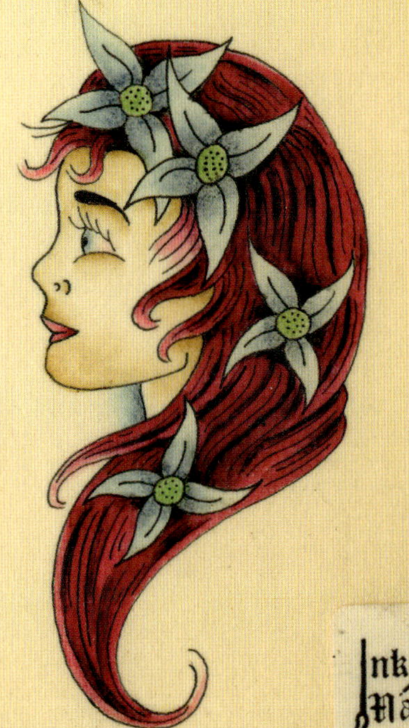
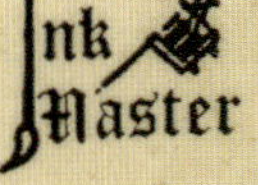
Ink
Master

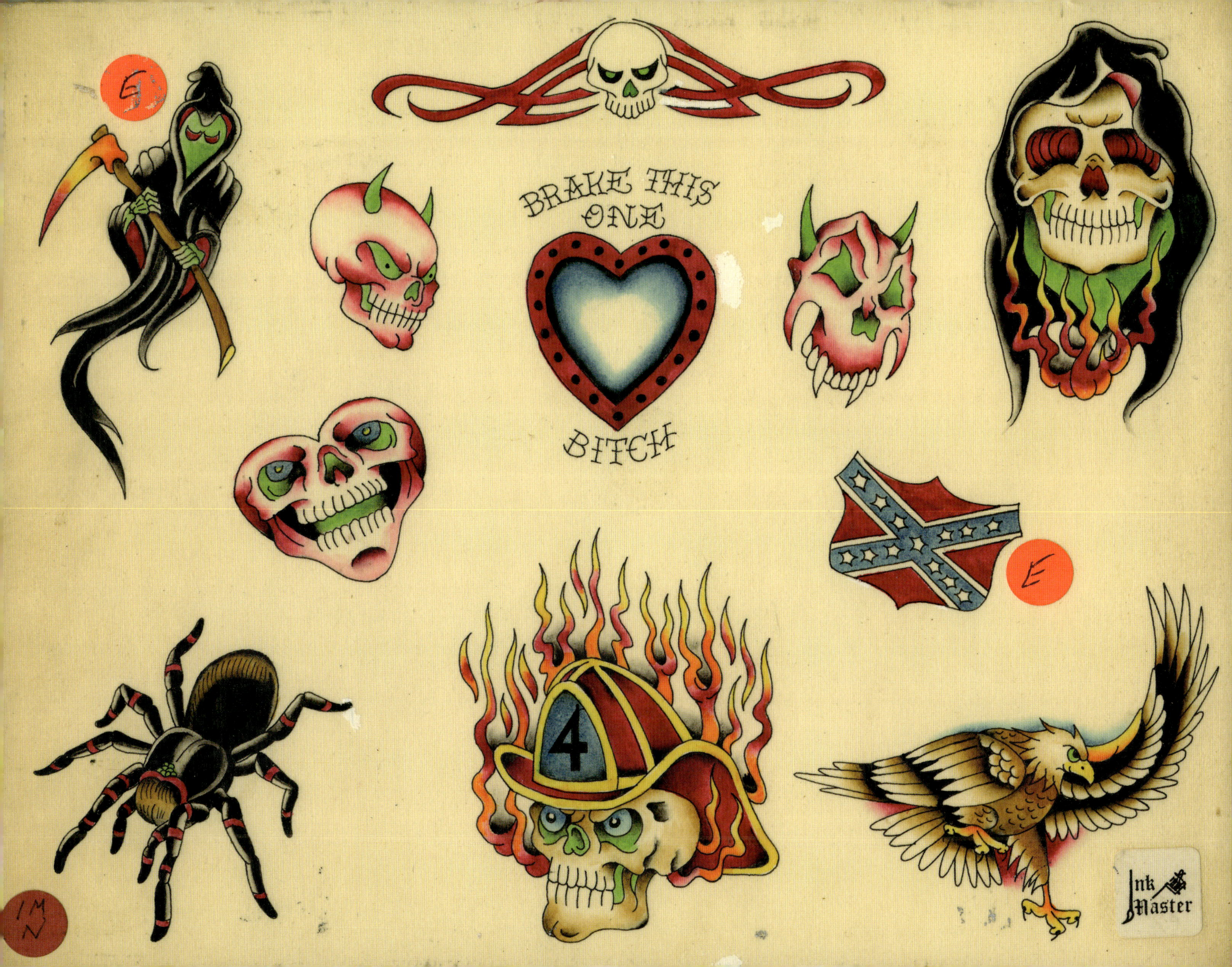
BRAKE THIS
ONE
BITCH
4
Ink Master

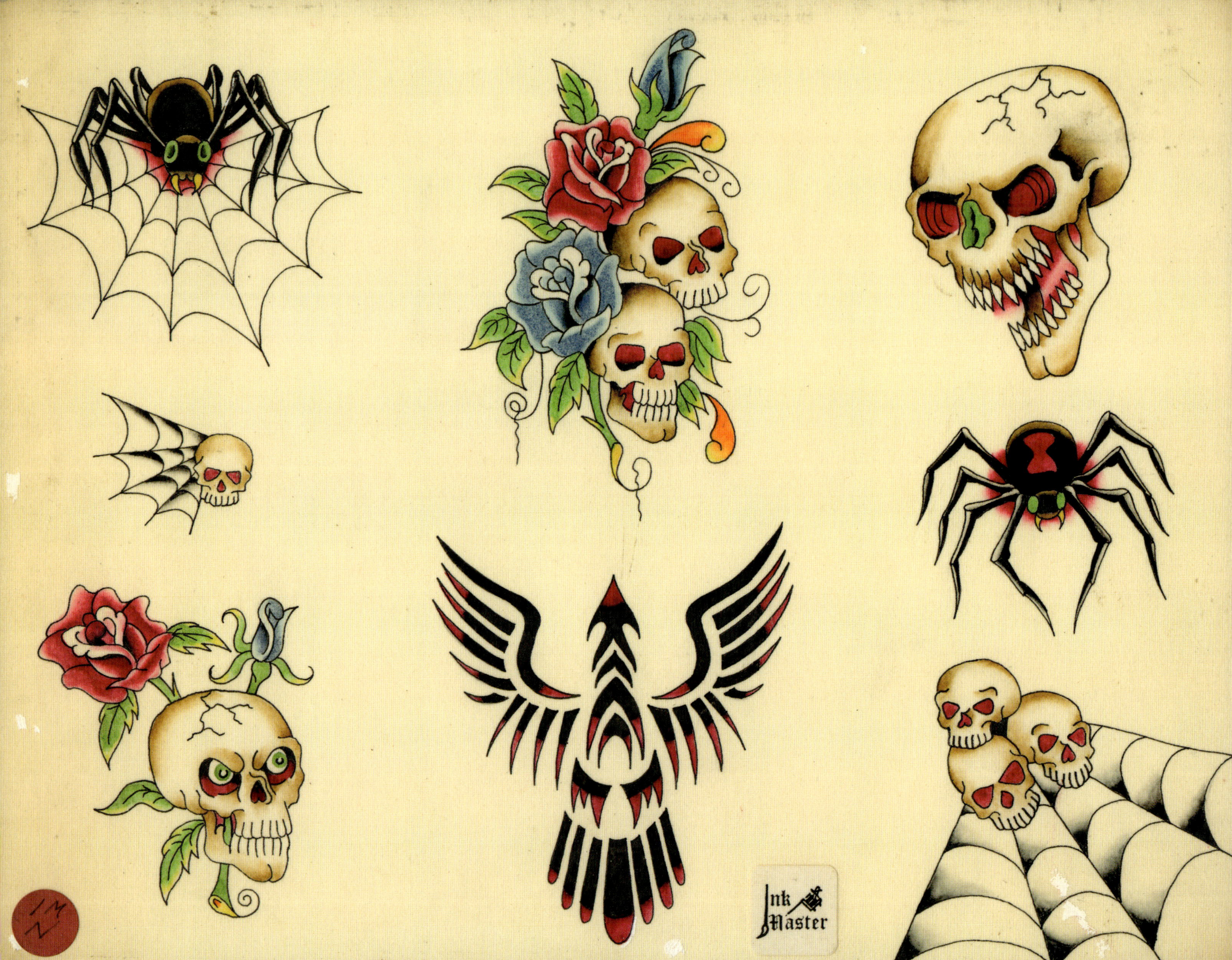
Ink Master

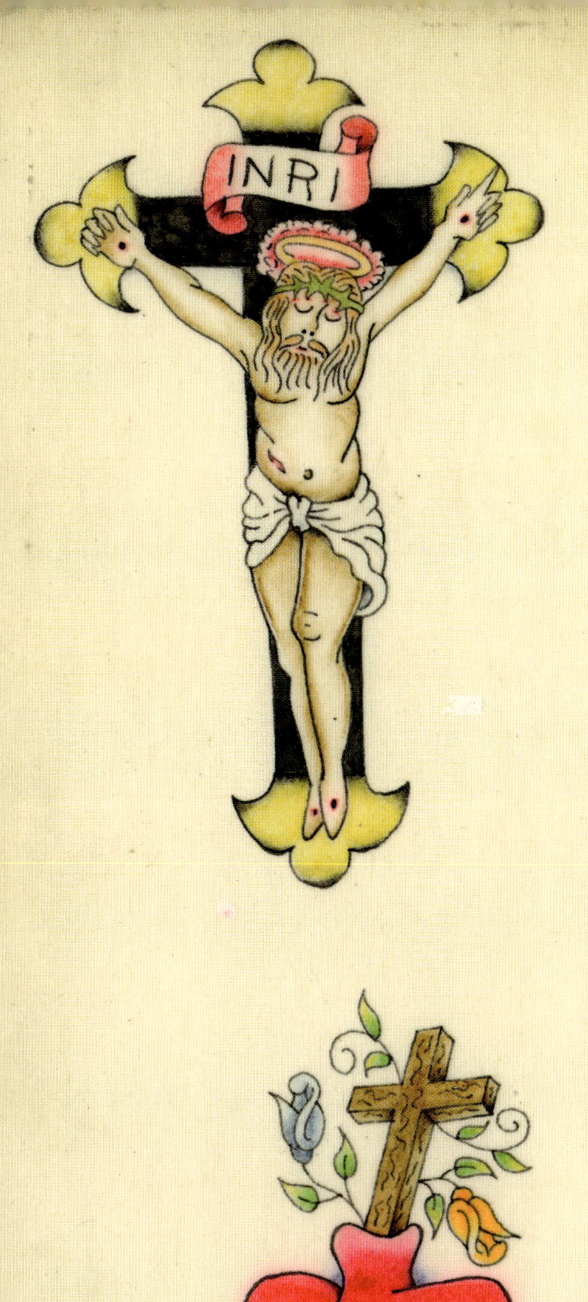
INRI

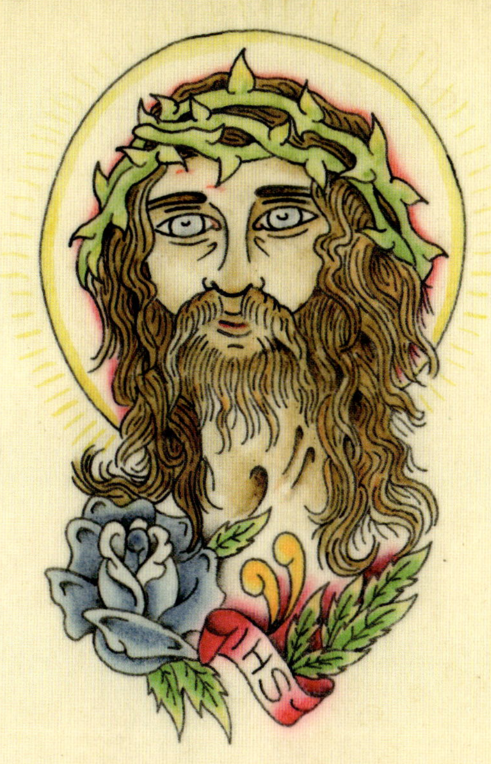
IHS

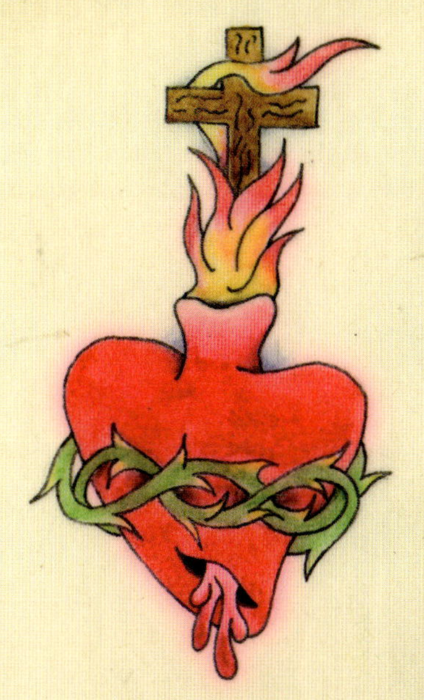

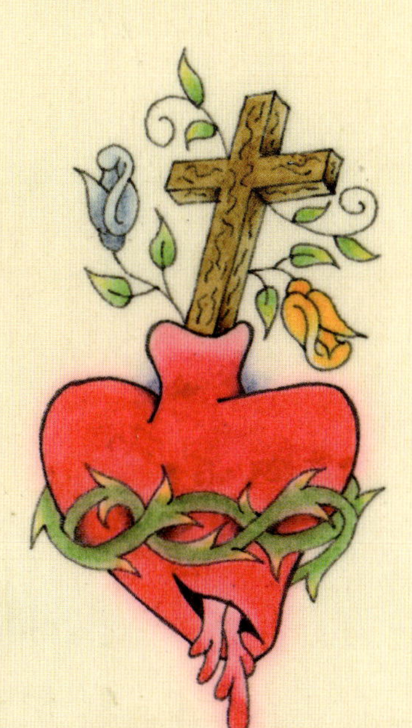

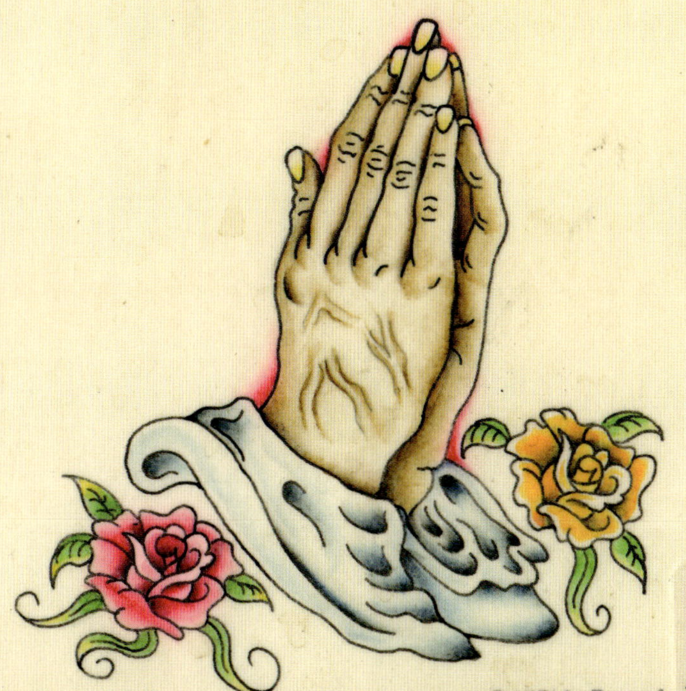

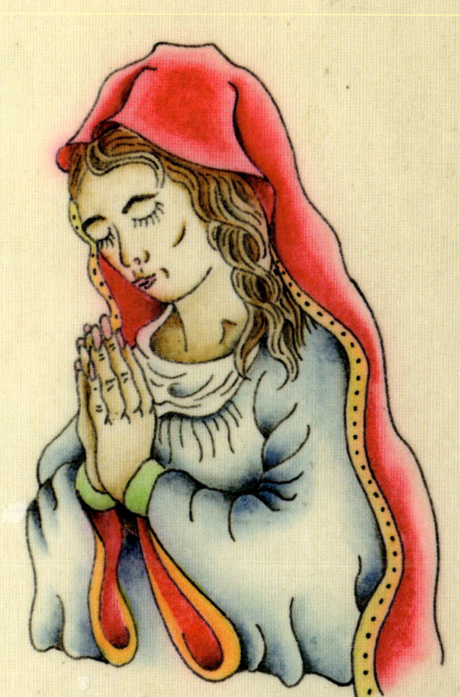

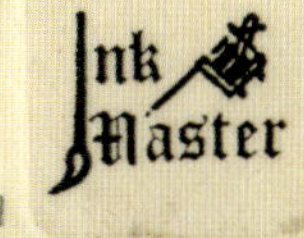
Ink
Master

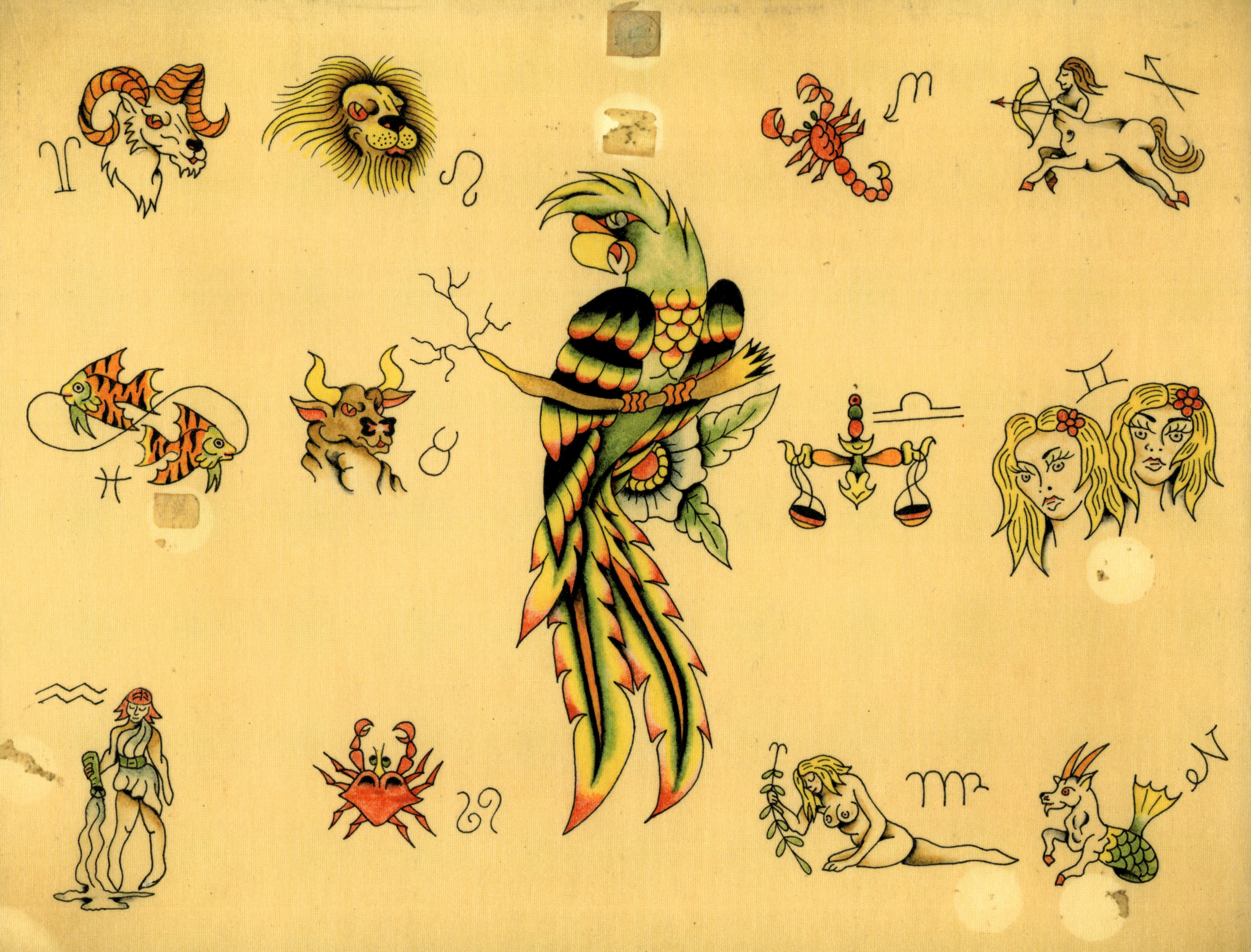

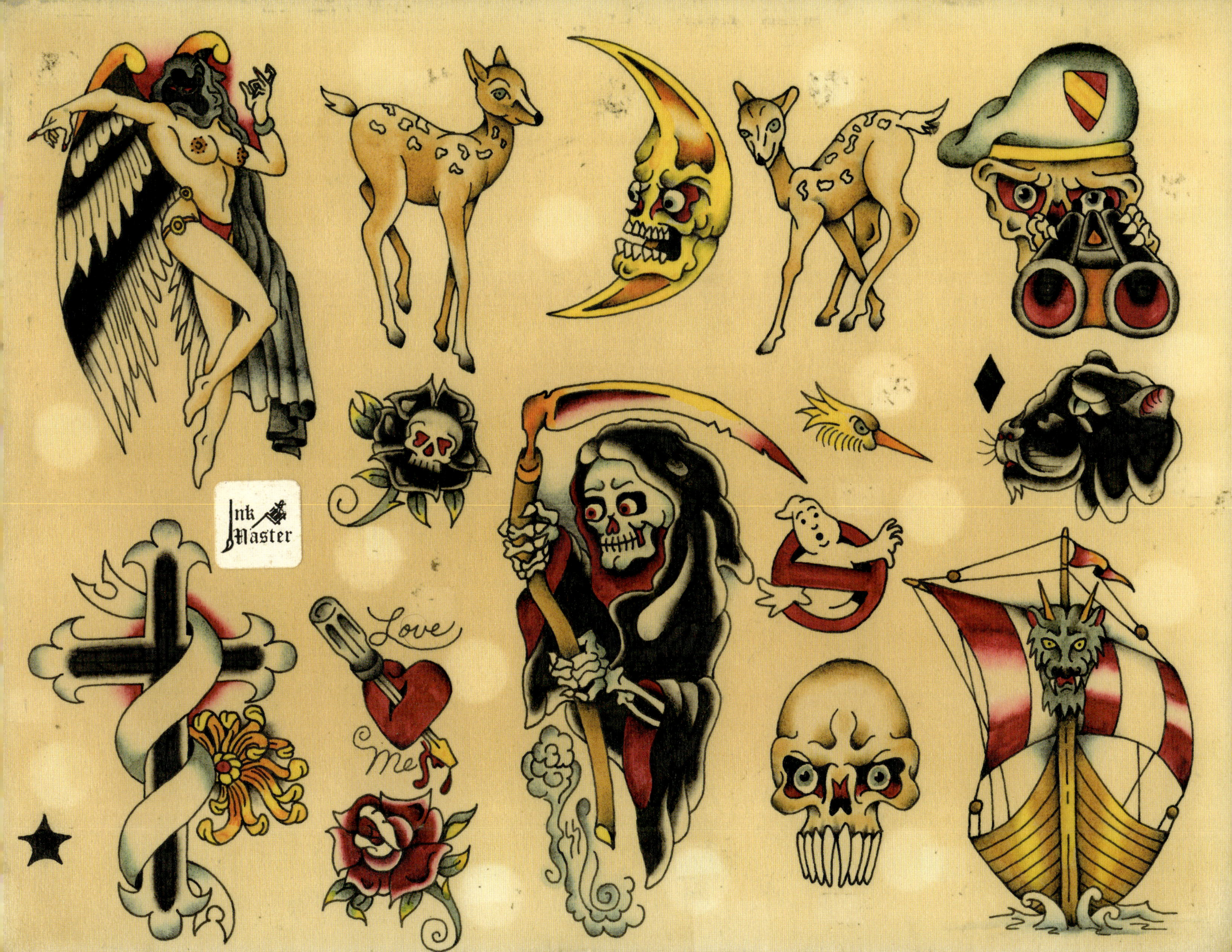
Ink Master
Love
Me

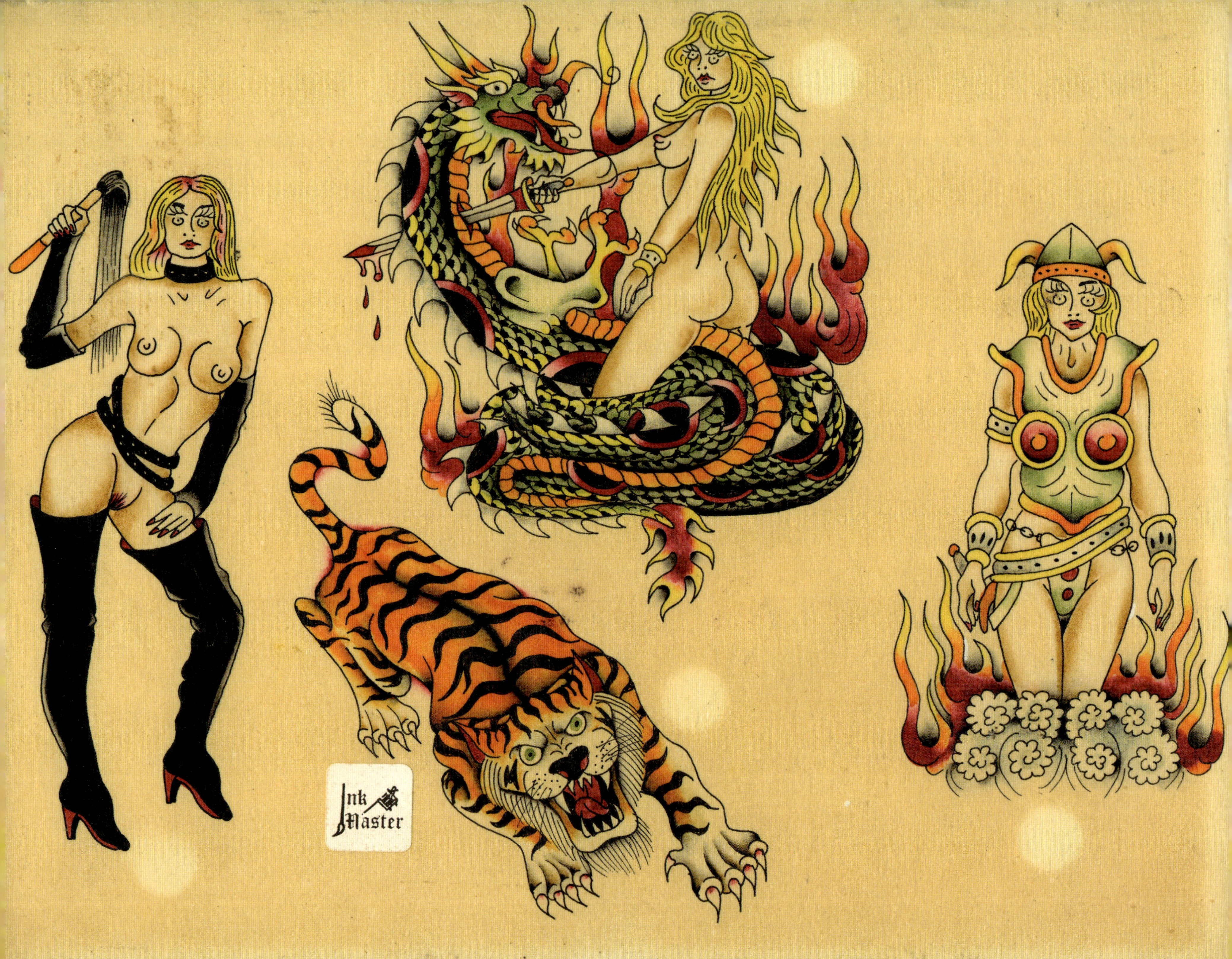
Ink Master

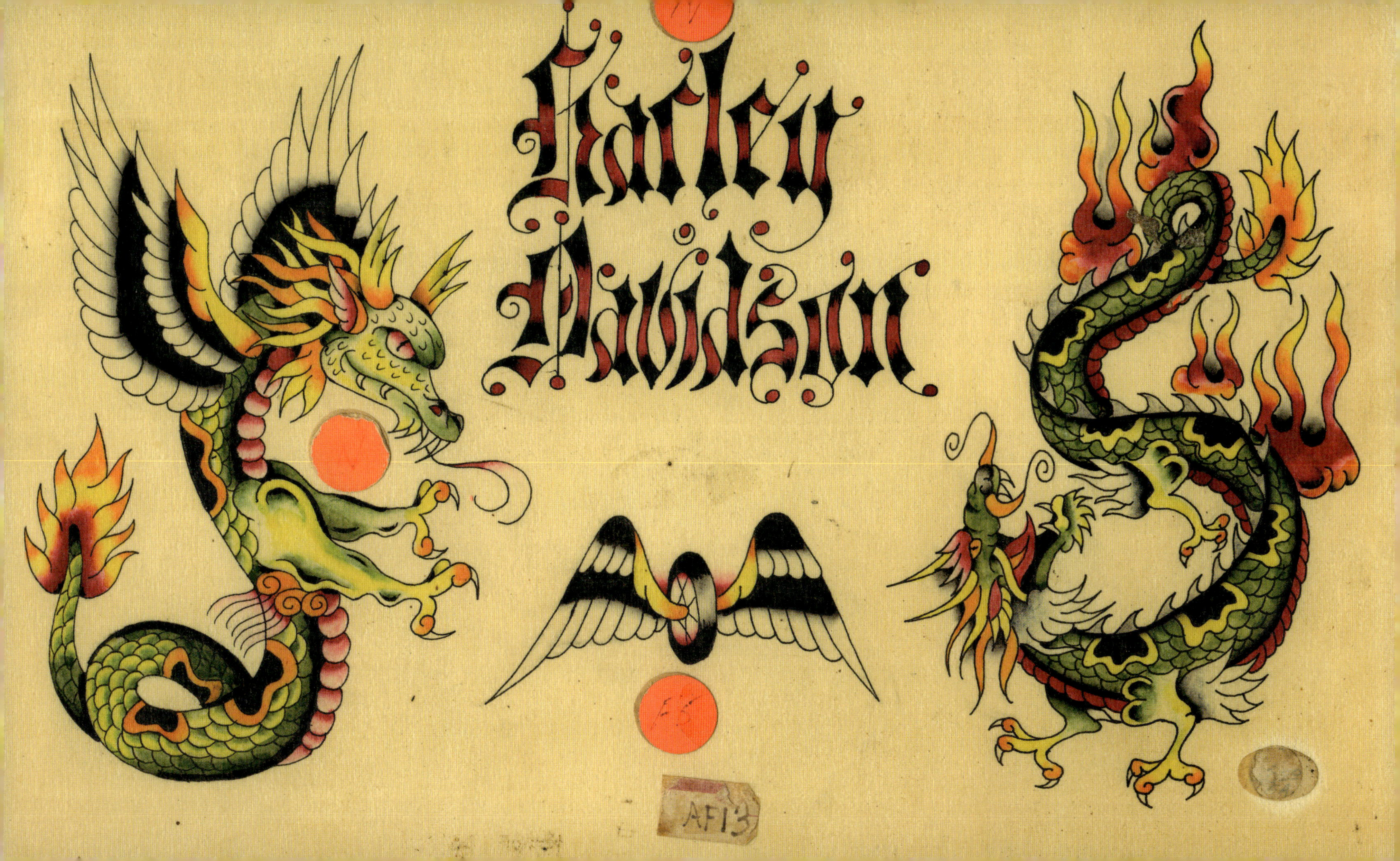
Harley
Davidson
AF13

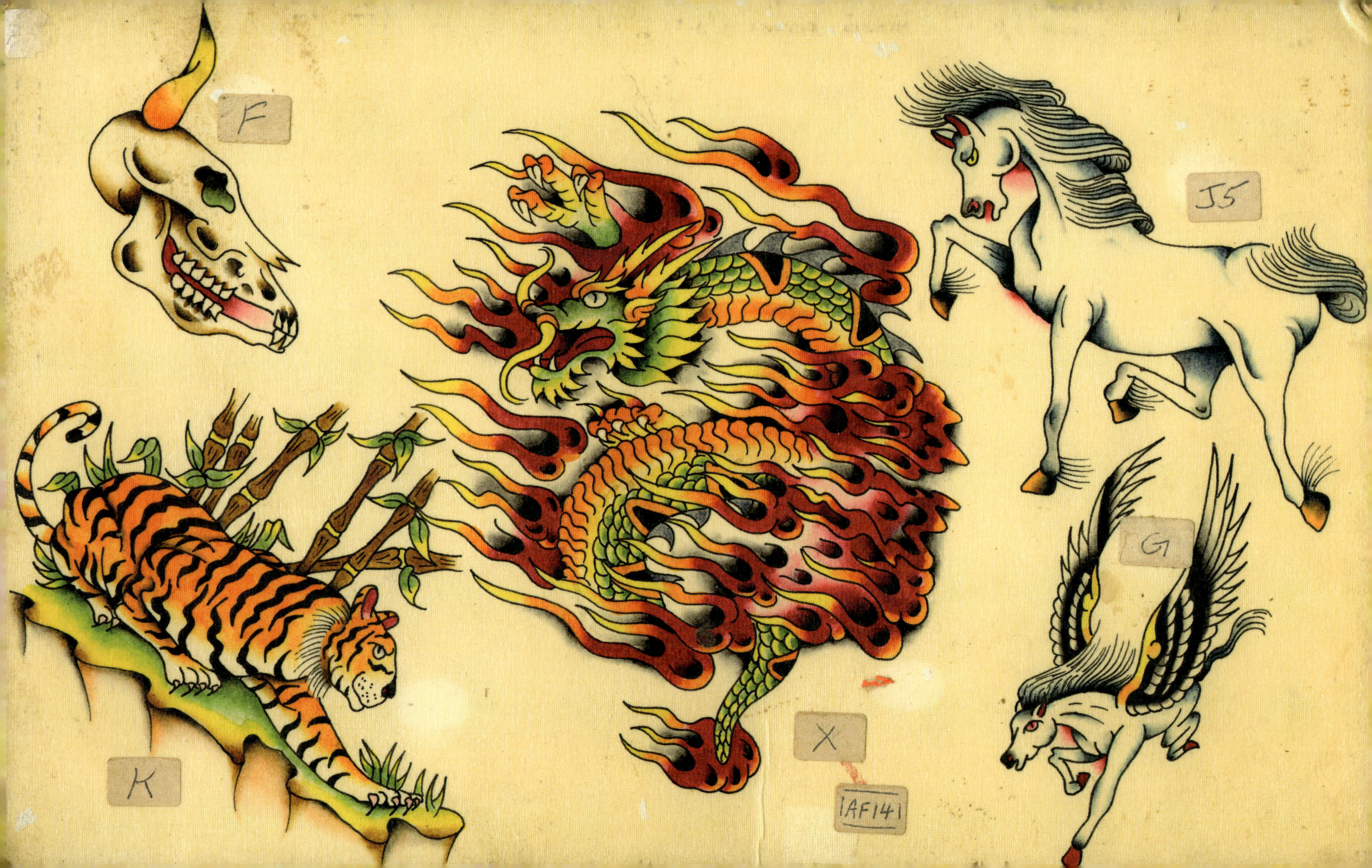
F
J5
G
X
K
AF141

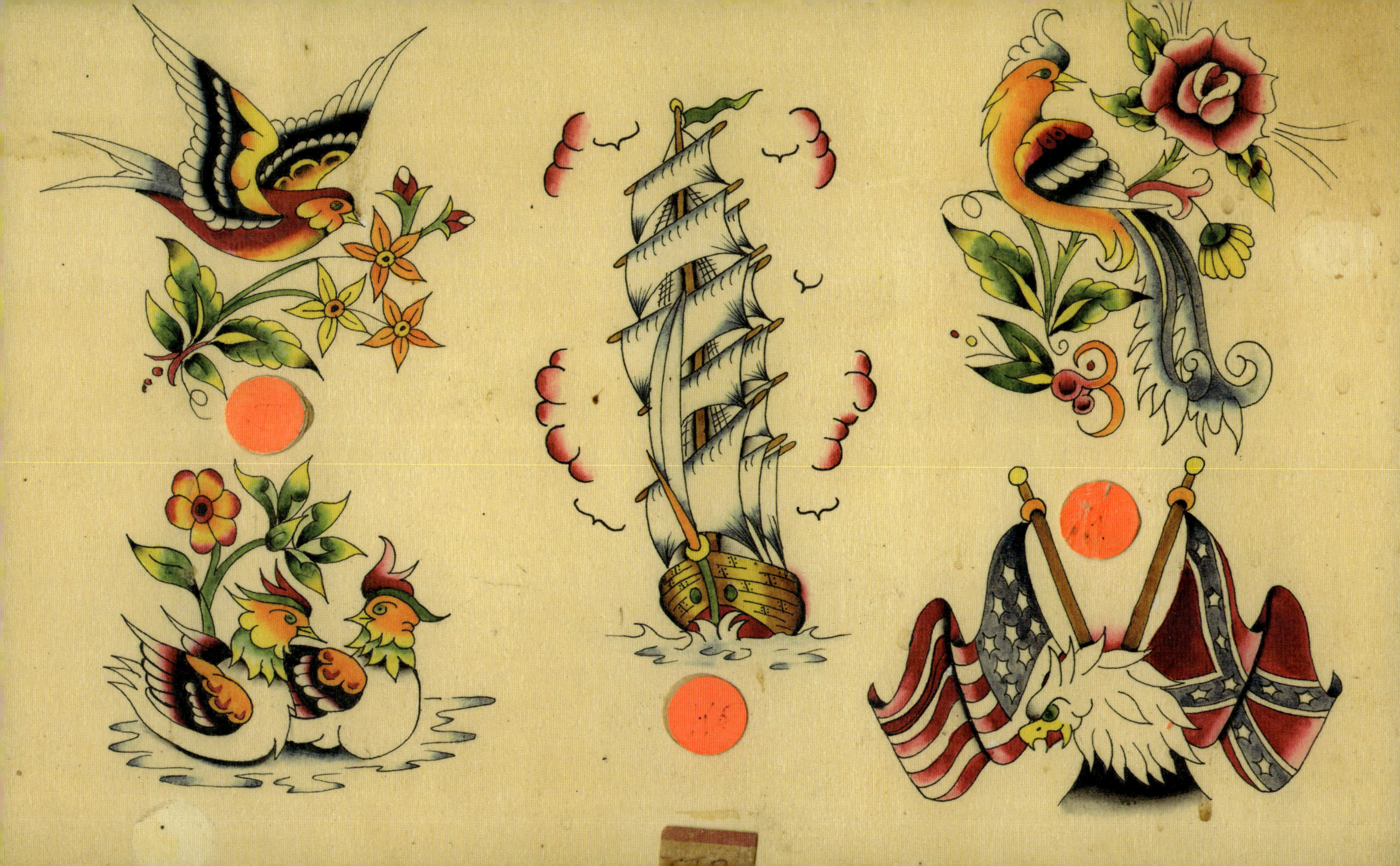

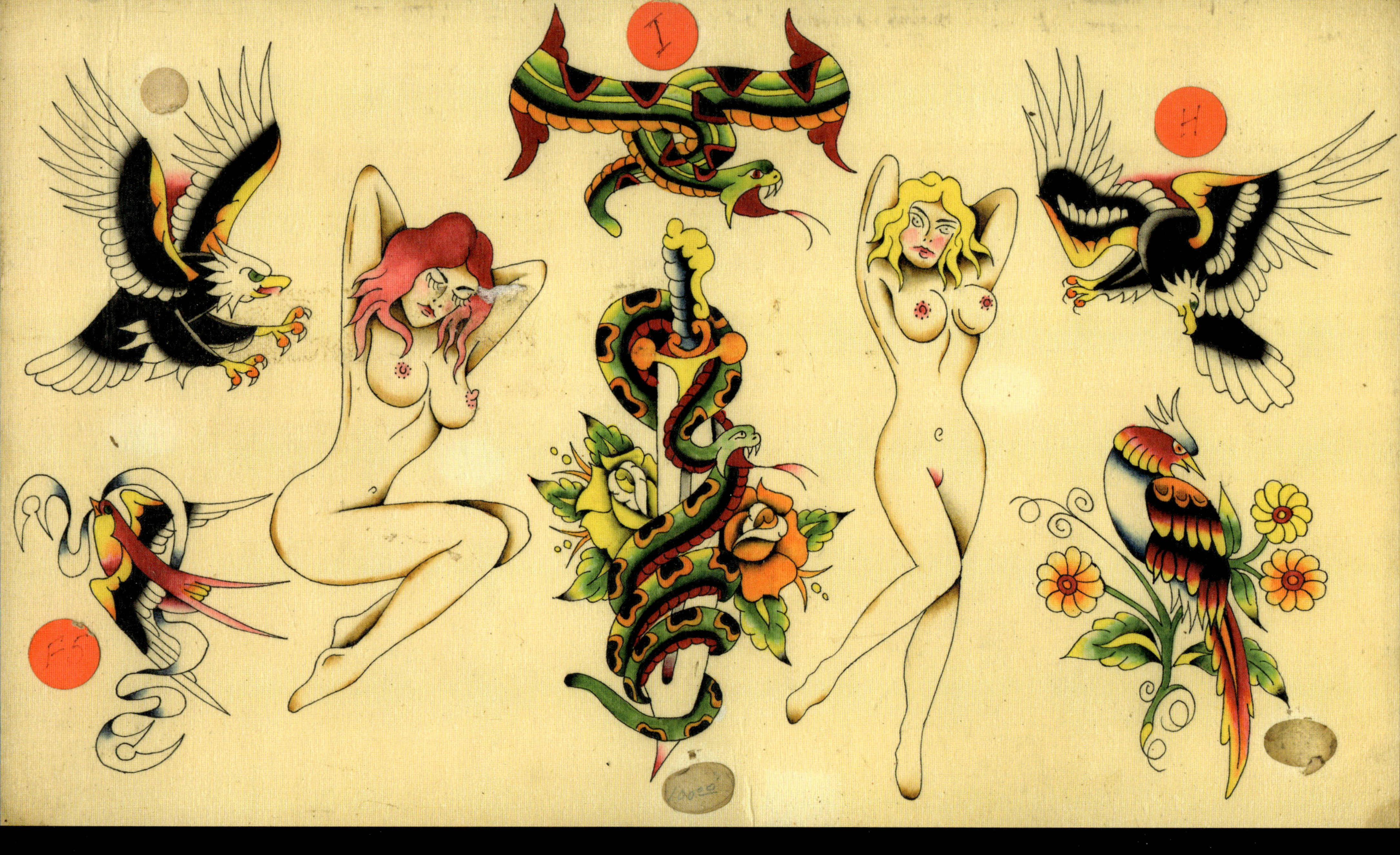
I
H
F5

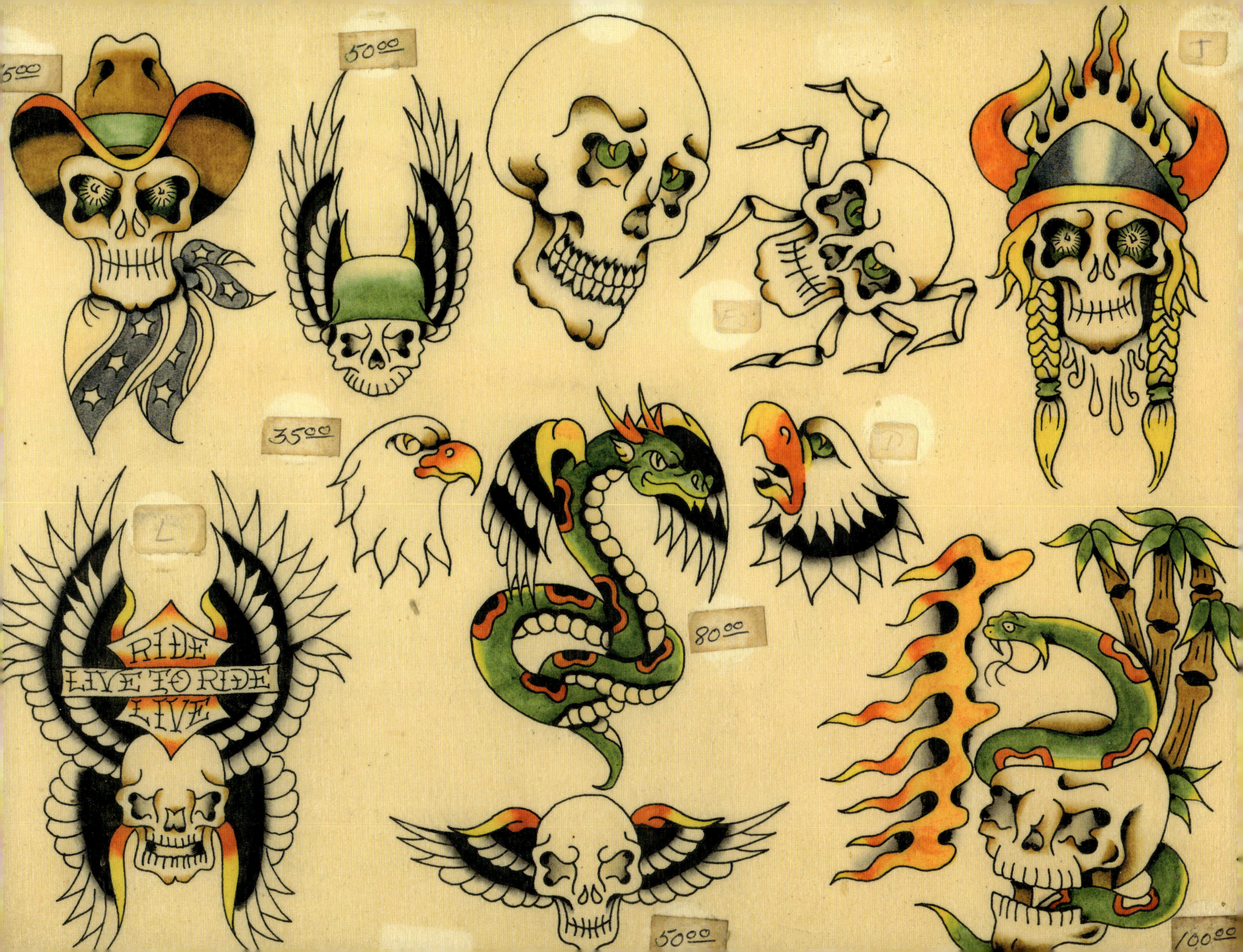

50⁰⁰
J
35⁰⁰
D
RIDE
LIVE TO RIDE
LIVE
L
80⁰⁰
50⁰⁰
100⁰⁰

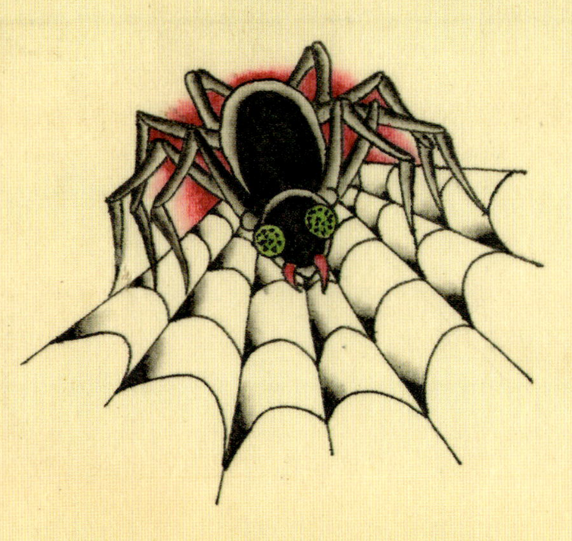

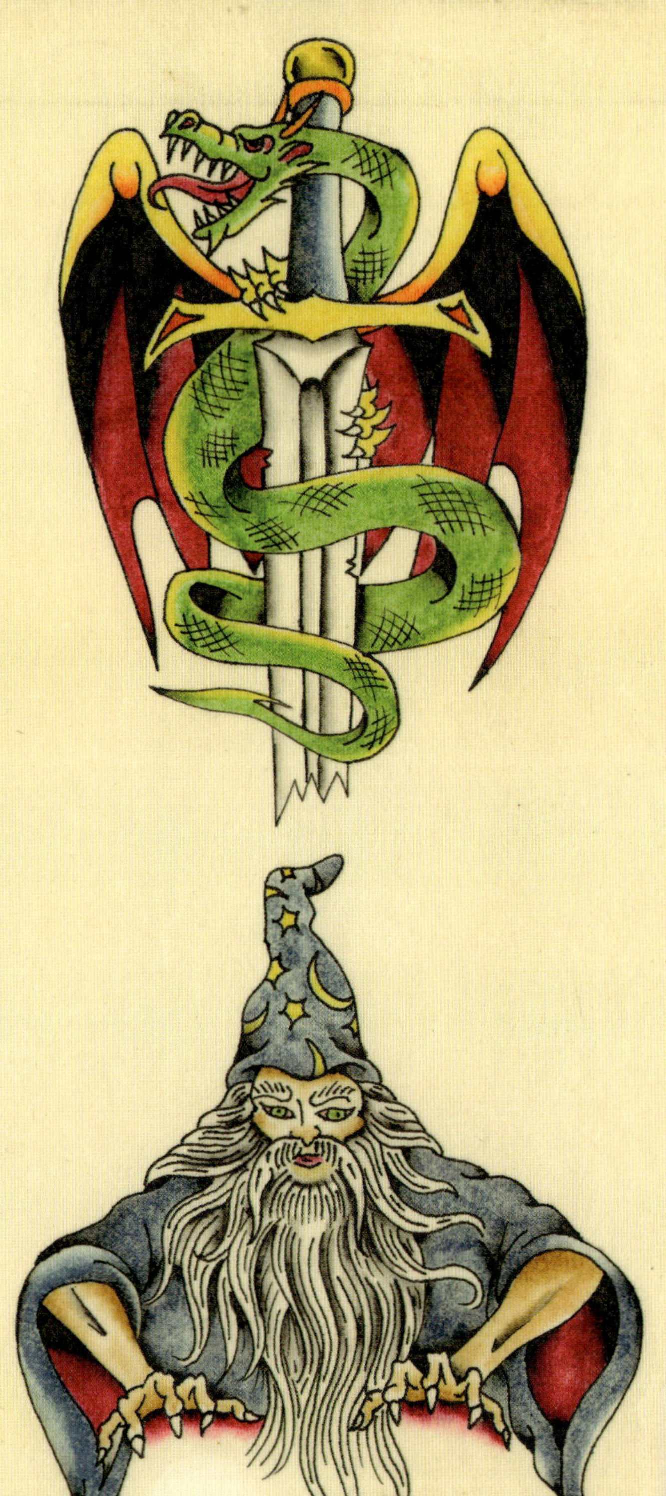

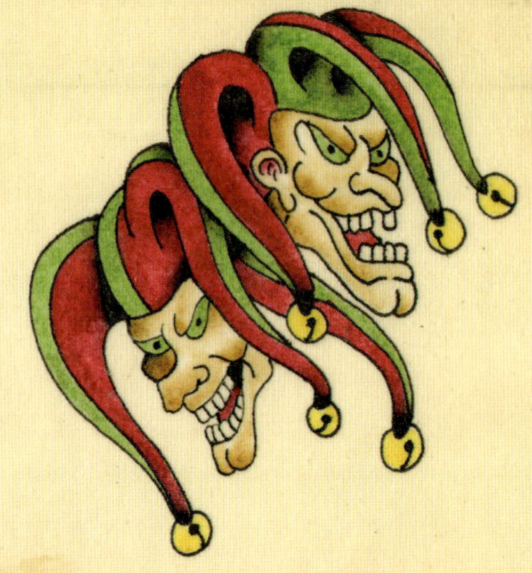

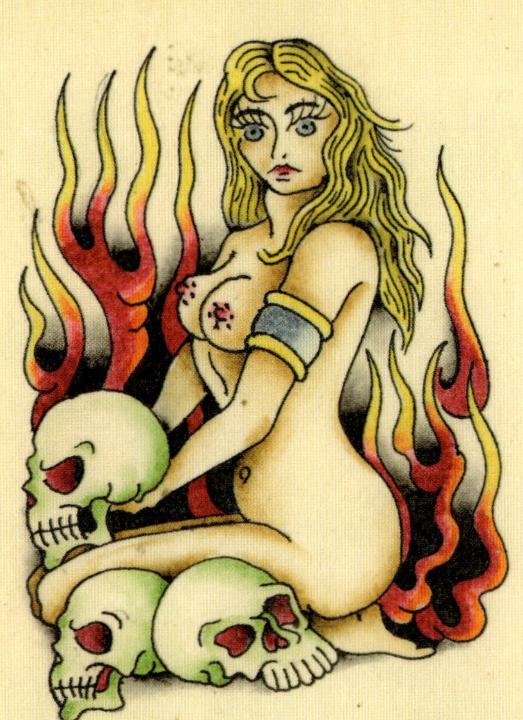

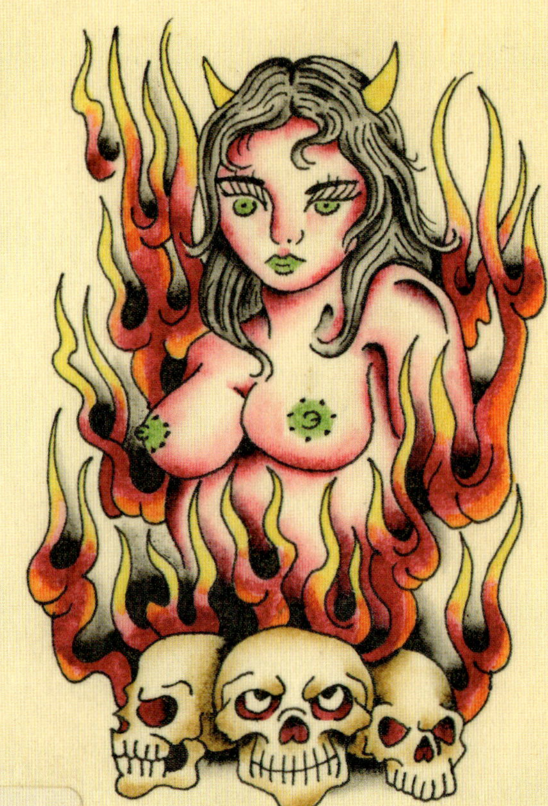

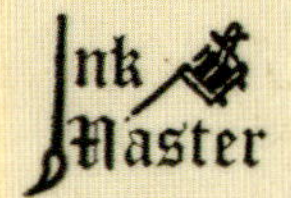
Ink
Master

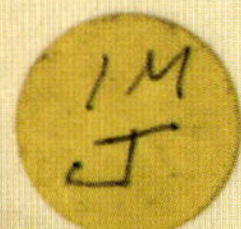
IM
J

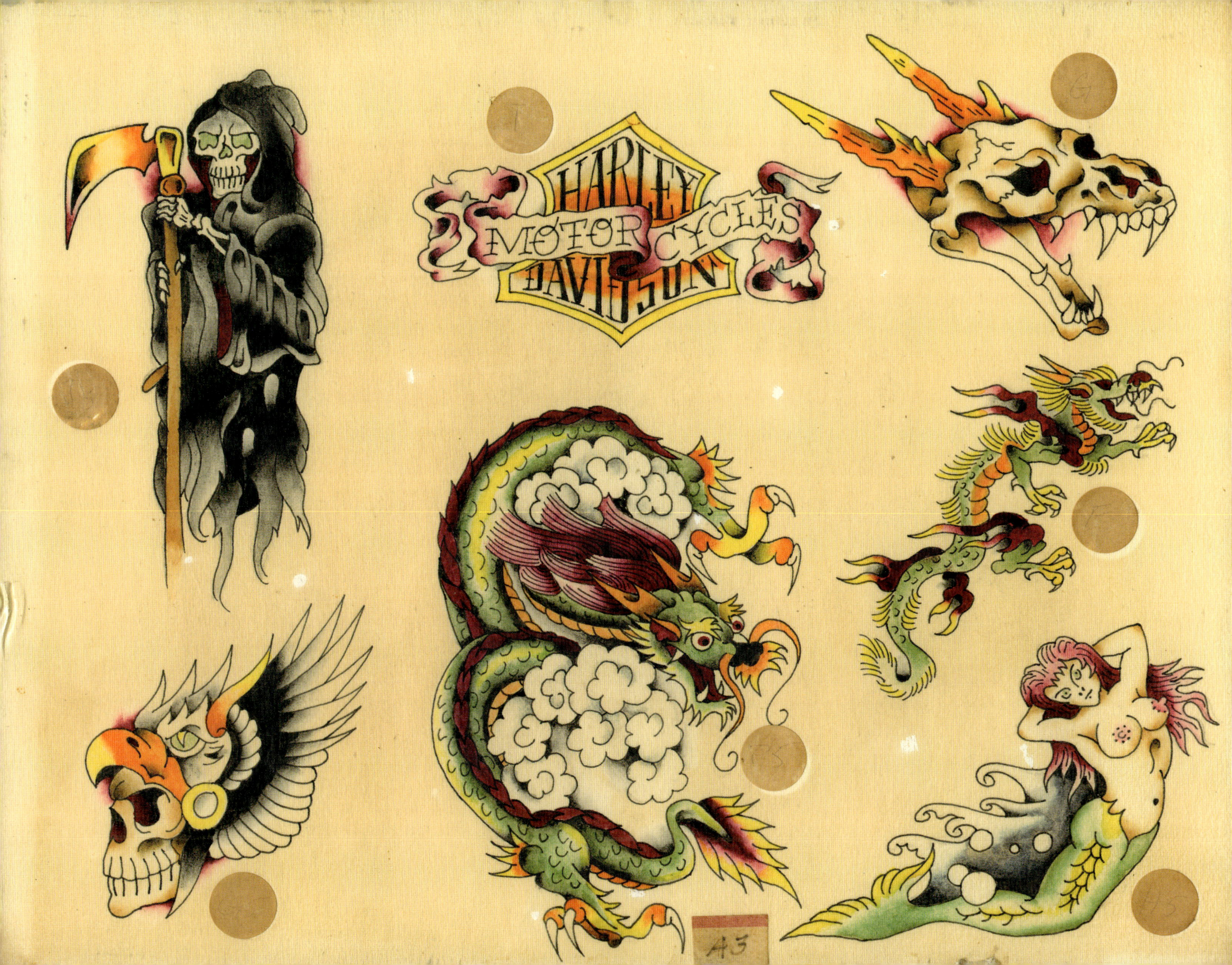
HARLEY
MOTOR CYCLES
DAVIDSON
A3

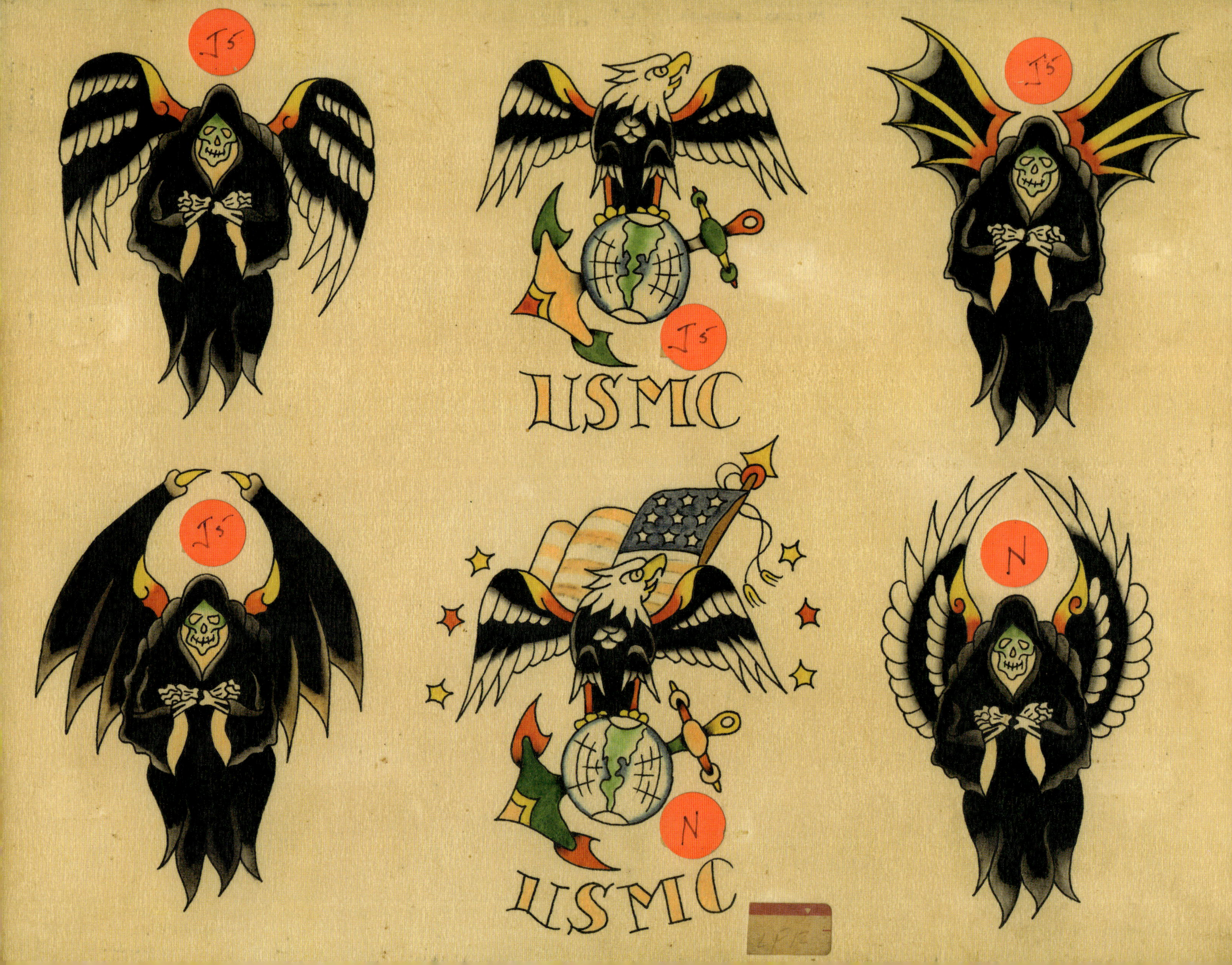
J5
J5
J5
USMC
J5
N
N
USMC

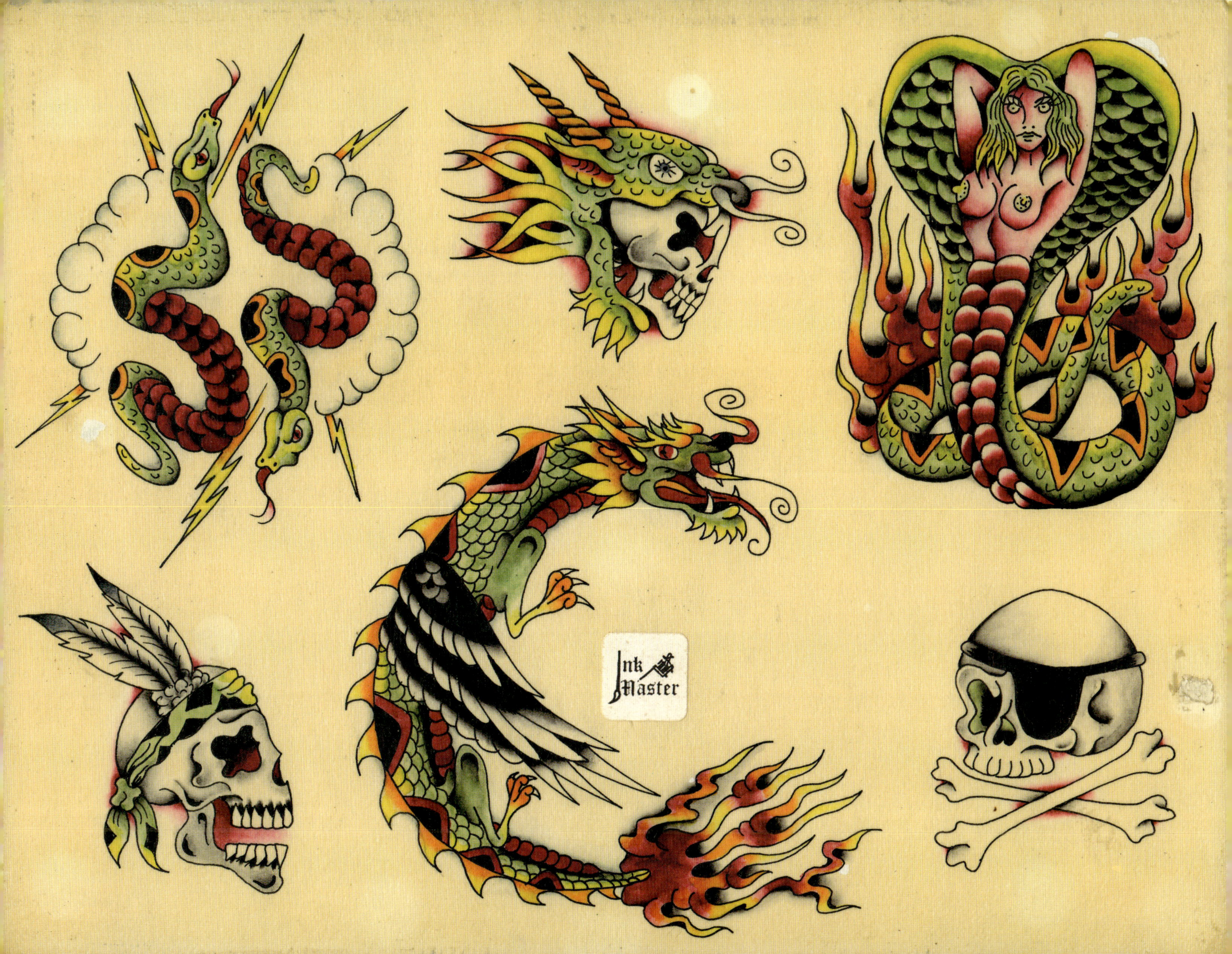
Ink Master

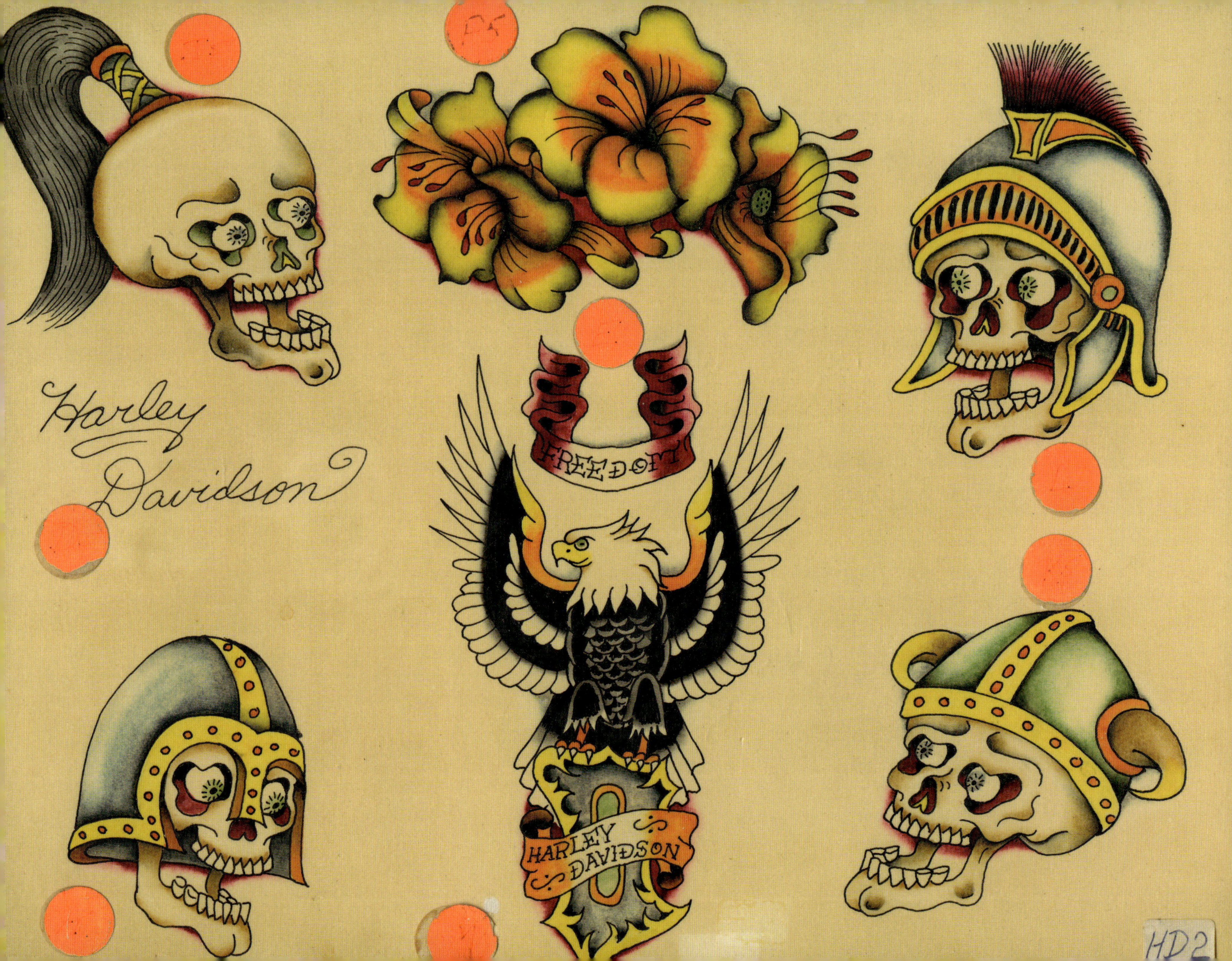
Harley Davidson
FREEDOM
HARLEY DAVIDSON
HD2

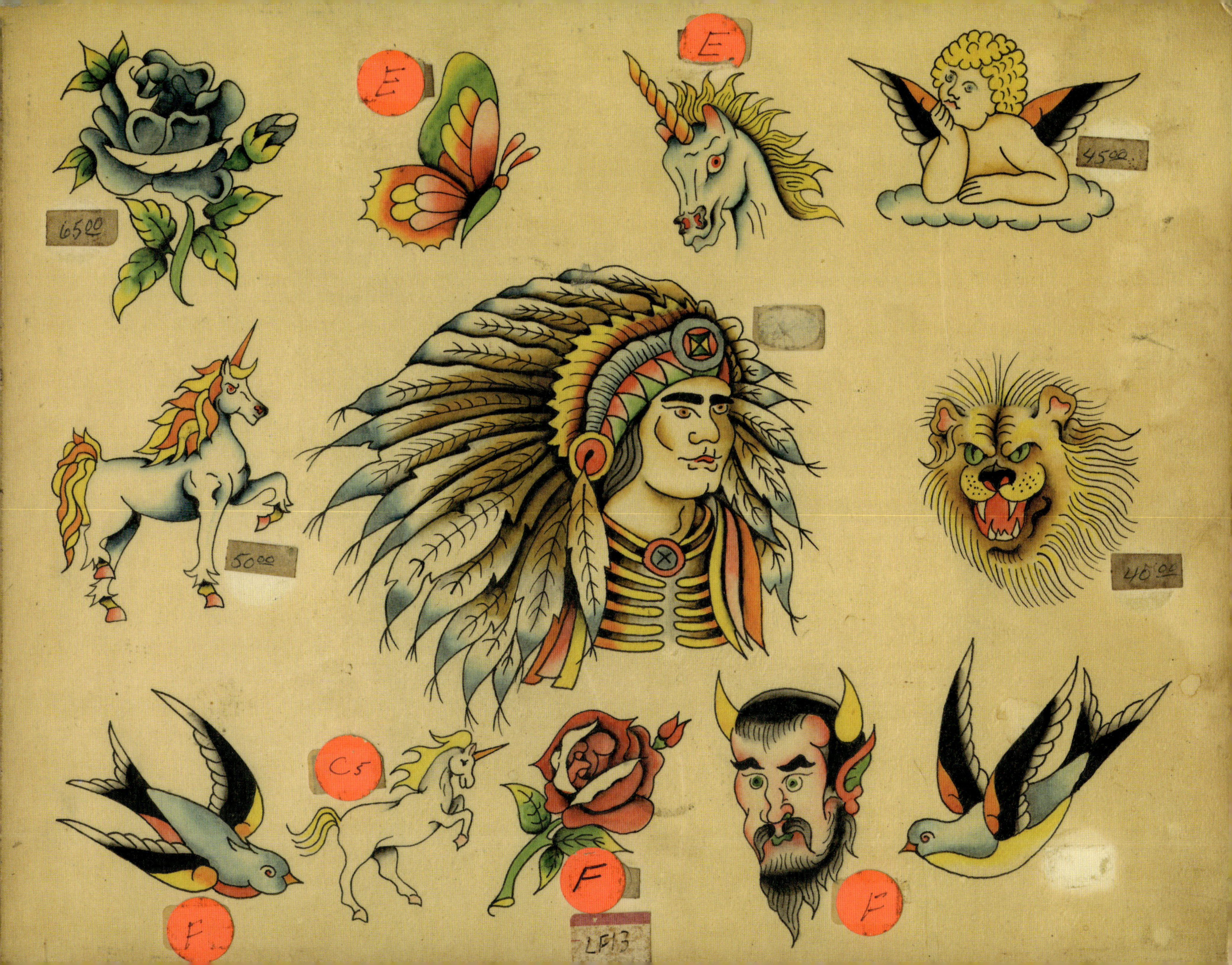

6500
E
E
4500
5000
4000
C5
F
F
F
F
LF13

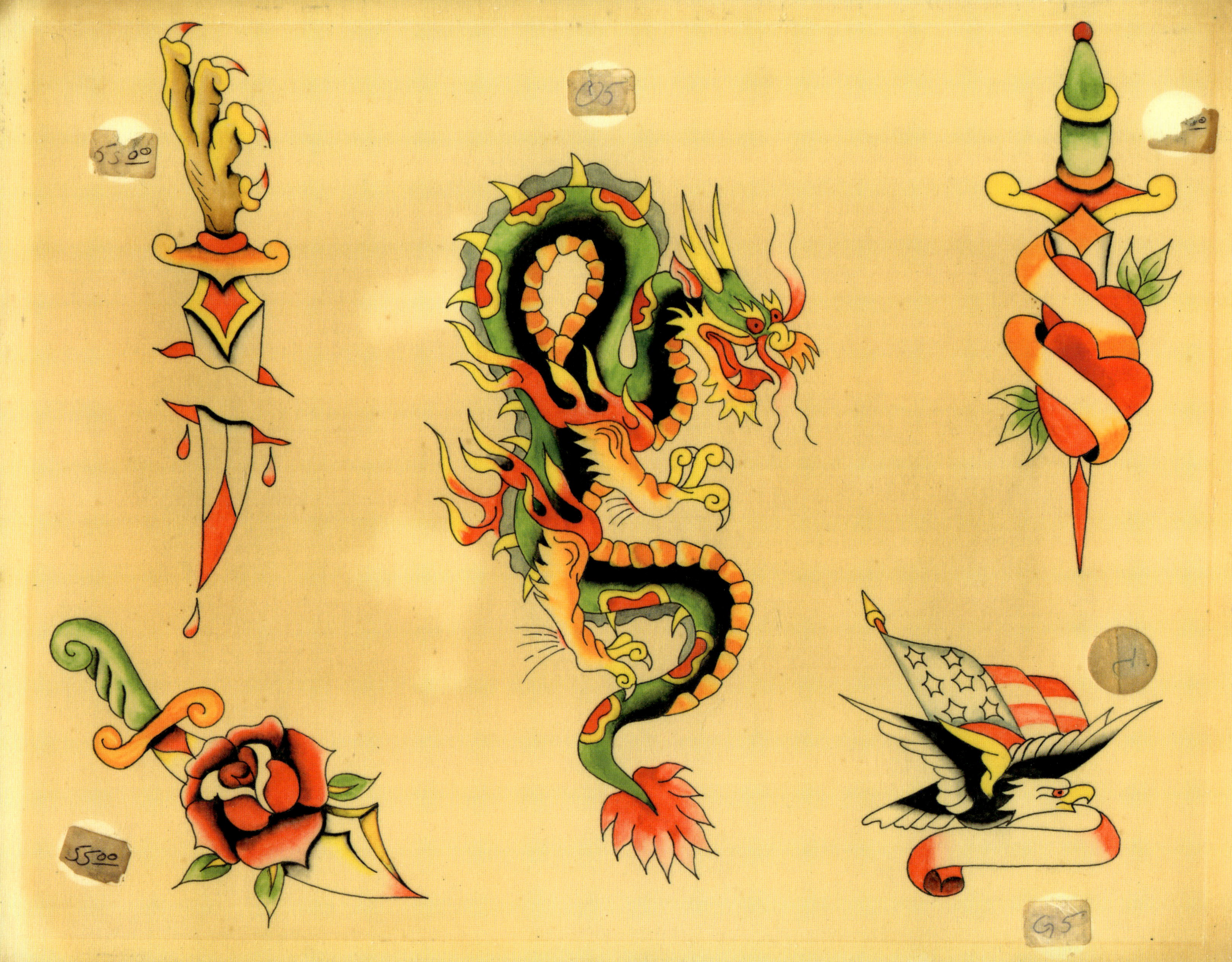
5500
5500
G5

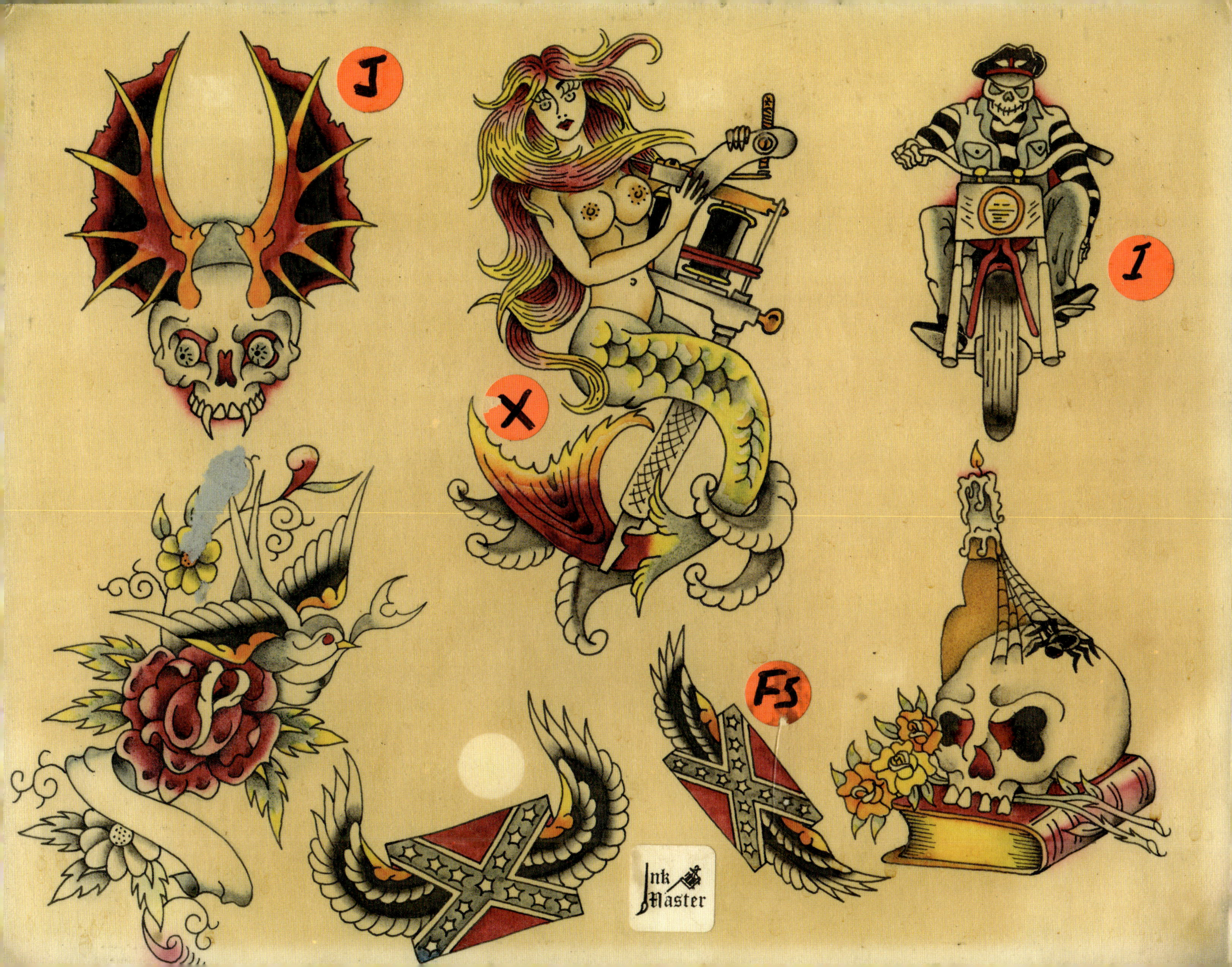
J
X
I
FS
Ink Master

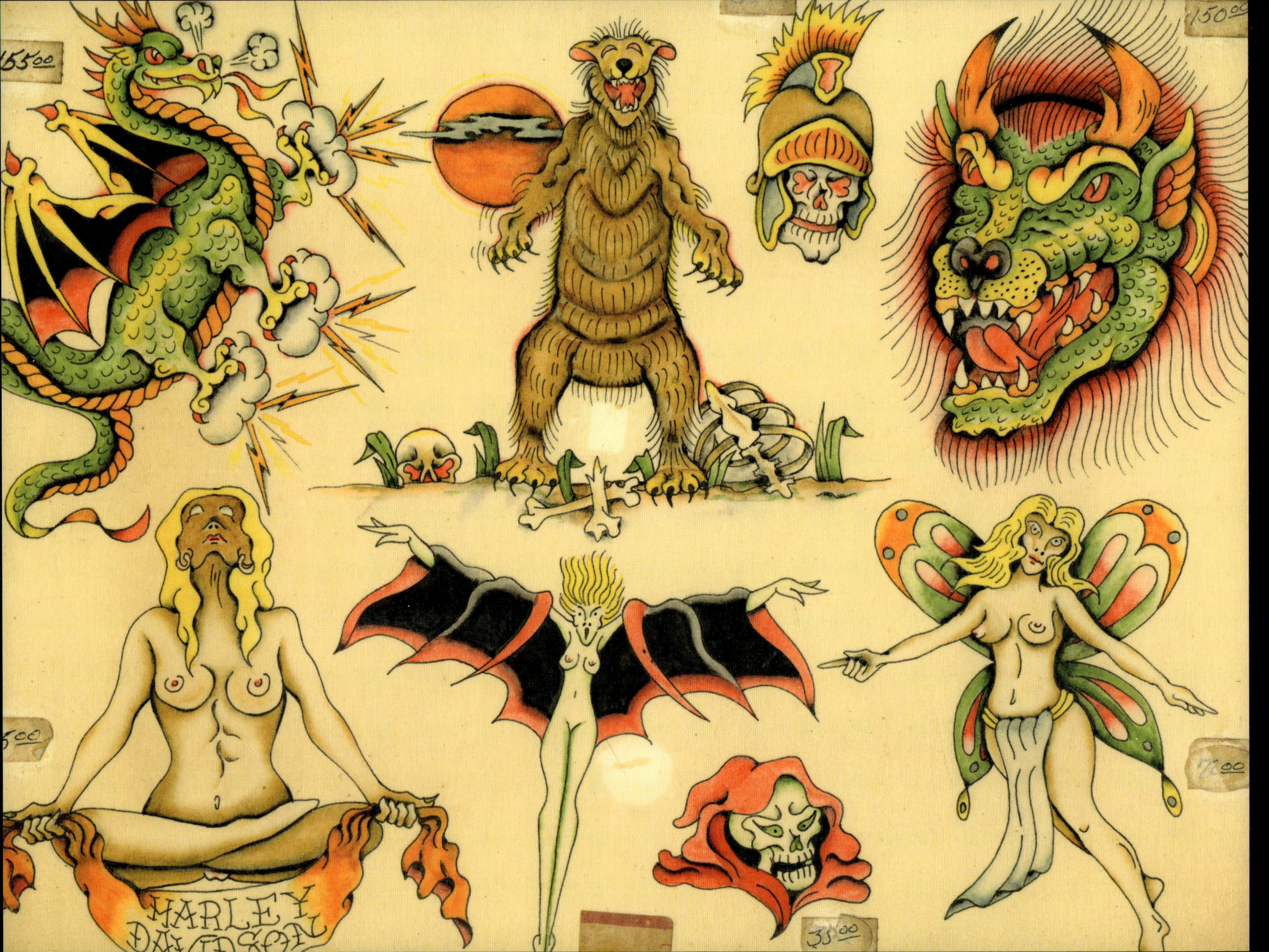
155 00
150 00
HARLEY
DAVIDSON
35 00

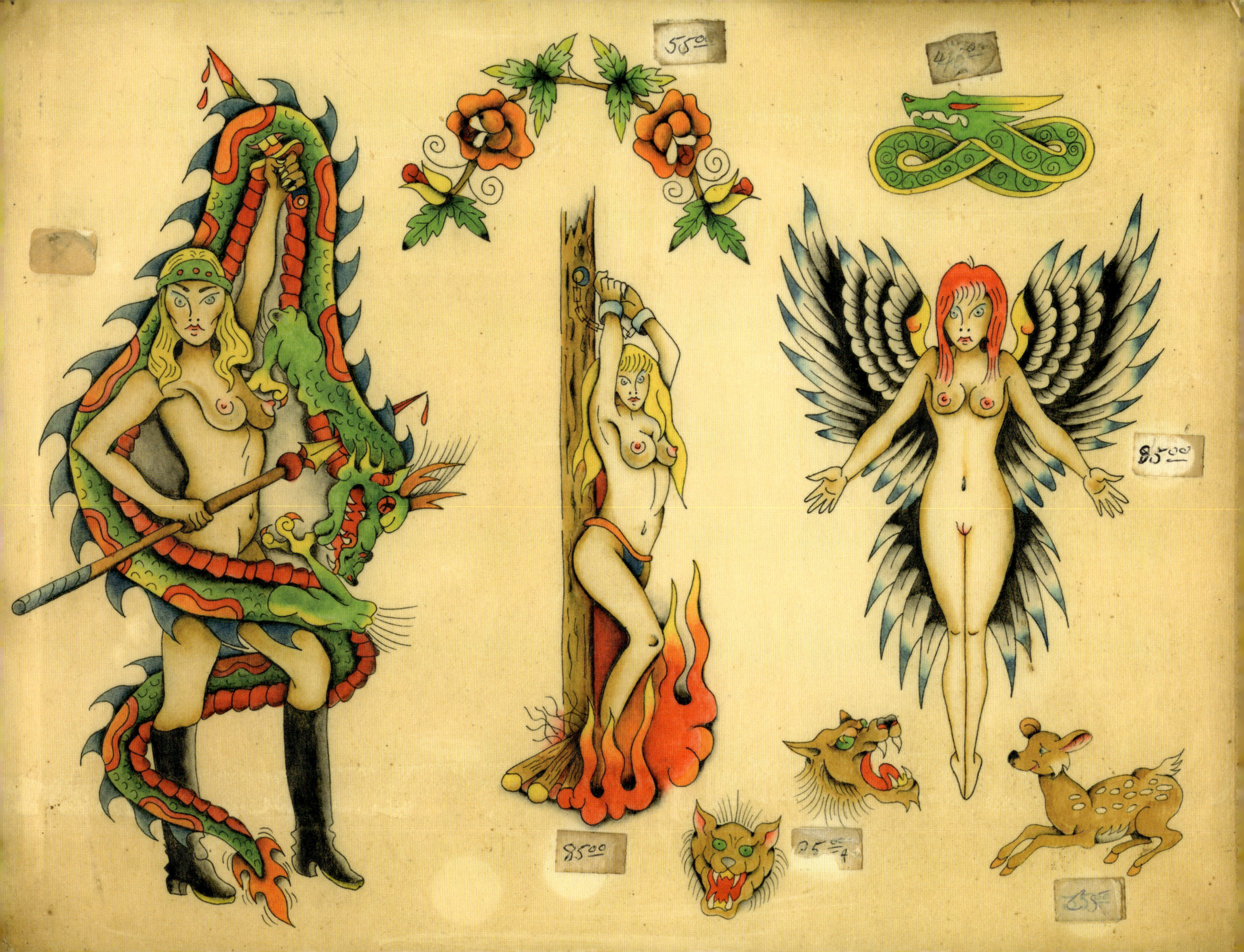

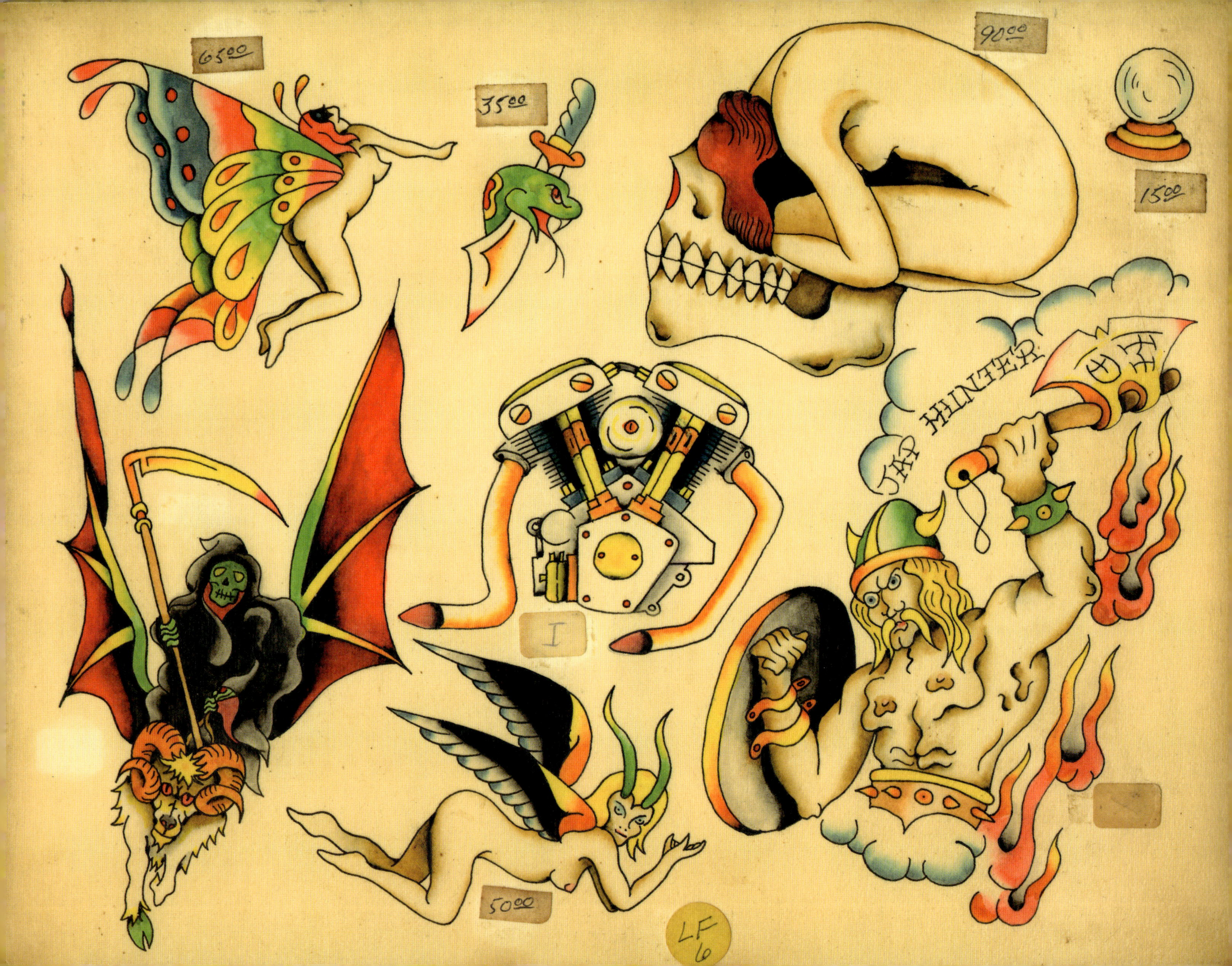

65.00
35.00
90.00
15.00
JAP HUNTER
I
50.00
LF 6

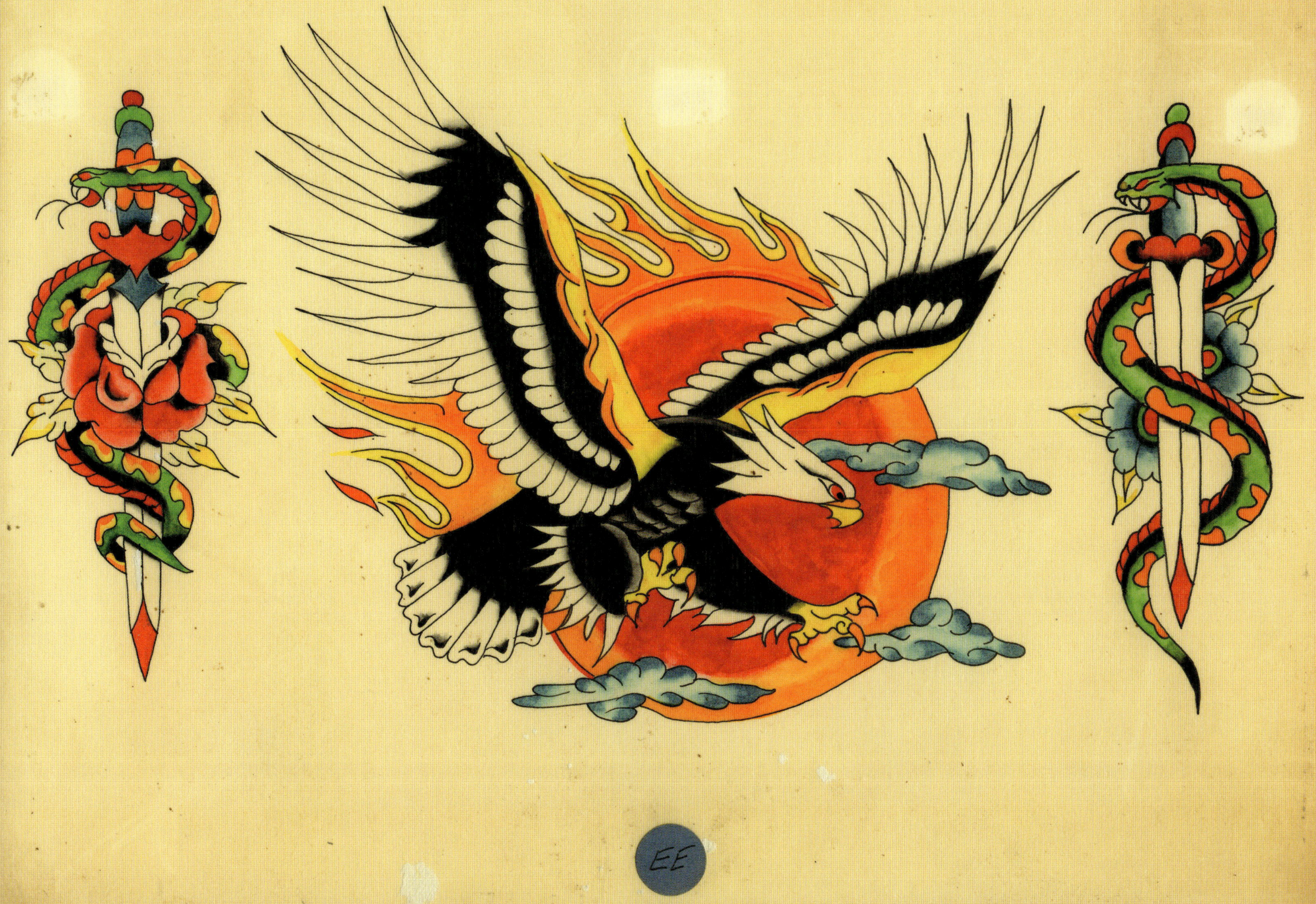

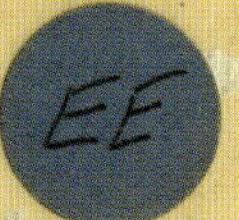
EE

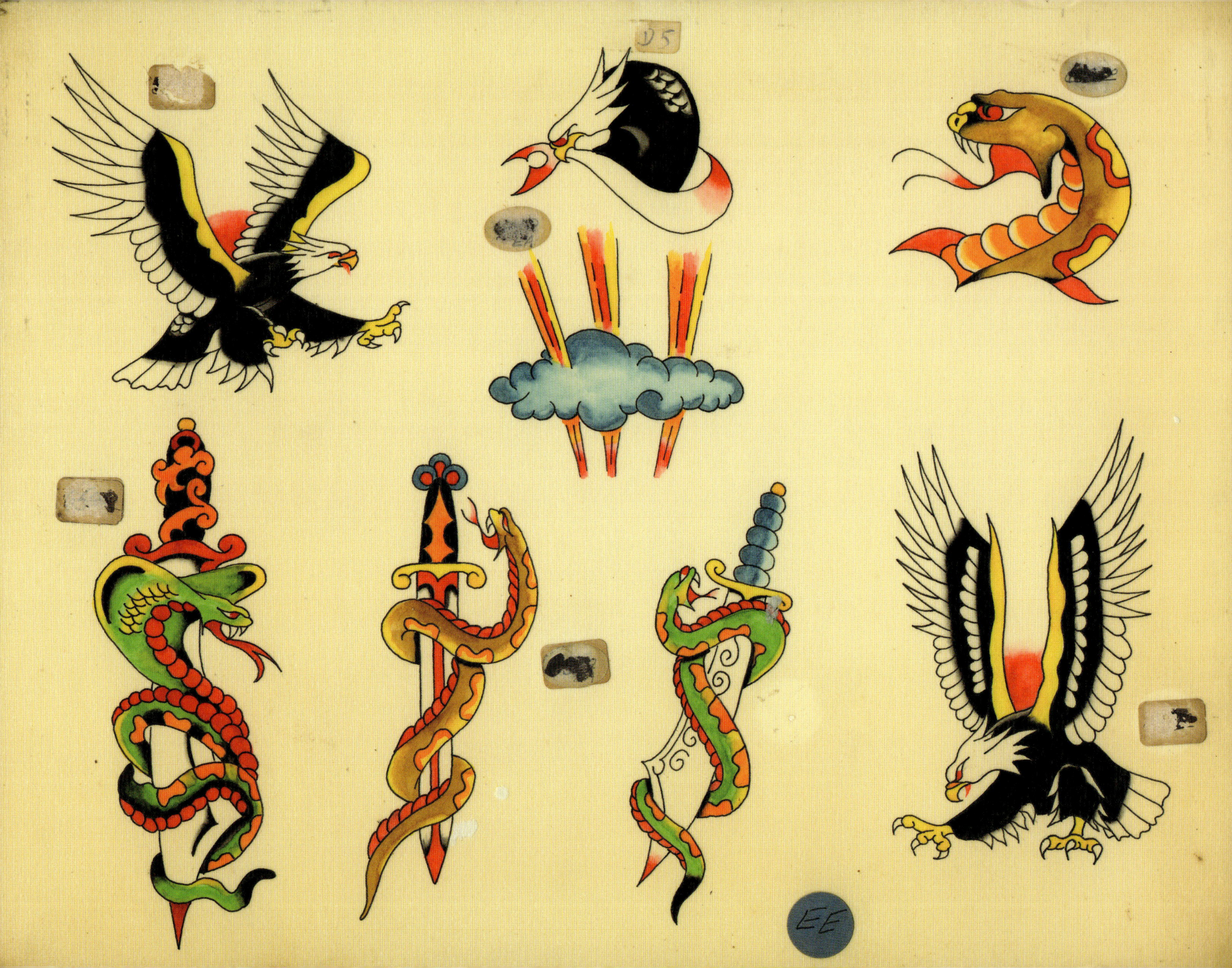
D5
EE

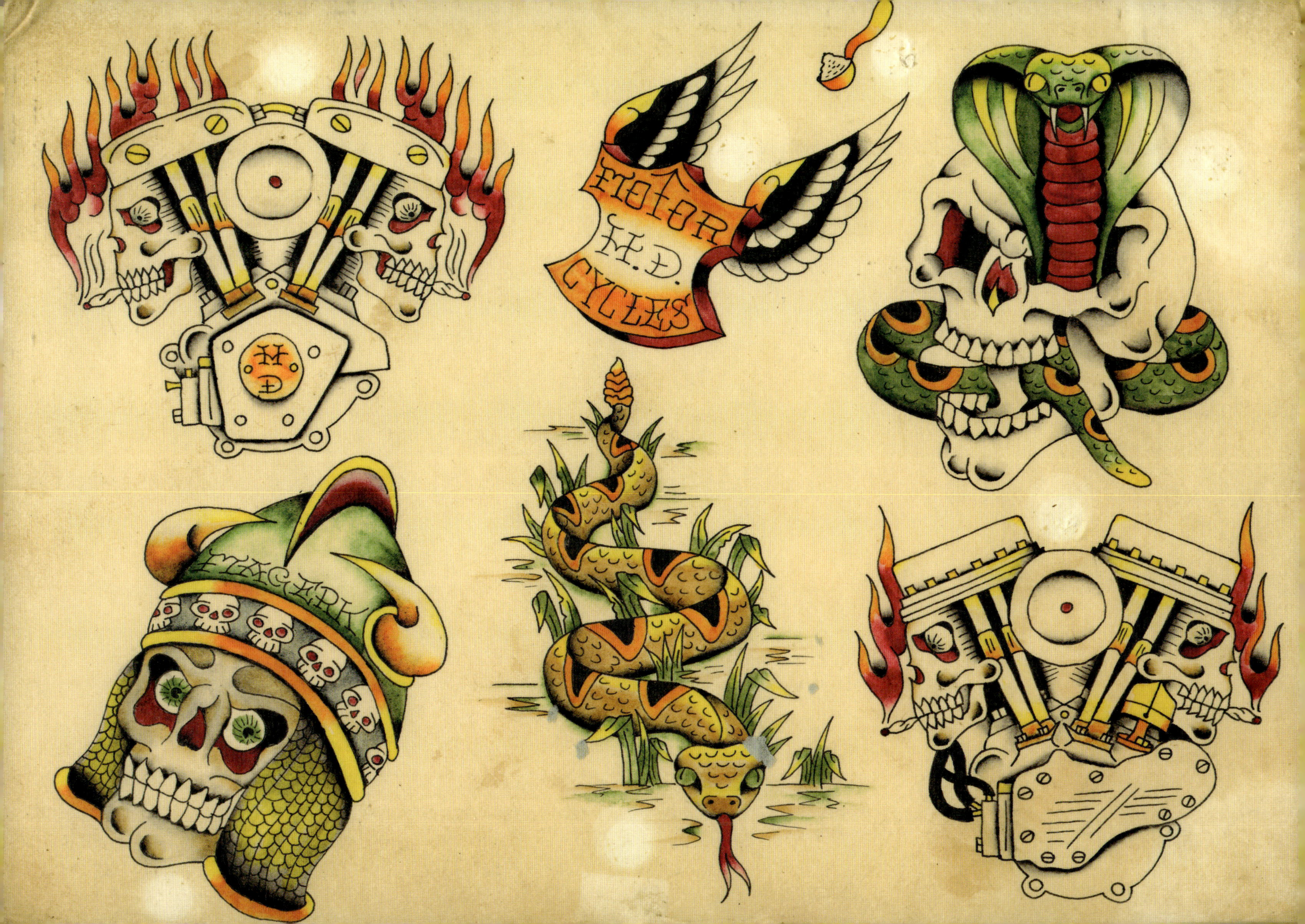
MOTOR
H.D.
CYCLES

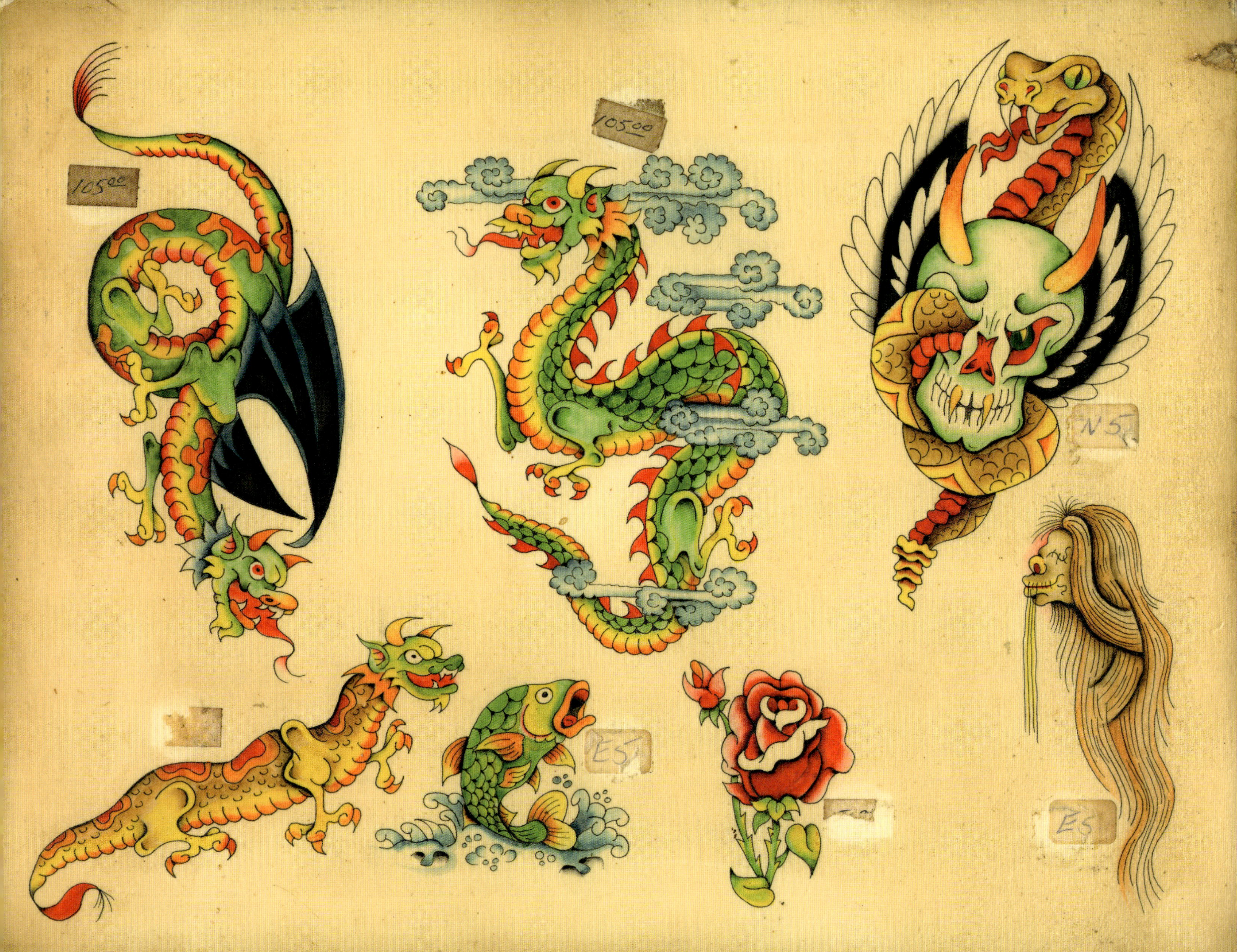
105^{00}
105^{00}
N5
E5
E5

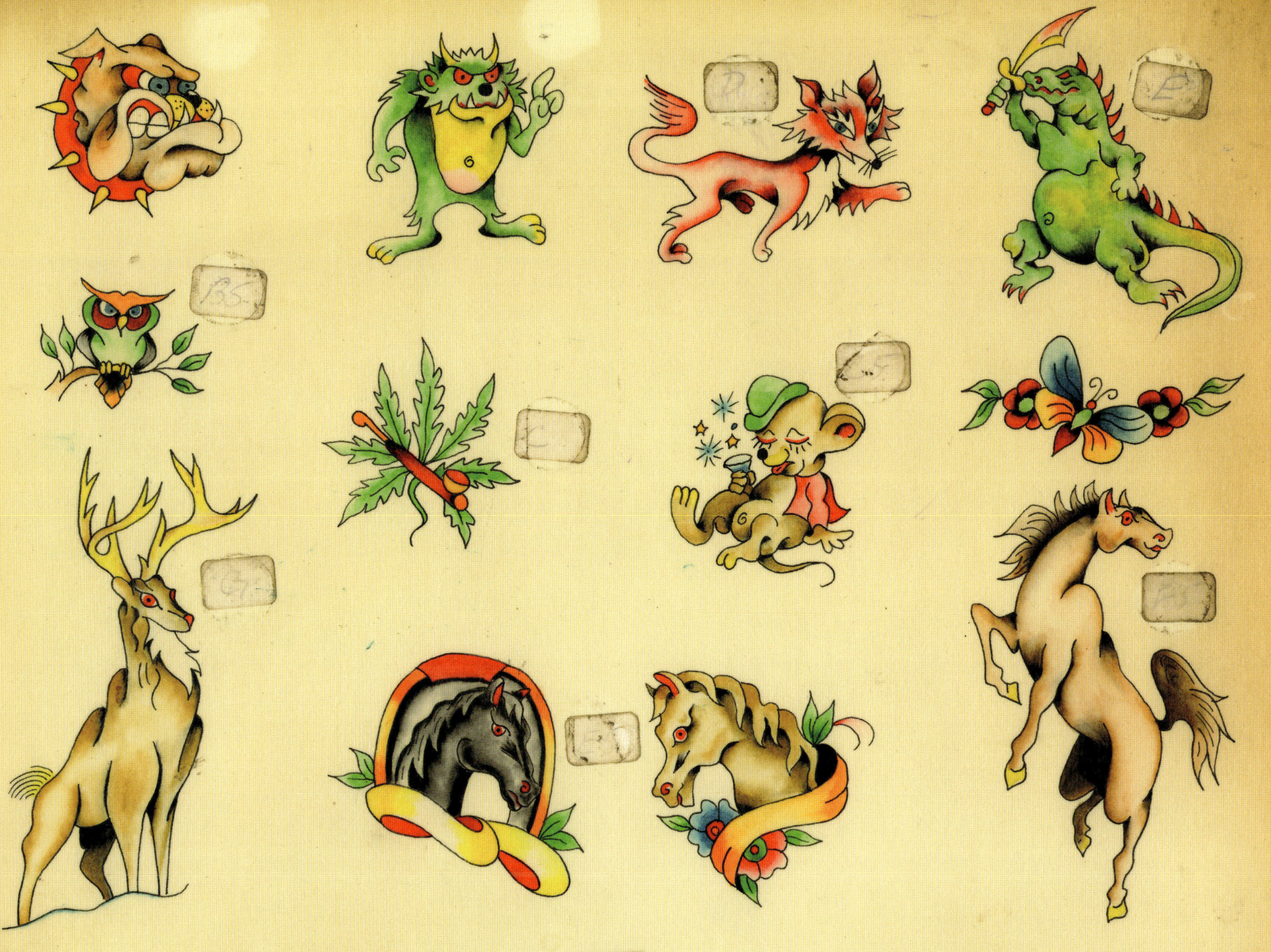
SM 5

FTY NUTS

35.00

45.00

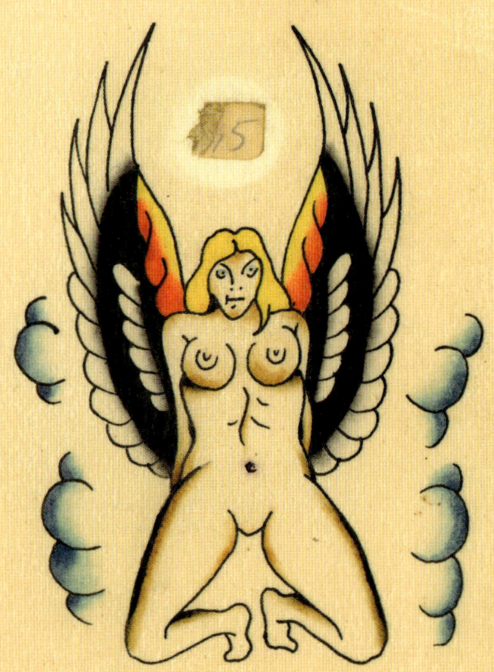

80.00

LF 7

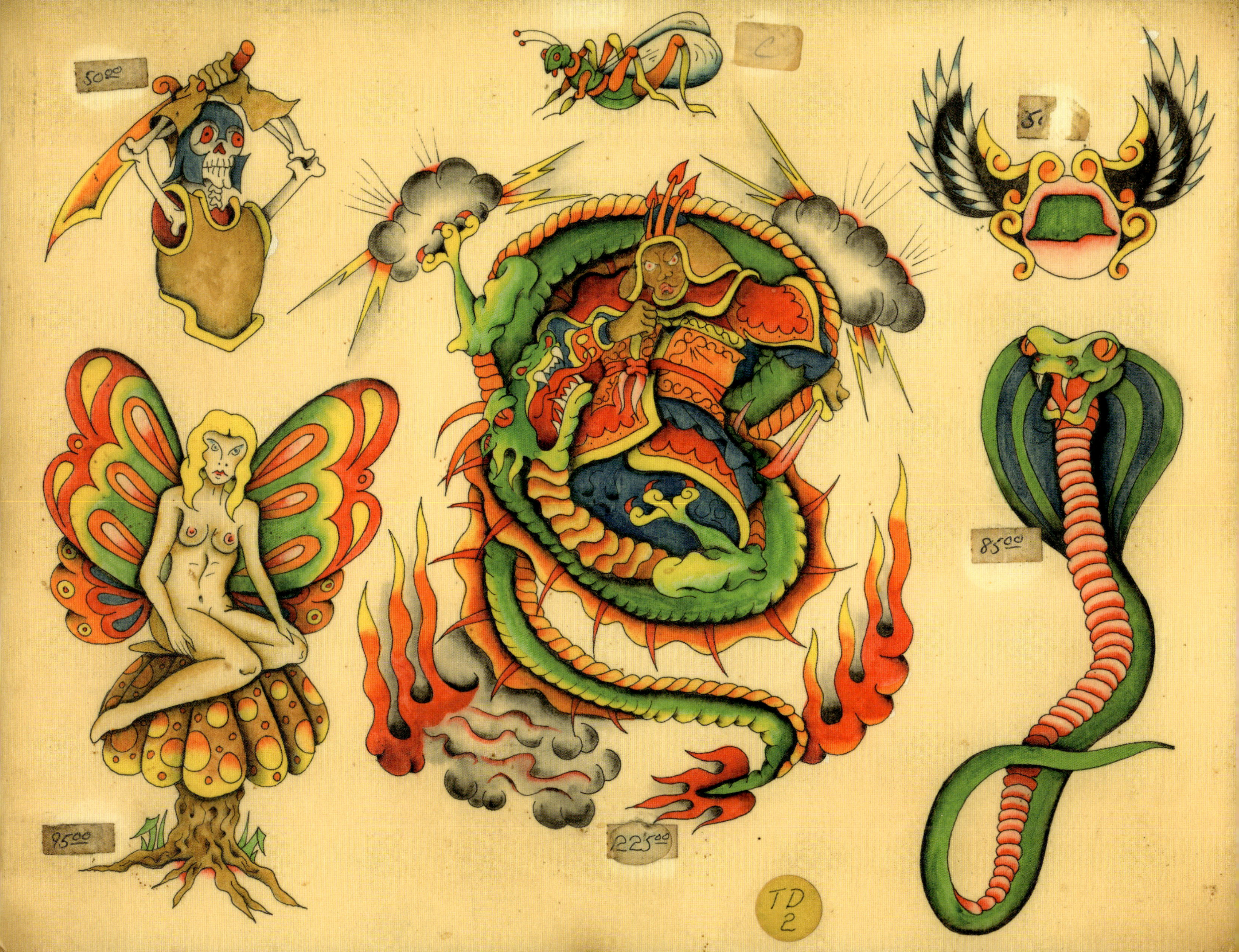

50.00
C
85.00
95.00
225.00
TD
2

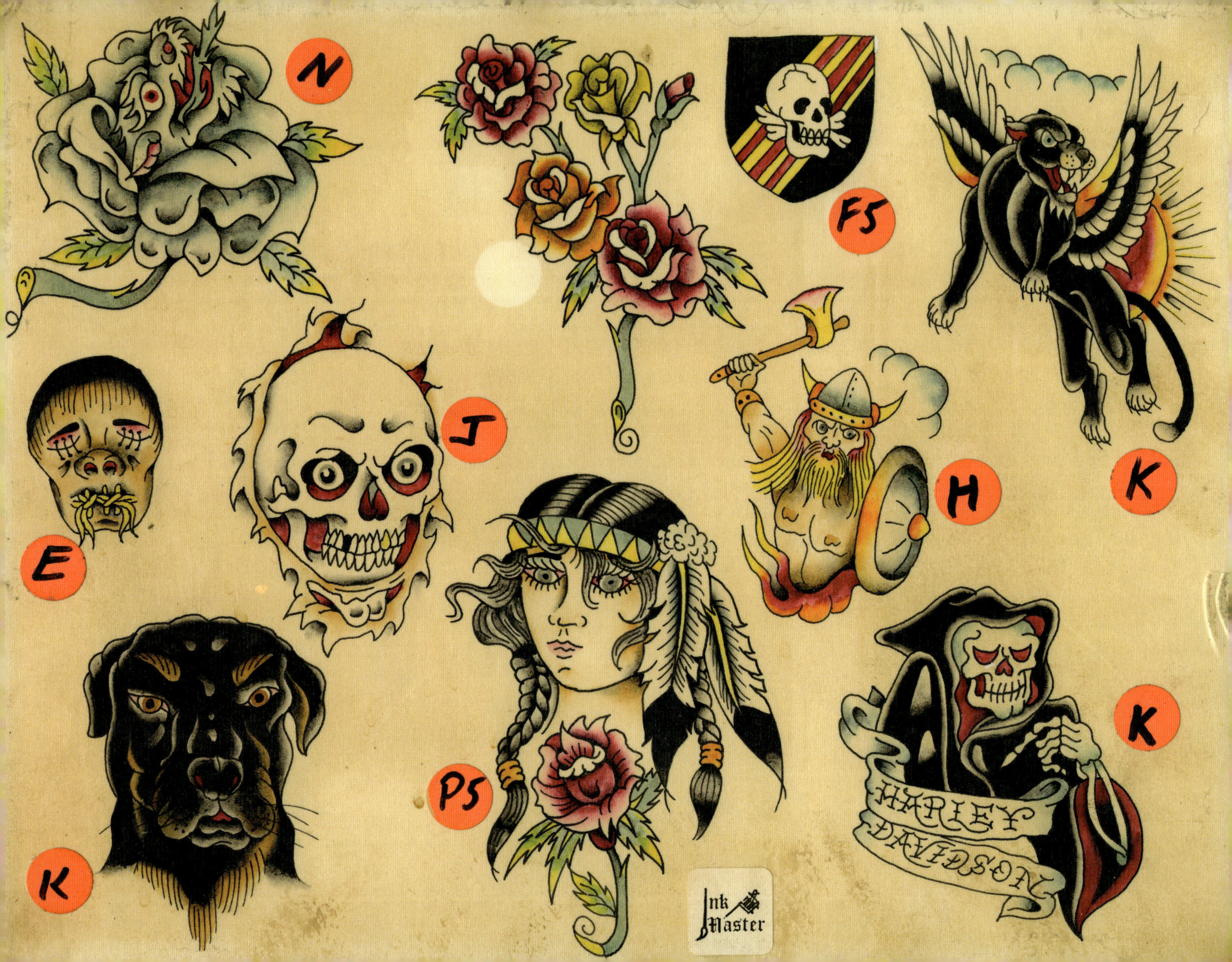

N
F5
J
H
K
E
K
P5
HARLEY
DAVIDSON
Ink Master

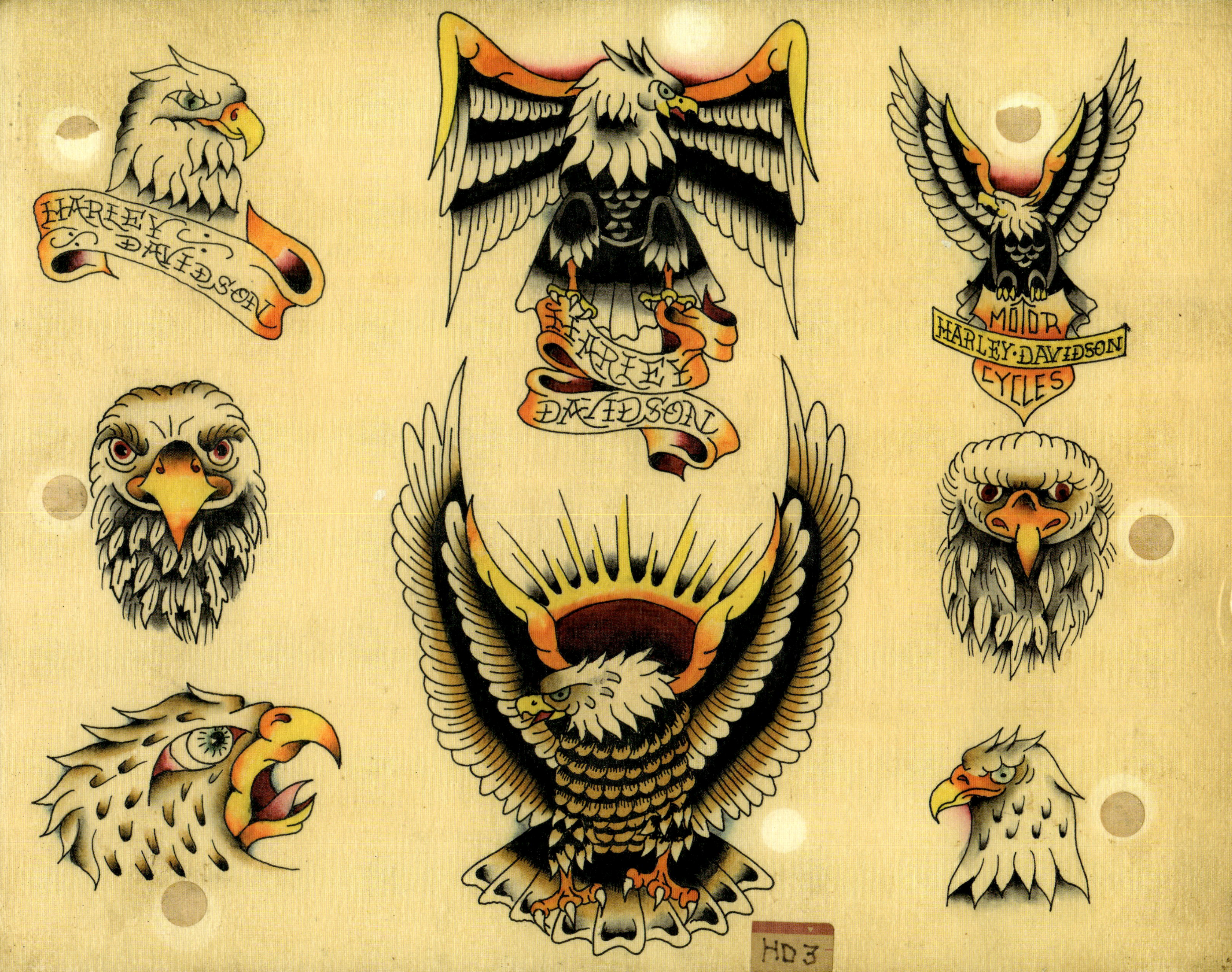
HARLEY DAVIDSON
HARLEY DAVIDSON
MOTOR
HARLEY·DAVIDSON
CYCLES
HD3

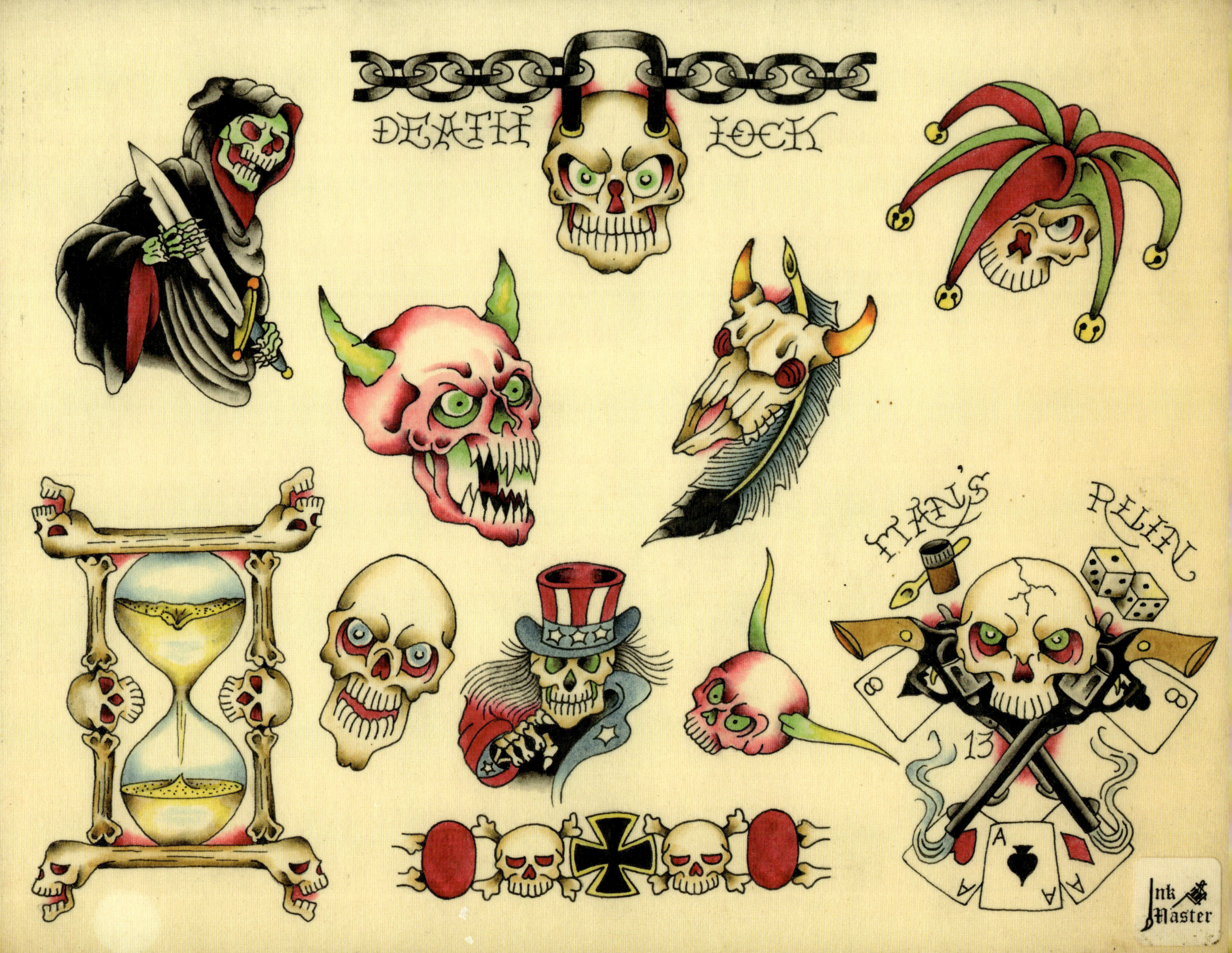
DEATH LOCK
MAN'S RUIN
13
Ink Master

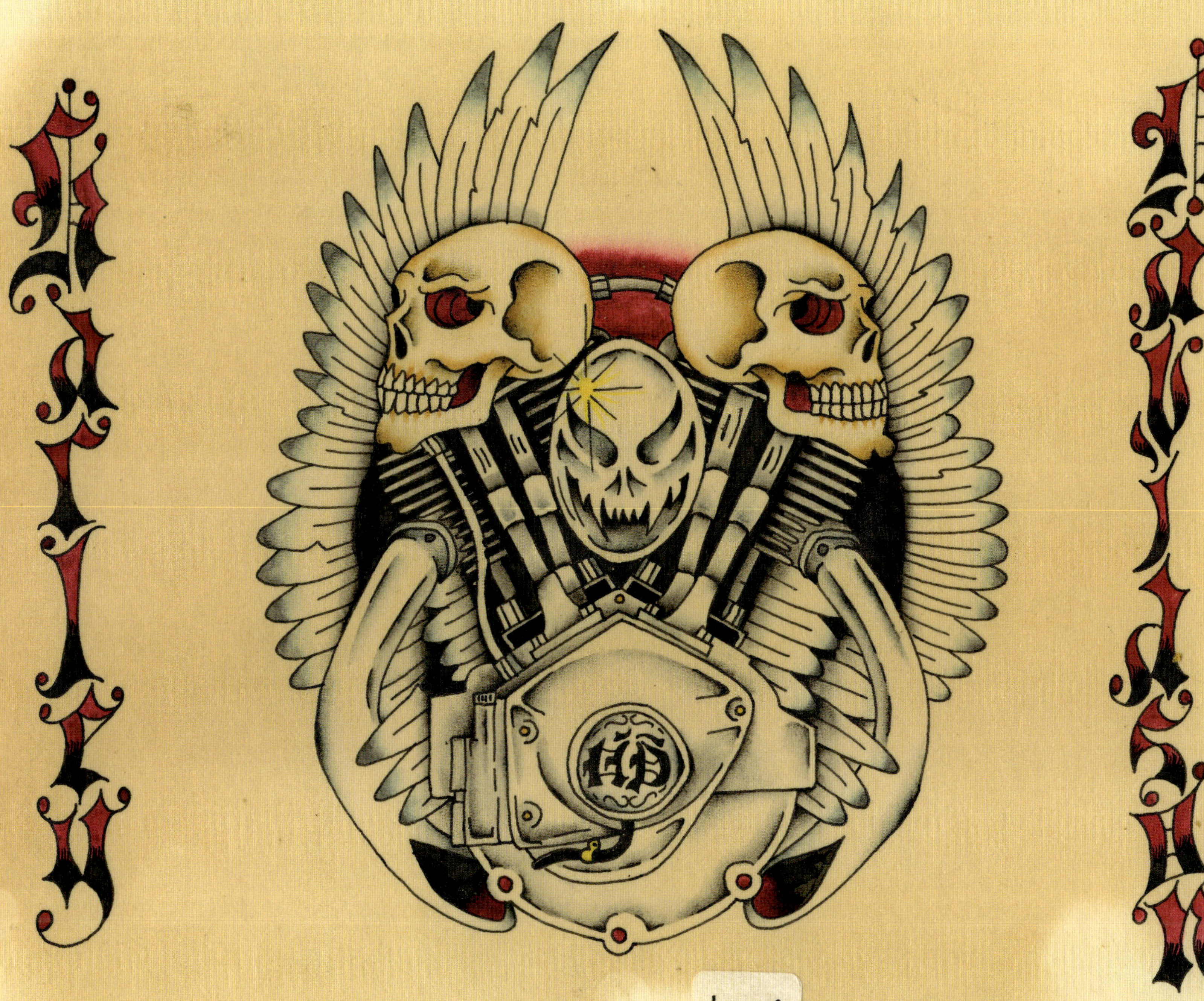
Harley
Davidson
Ink Master

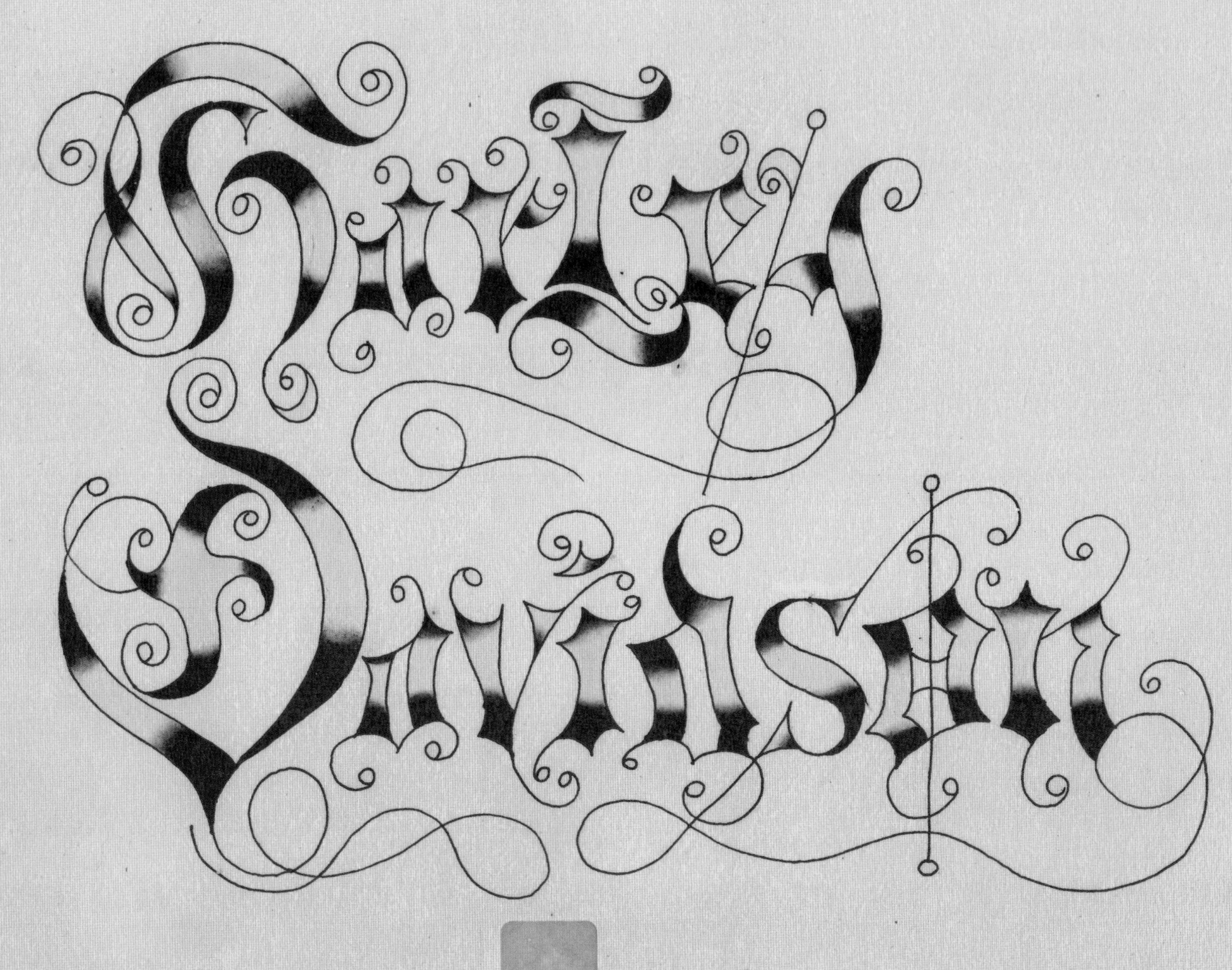

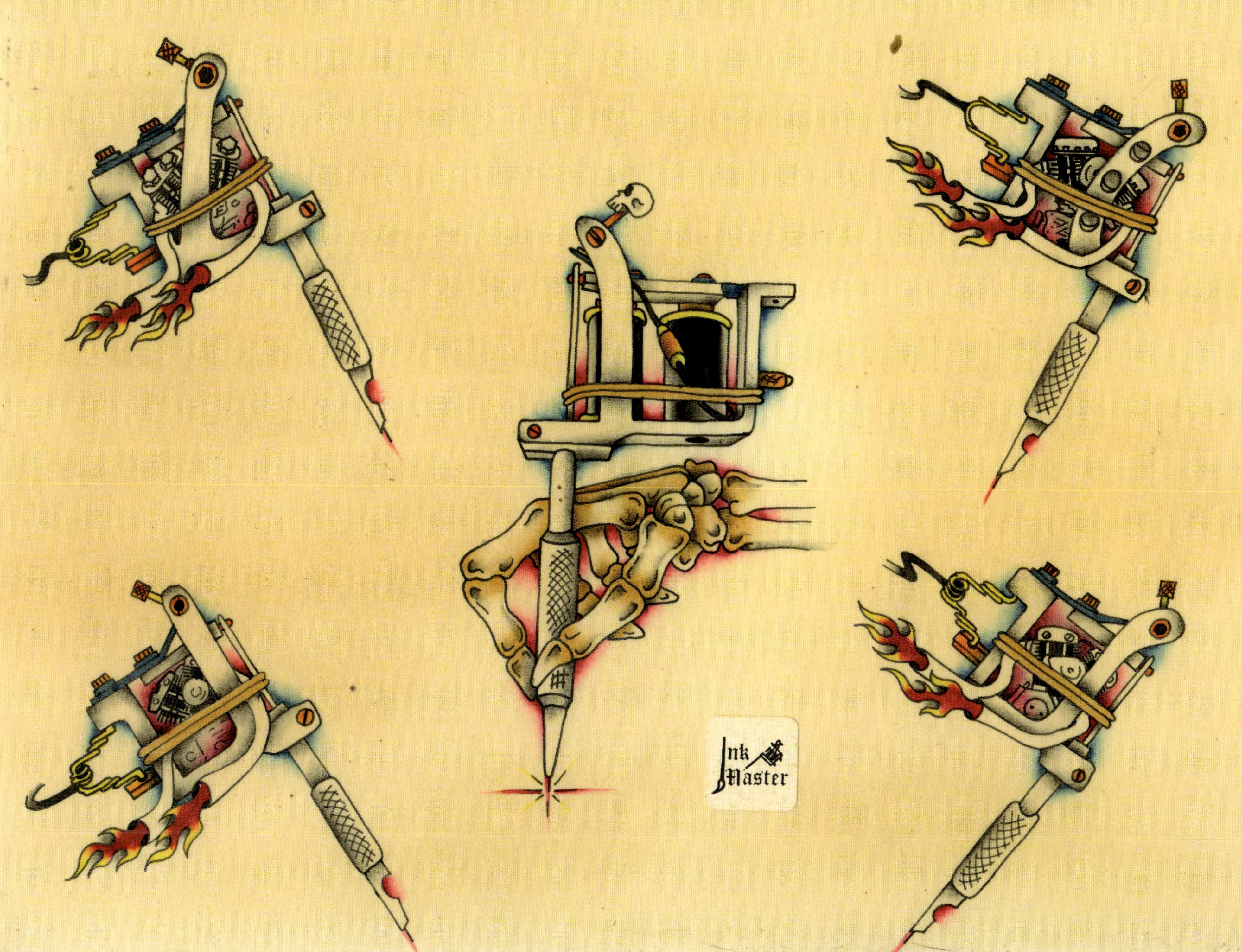
Ink
Master

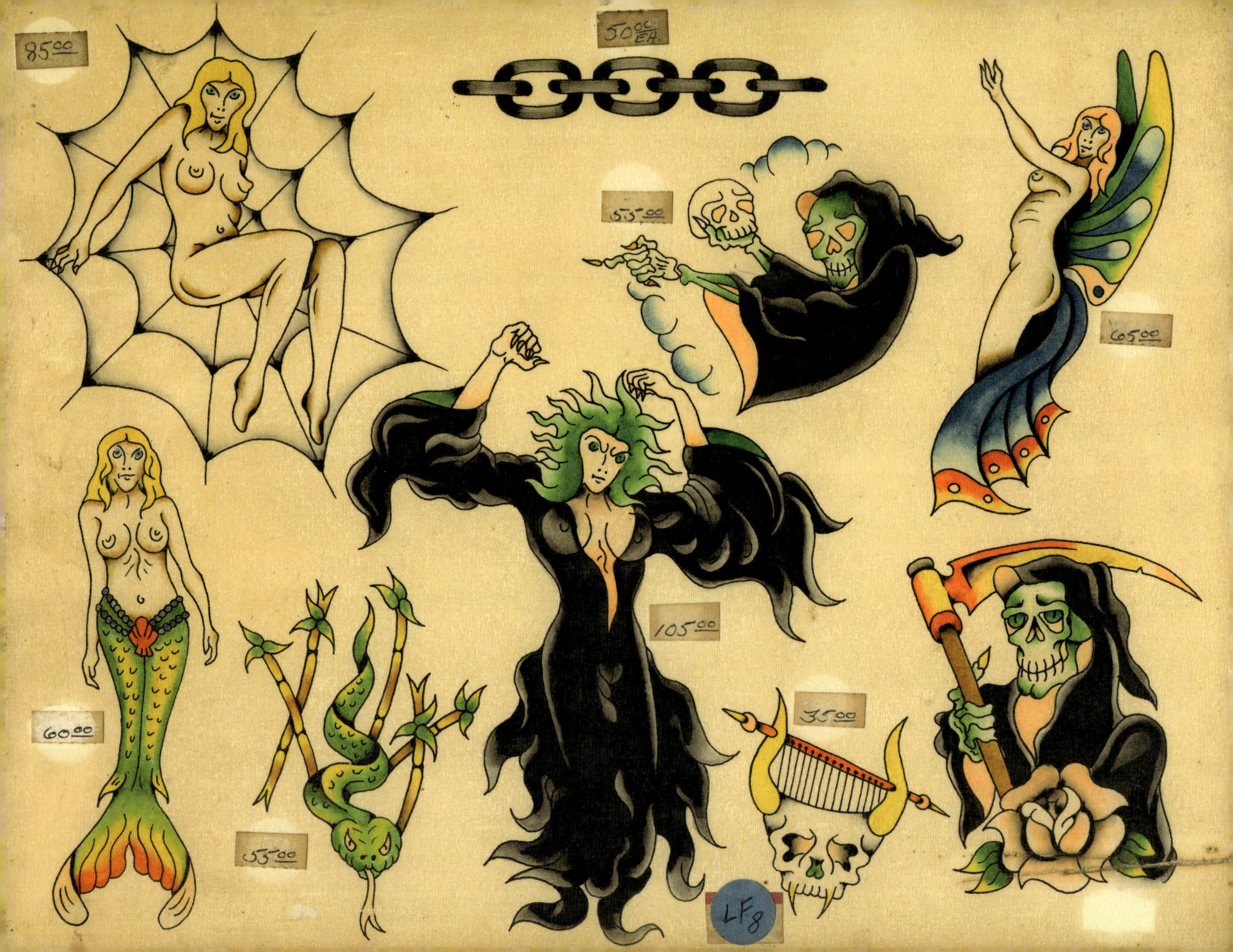
85.00
50.00 EA
55.00
65.00
105.00
60.00
35.00
55.00
LF8

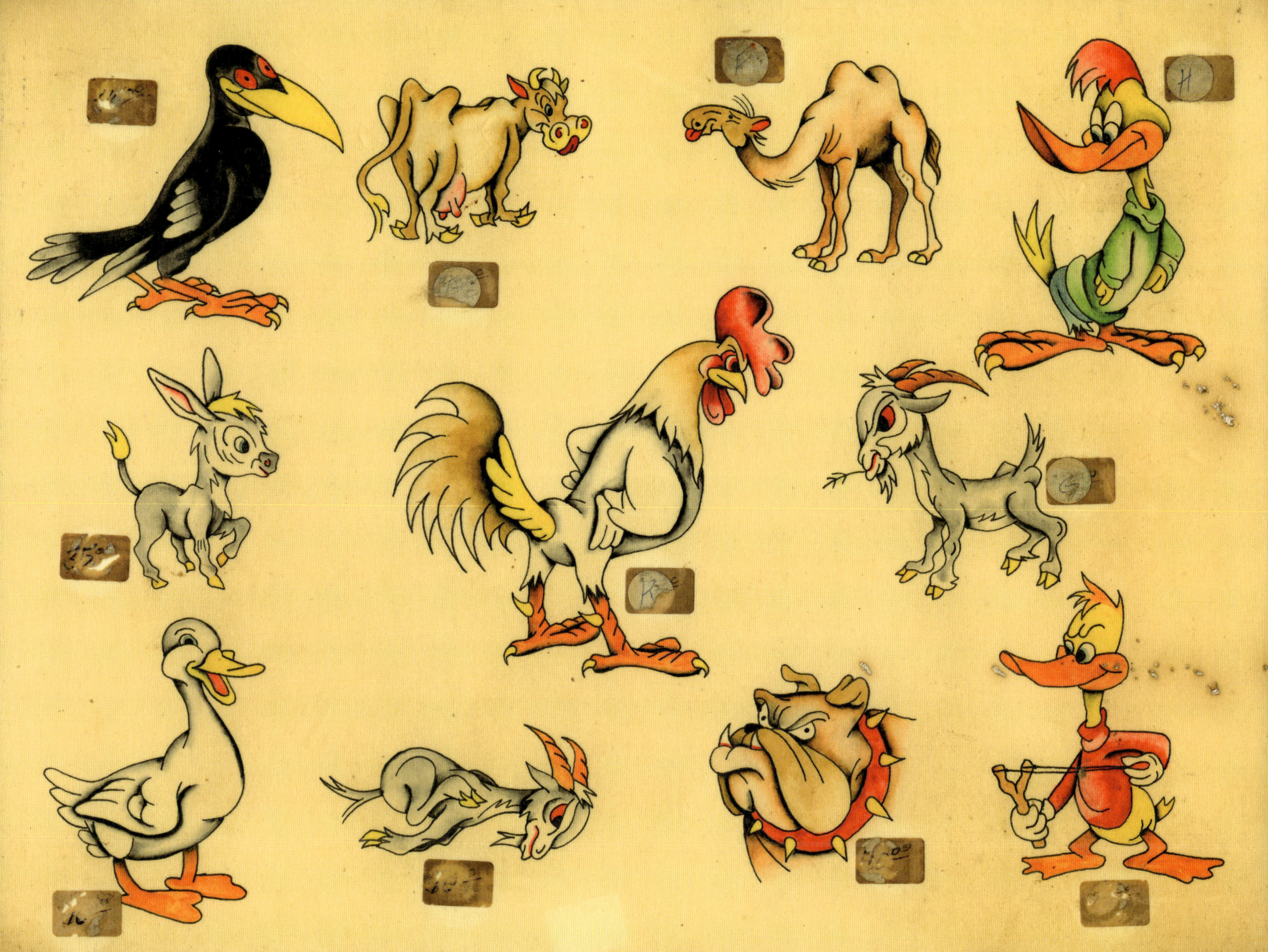

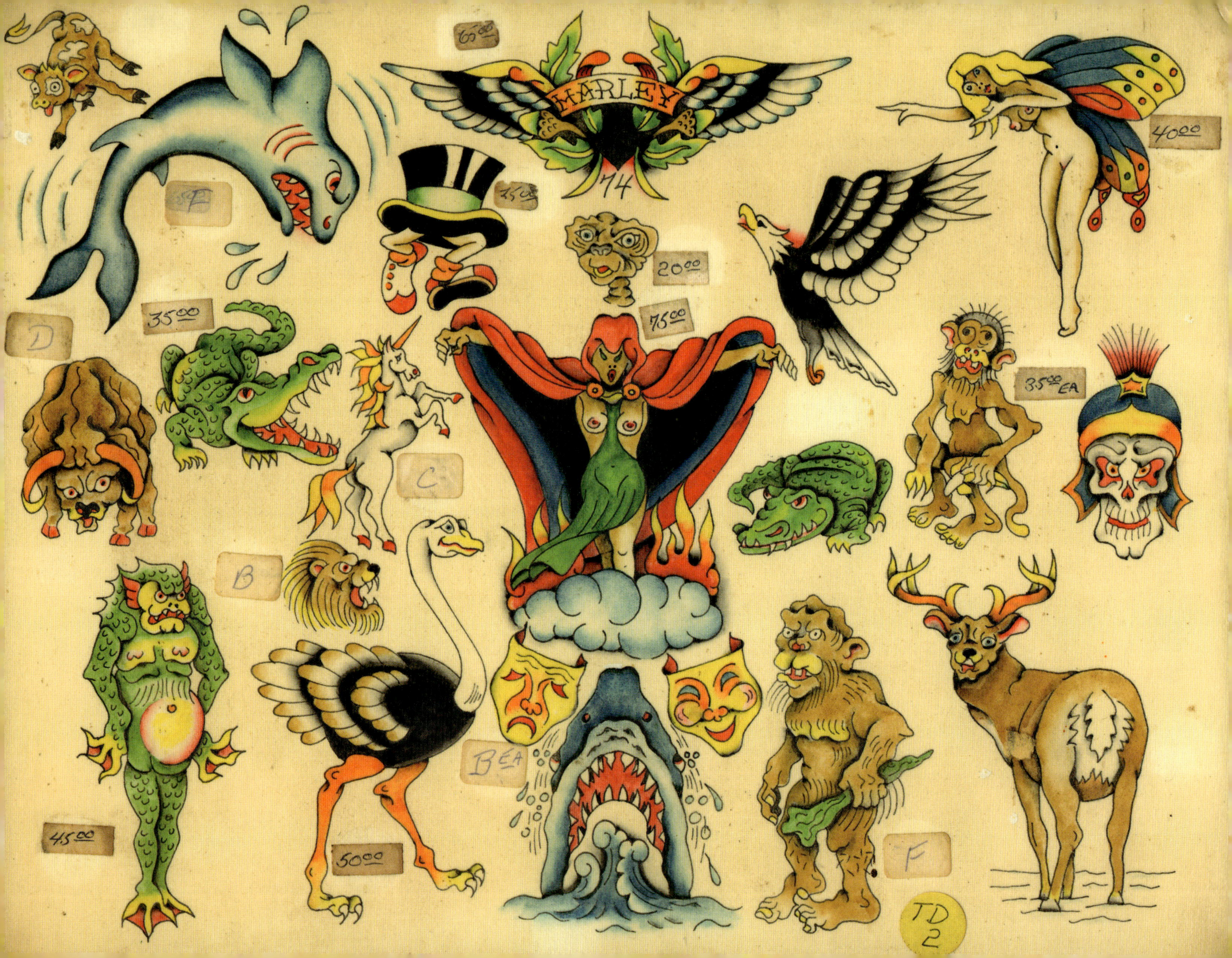
HARLEY
74
40.00
20.00
75.00
35.00
D
35.00 EA
C
B
45.00
50.00
B EA
F
TD
2

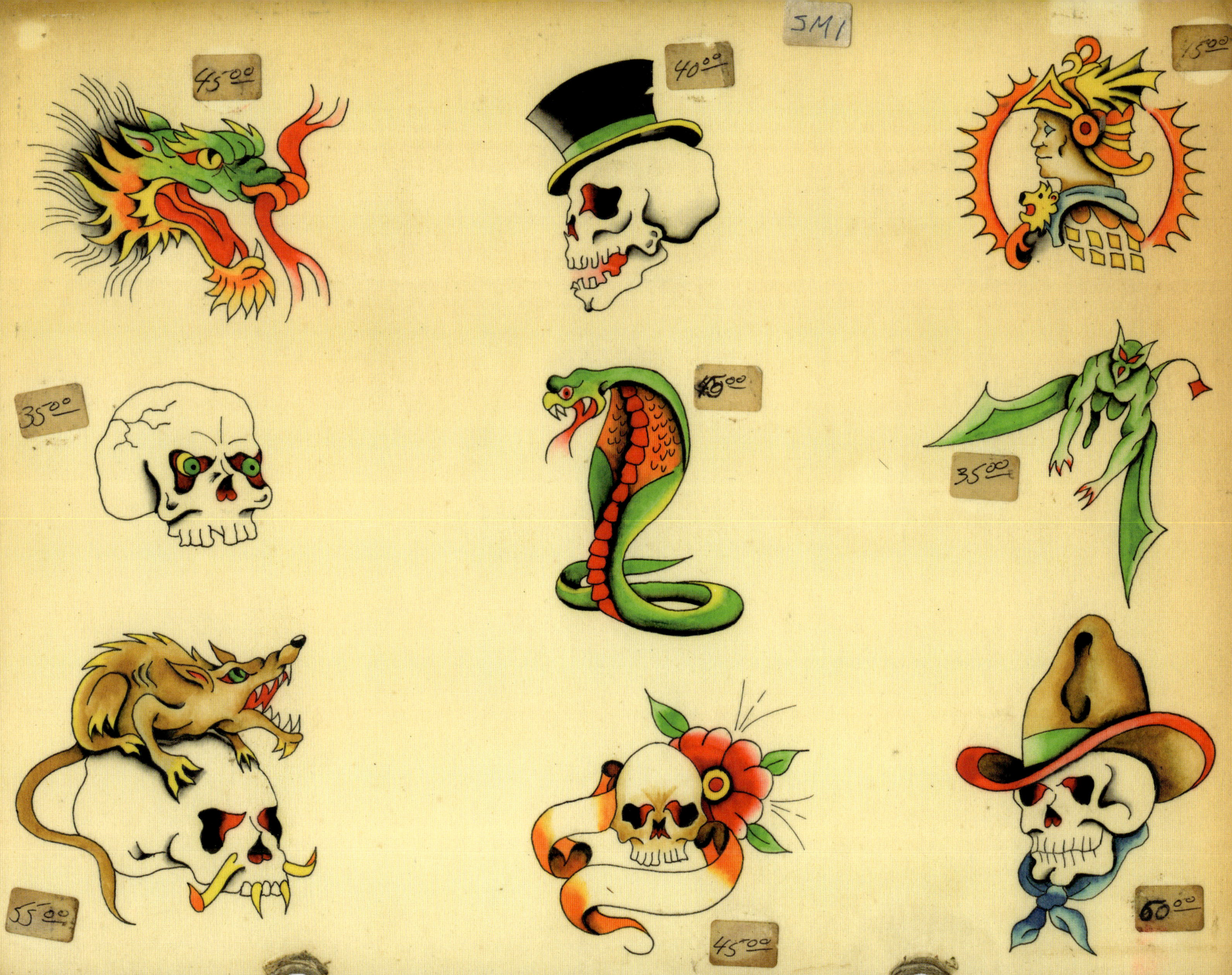
SM1
45 00
40 00
15 00
35 00
35 00
55 00
45 00
60 00

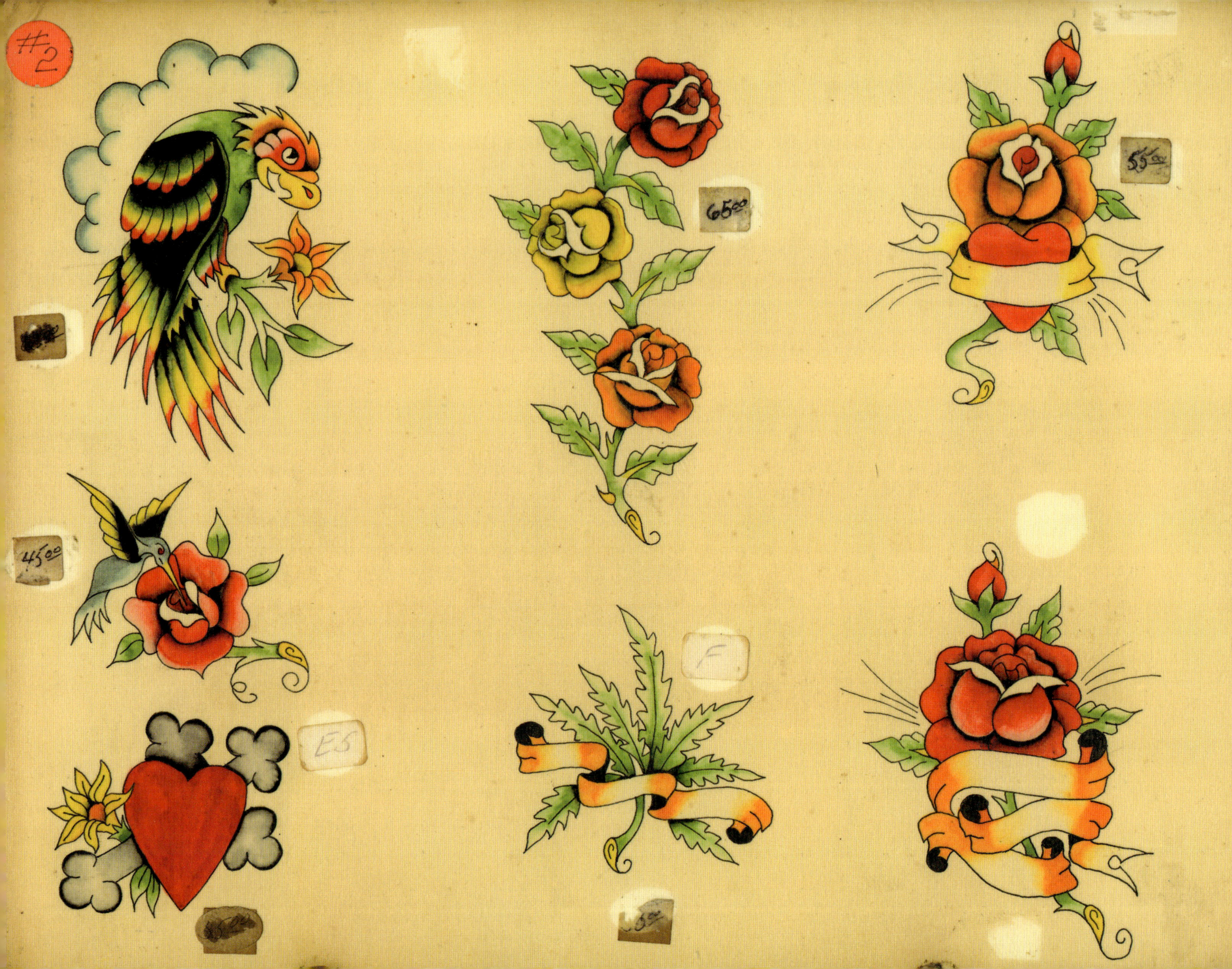
#2
6500
5500
4500
F
ES

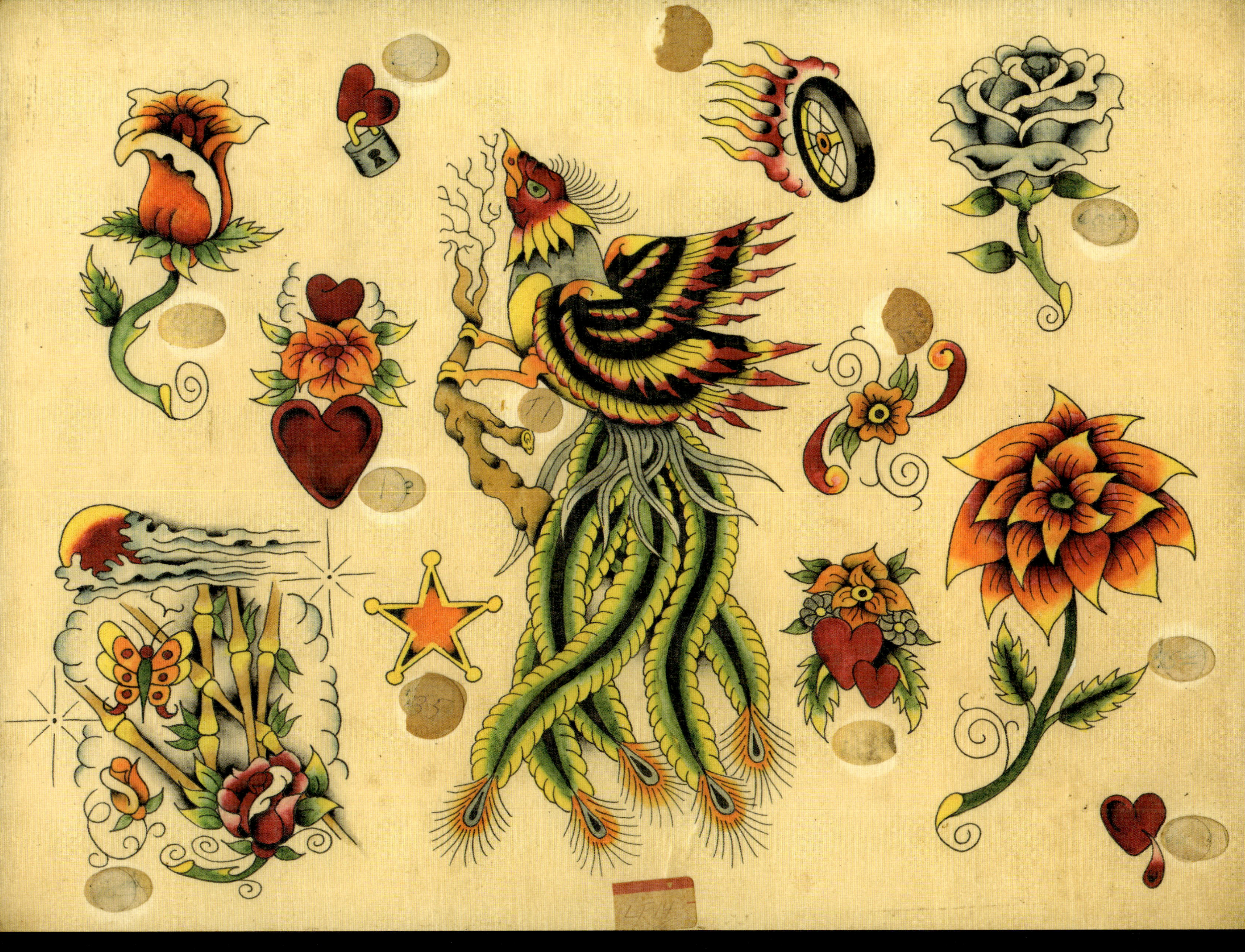

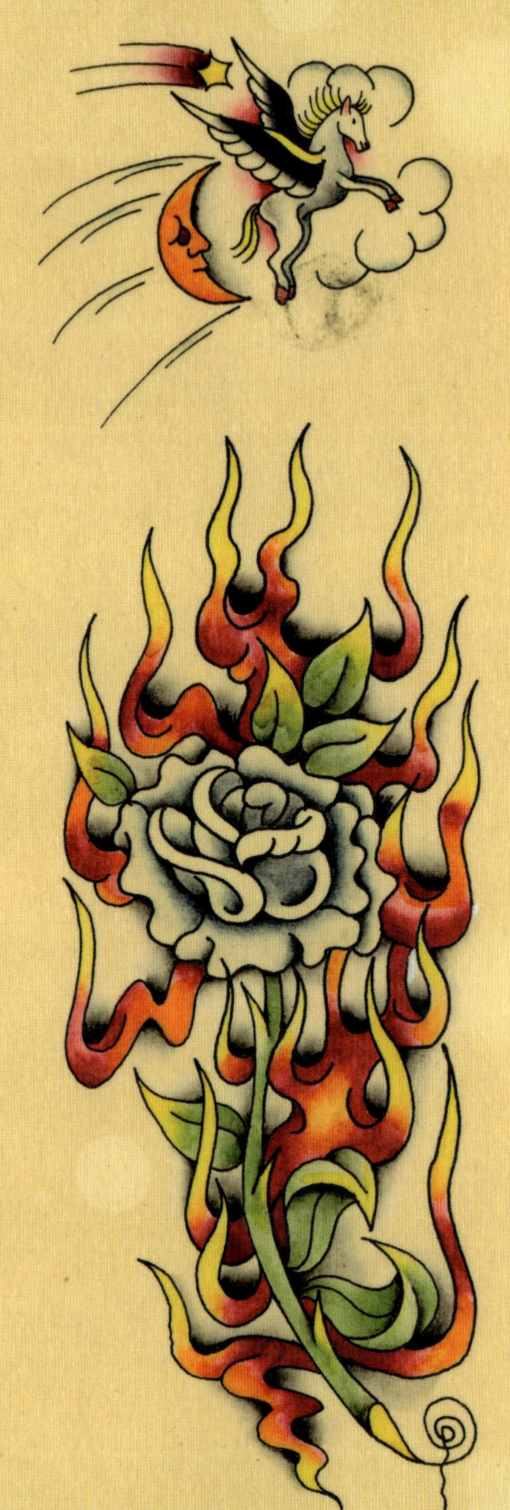

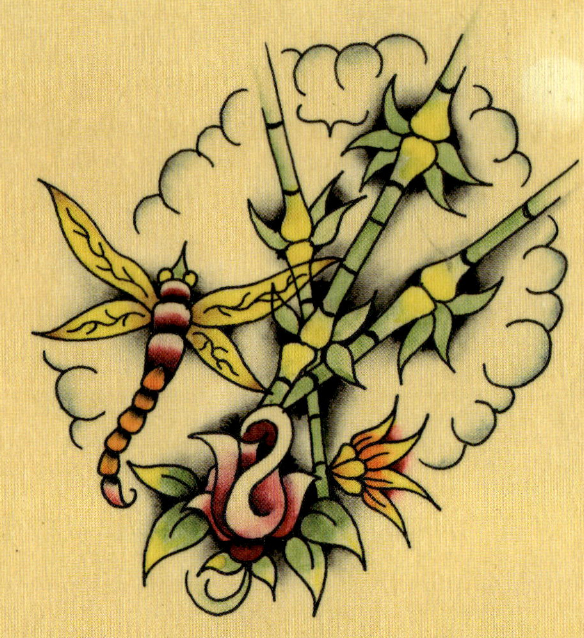

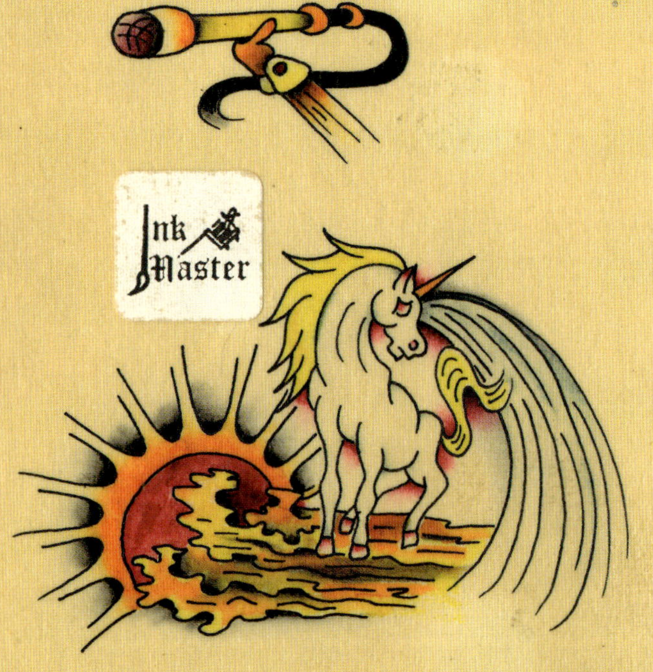
Ink Master

40.00

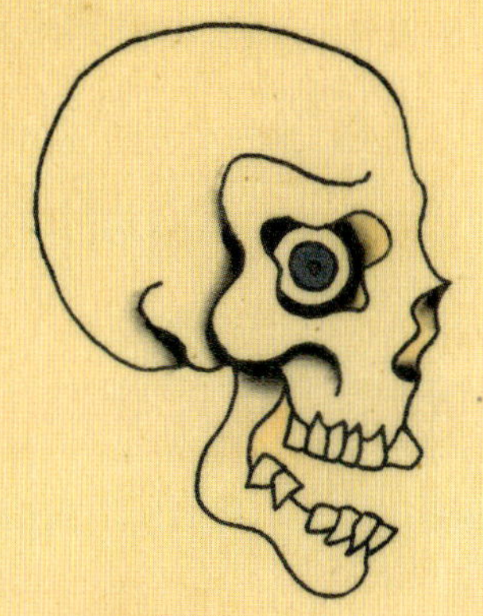

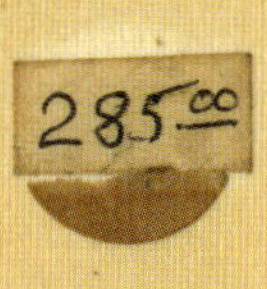

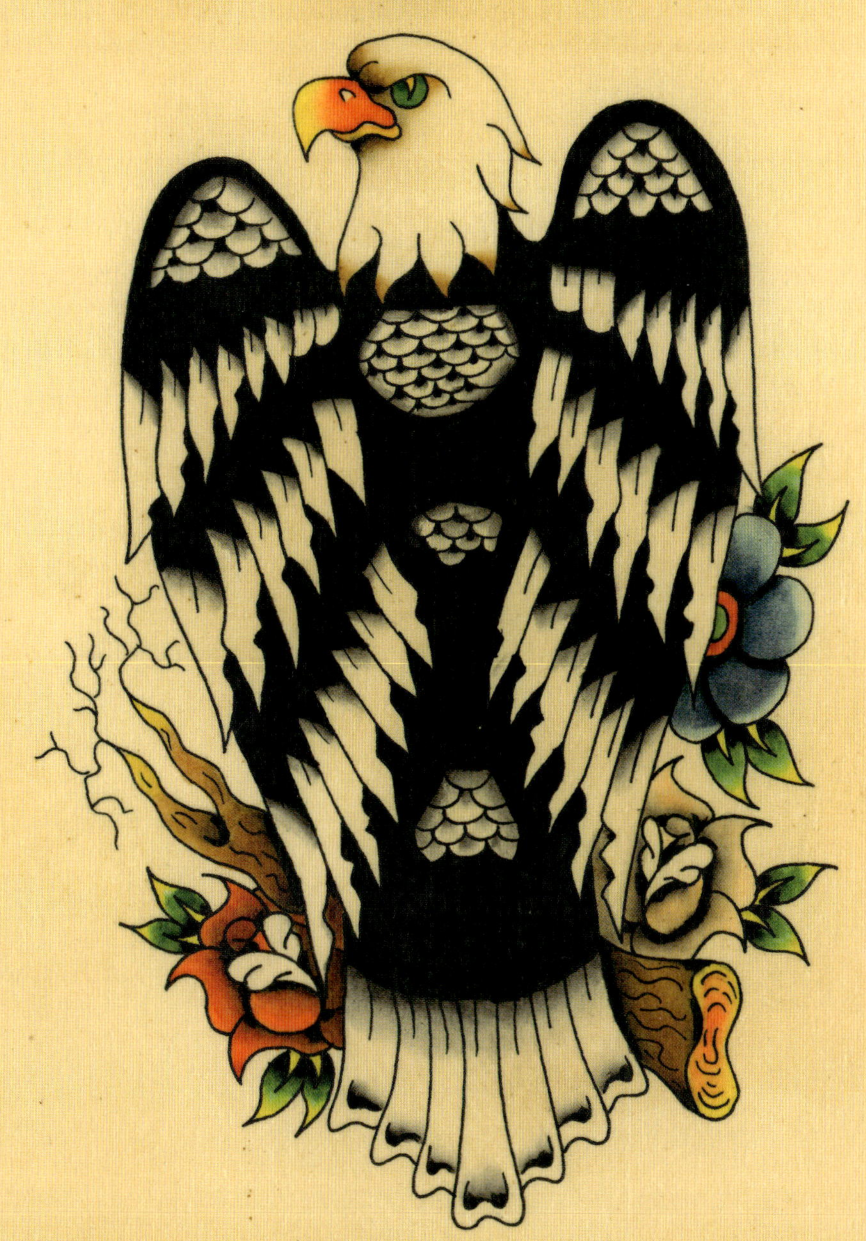

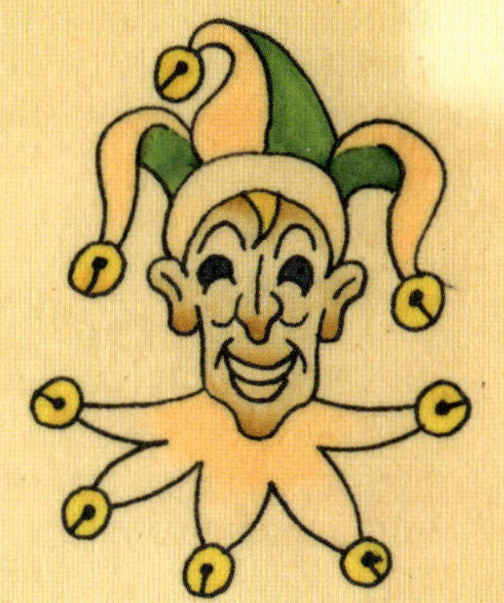

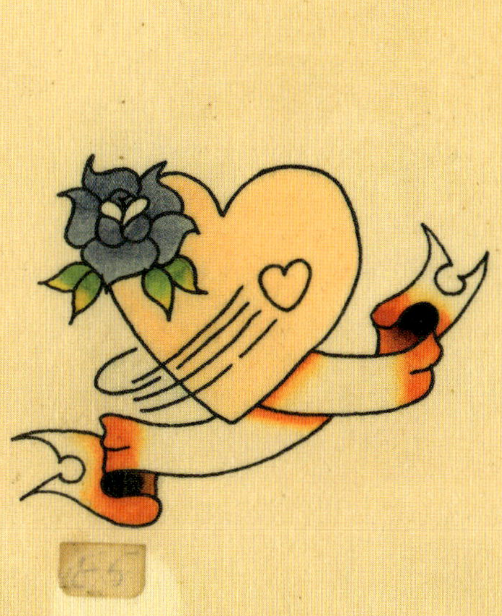

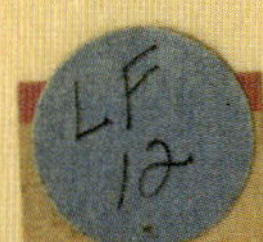

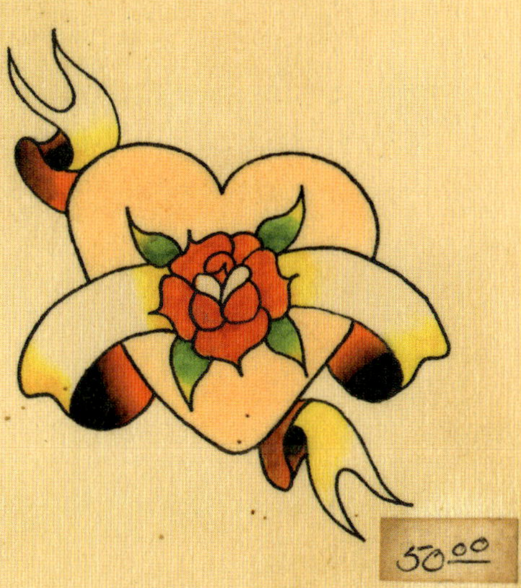

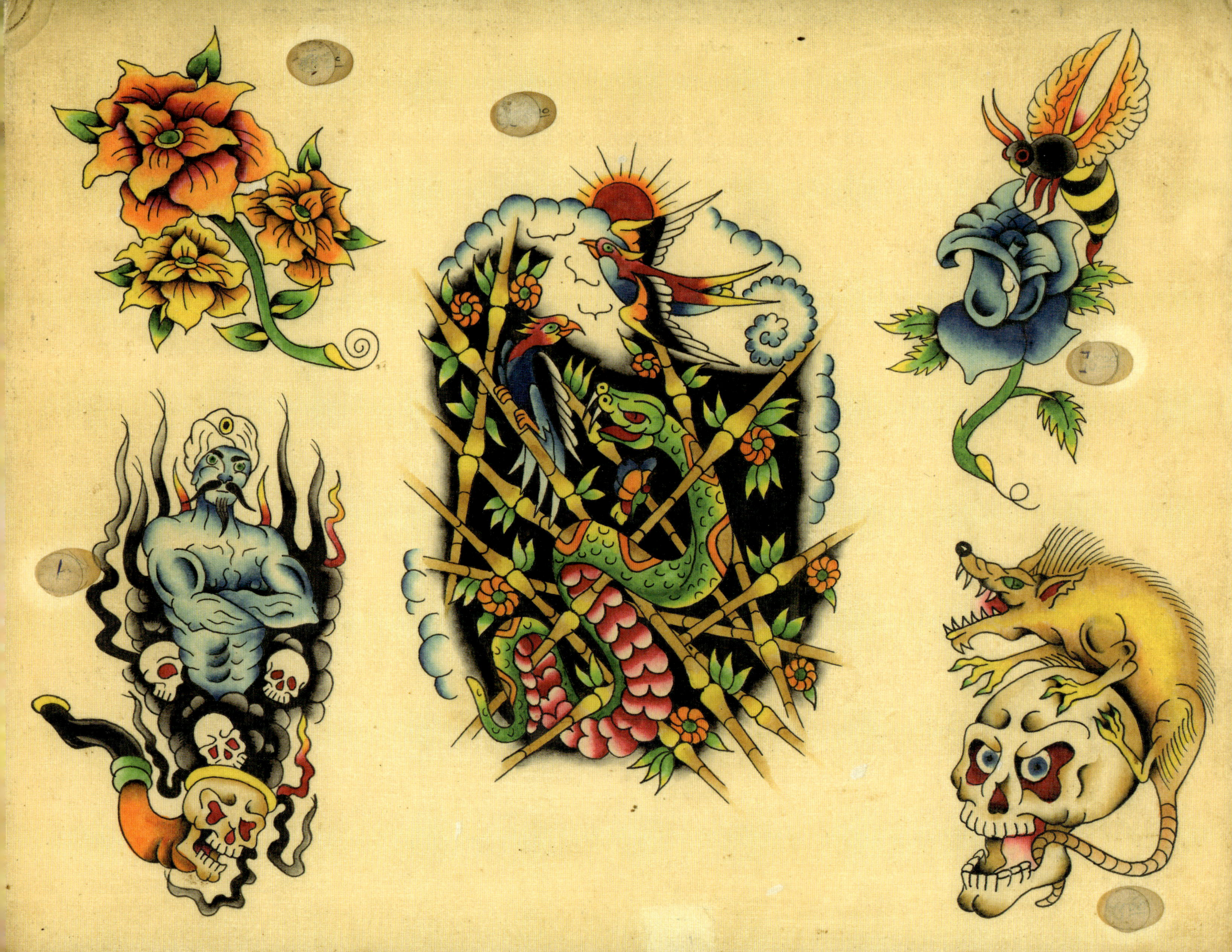

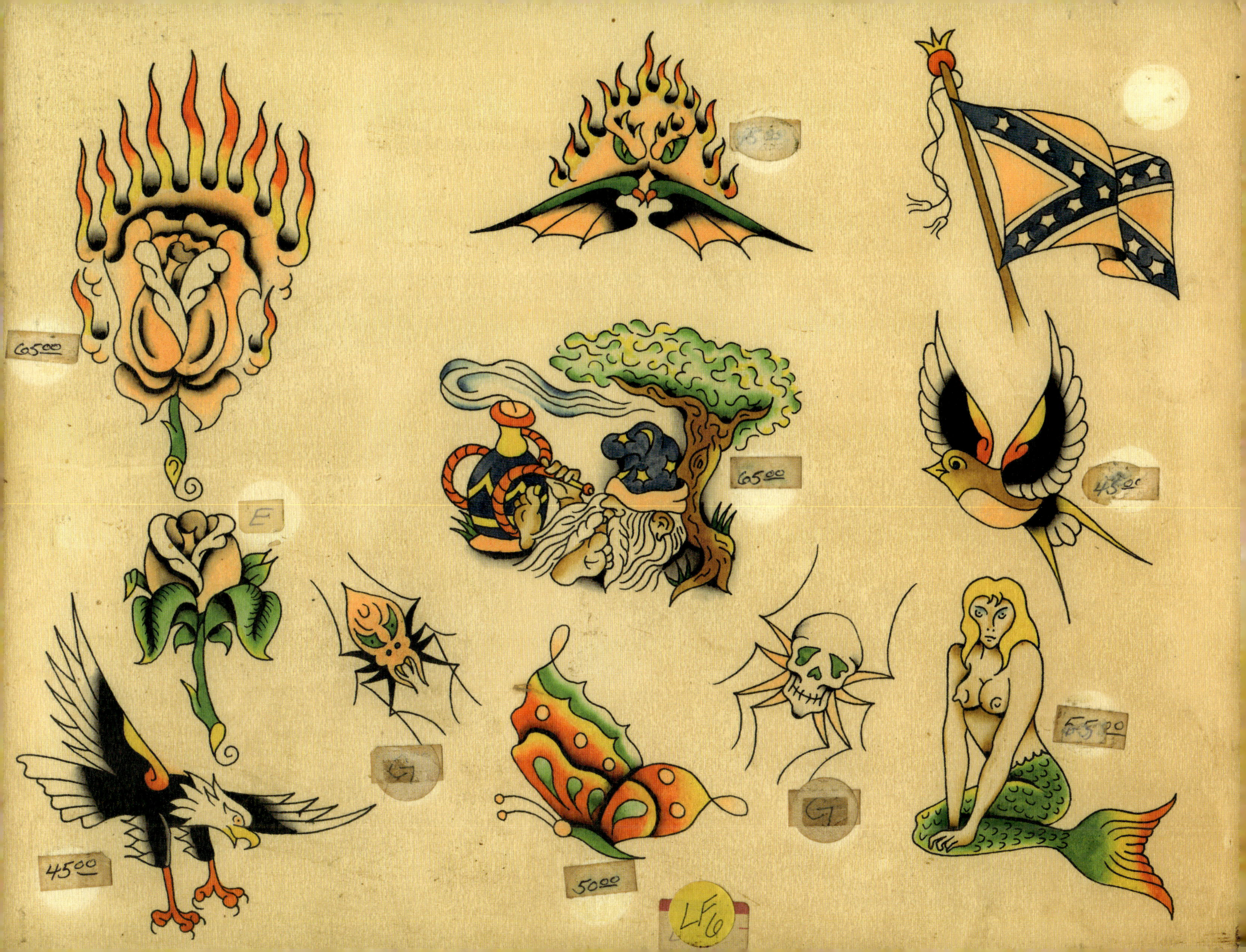
6500
6500
4500
E
G
G
4500
5000
5500
LF6

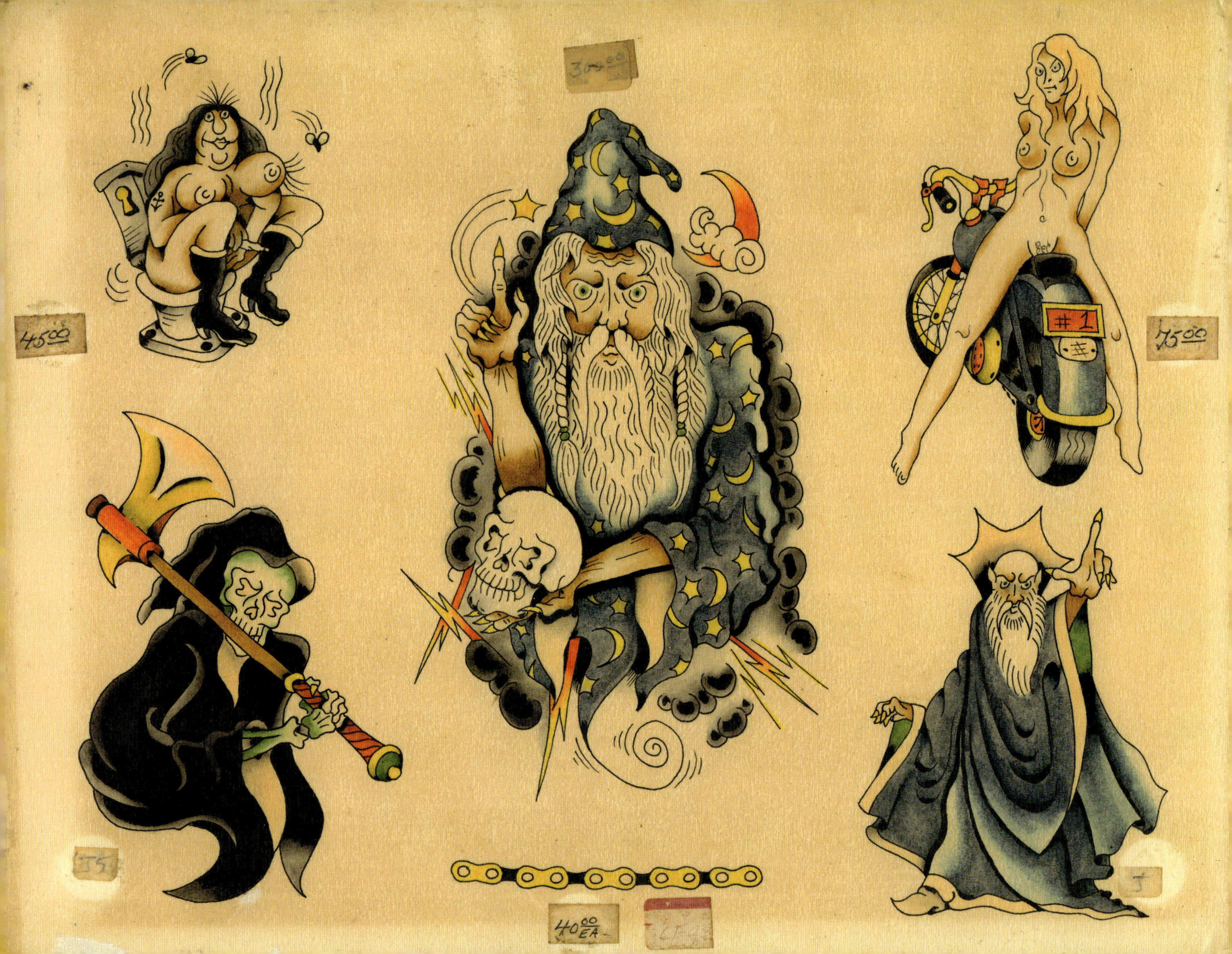
45^{00}
#1
75^{00}
40^{00} EA.

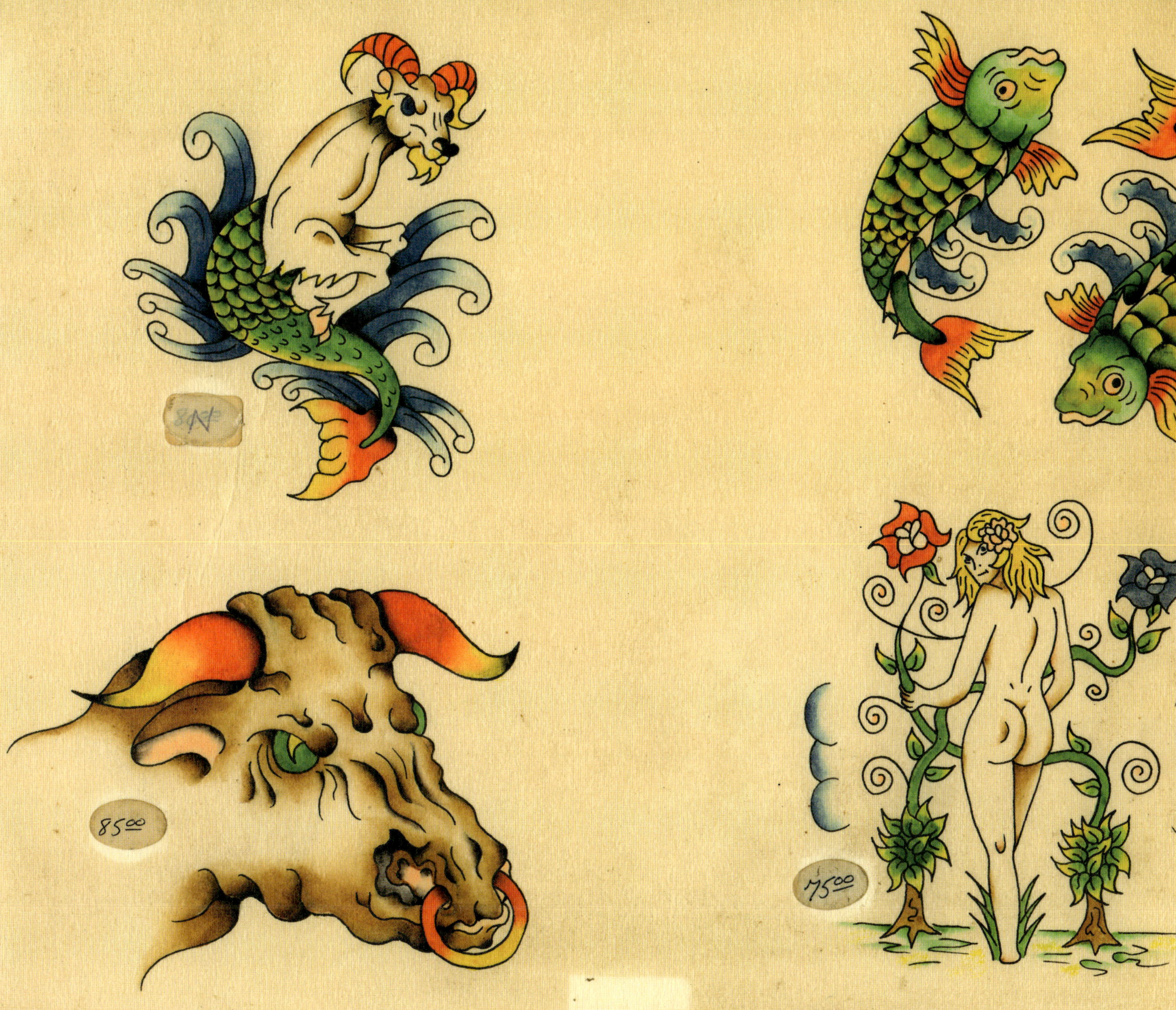

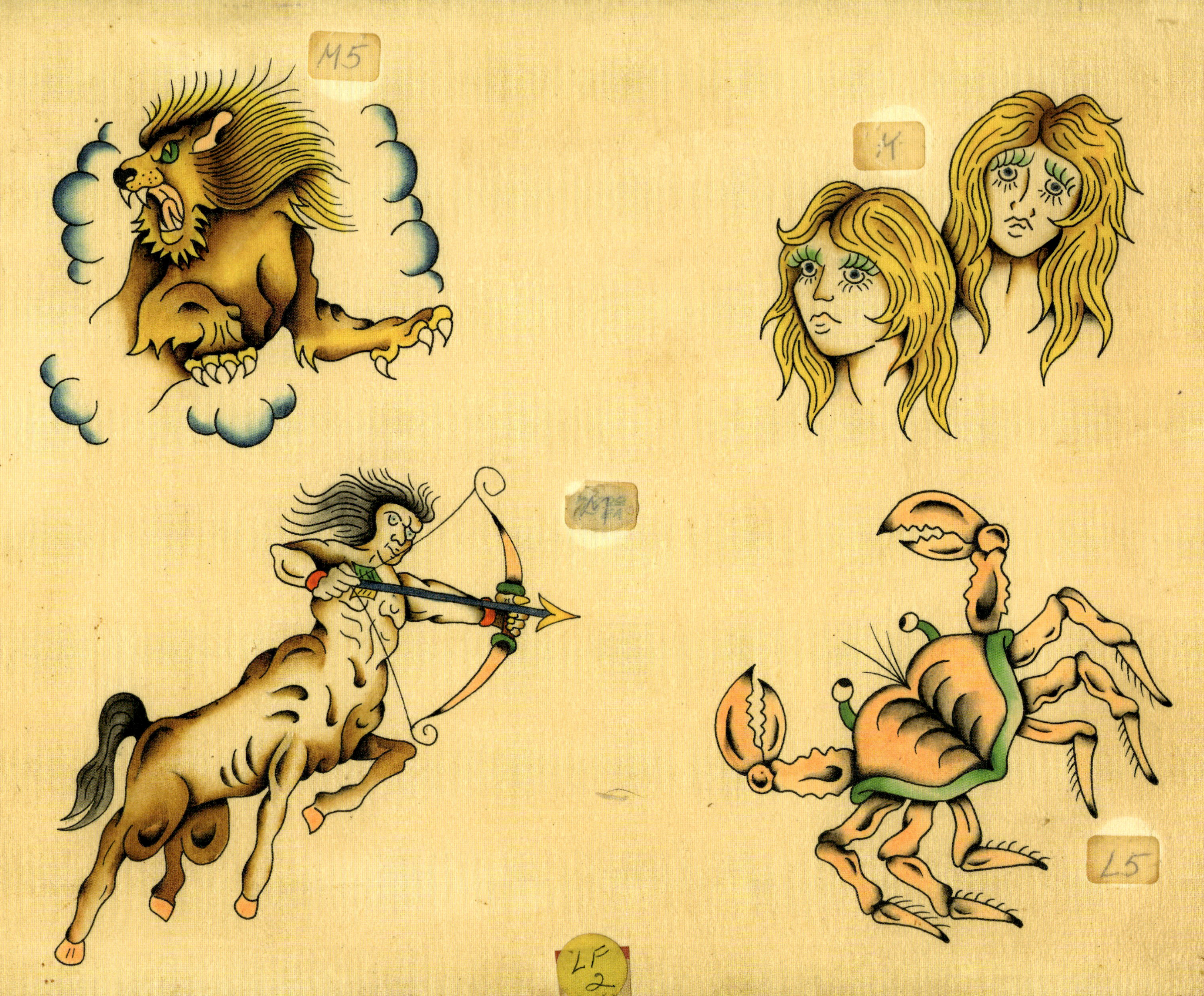
M5
L5
LF 2

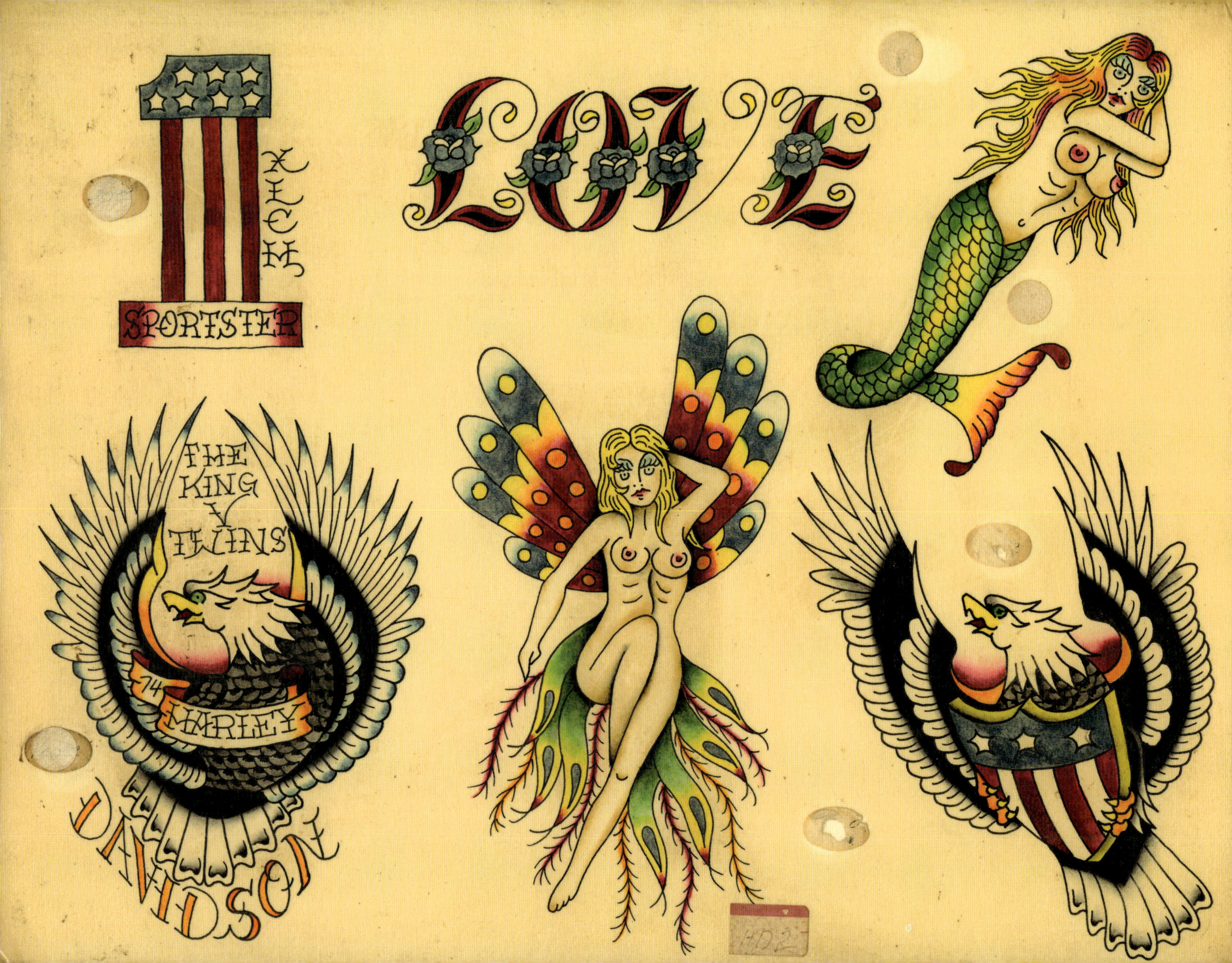
LOVE
1
XLCH
SPORTSTER
THE KING V TWINS
74
HARLEY
DAVIDSON
HD2

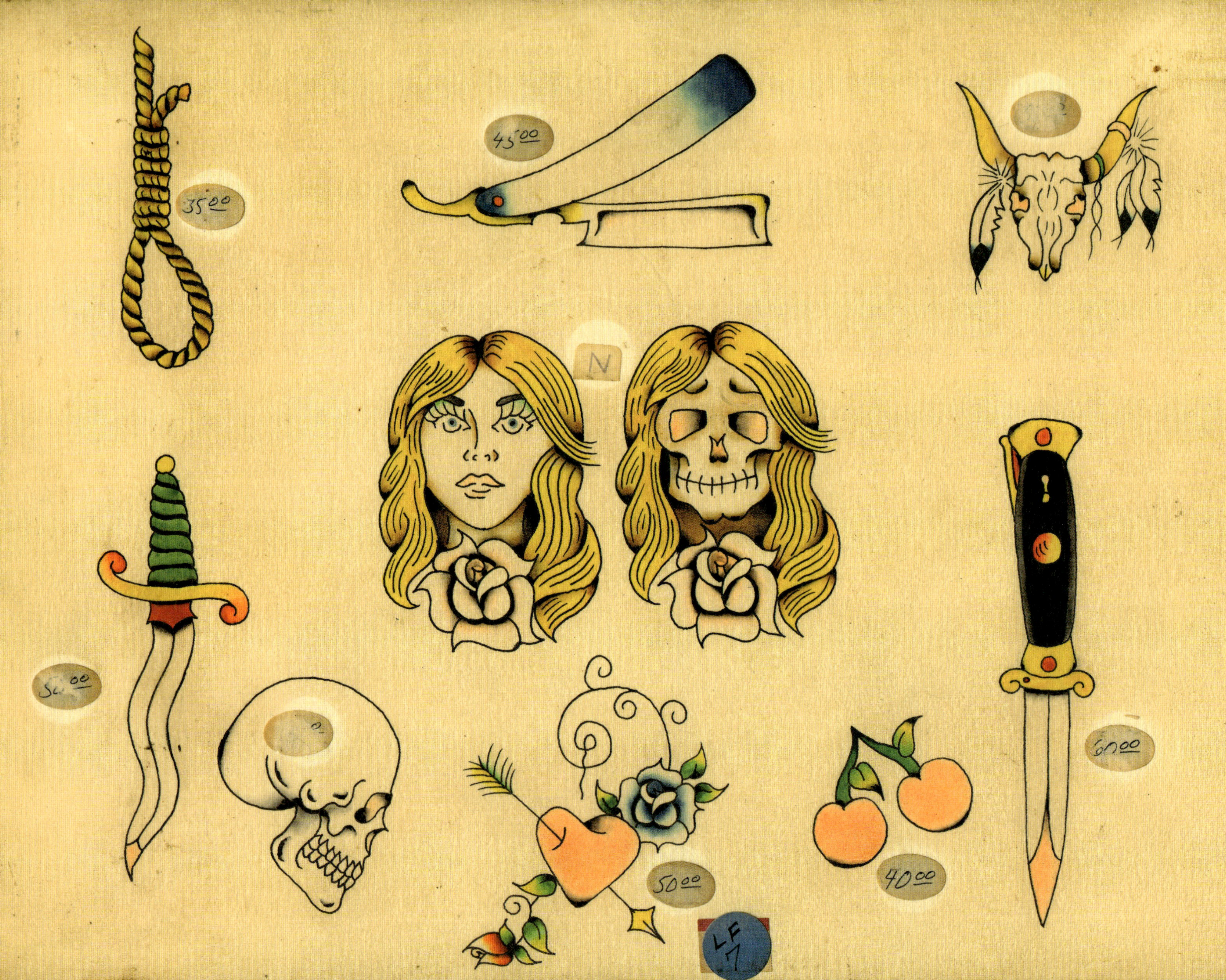
35 00
45 00
N
50 00
40 00
LF
7

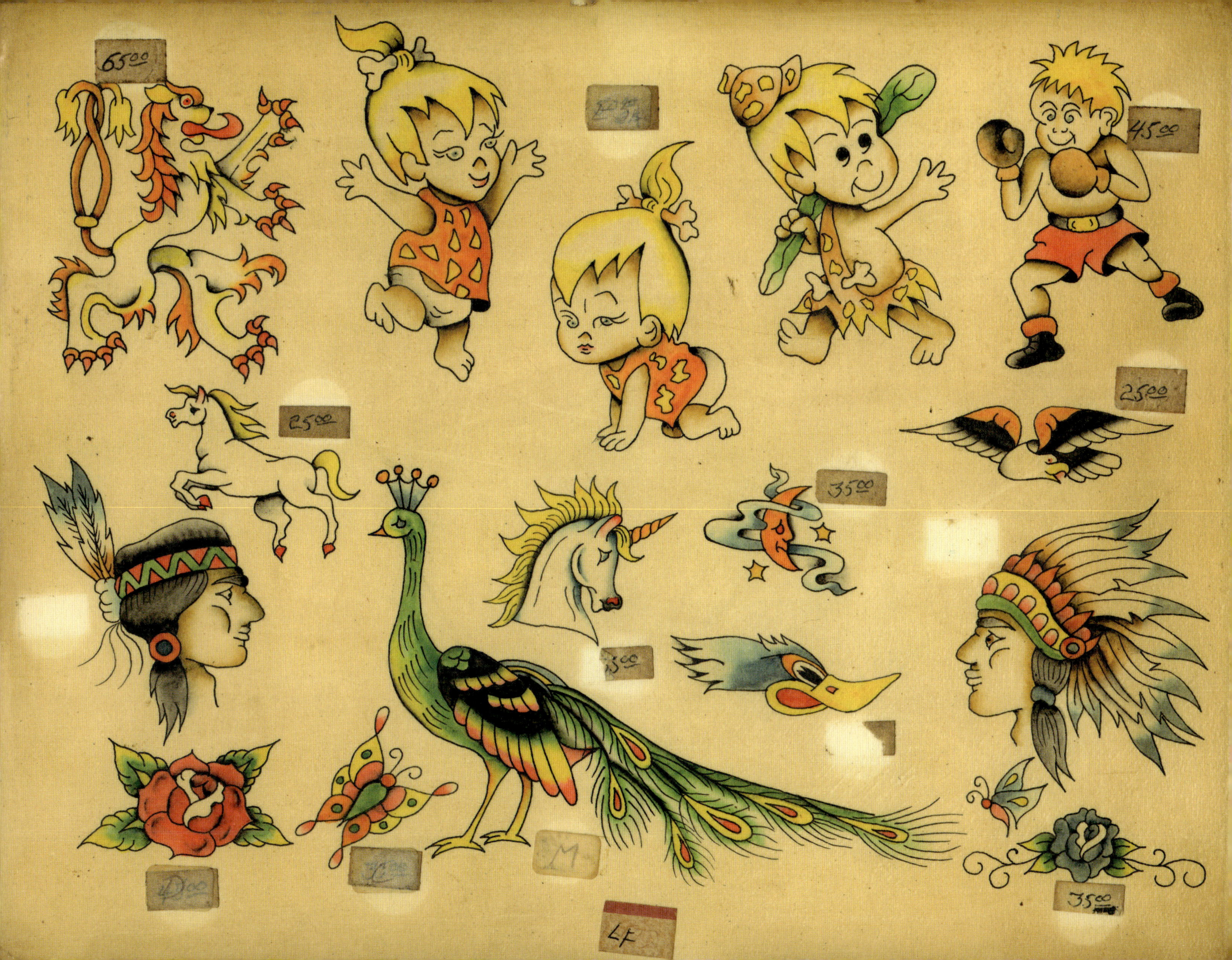

6500
4500
2500
2500
3500
3500
4F

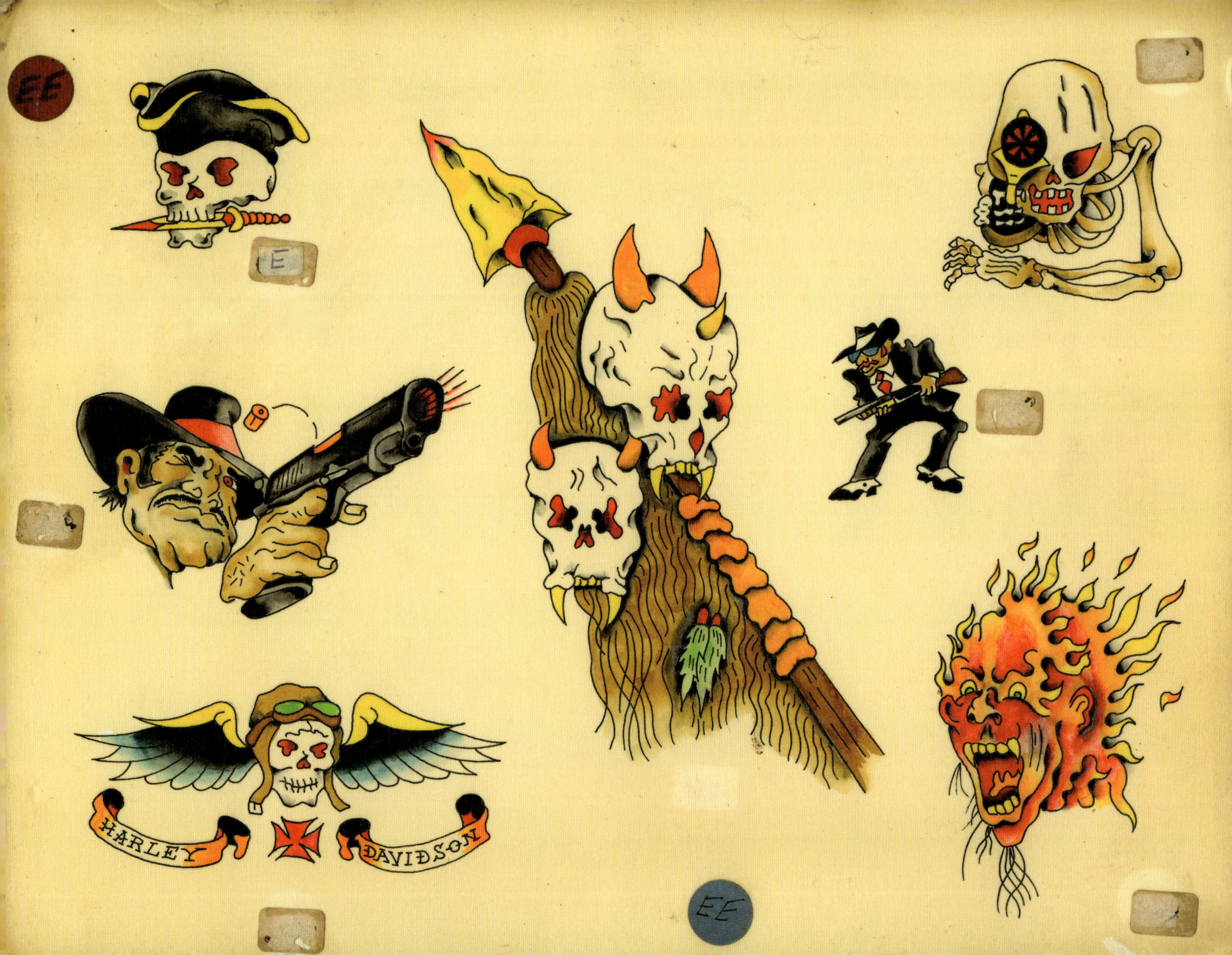
EE
E
HARLEY
DAVIDSON
EE

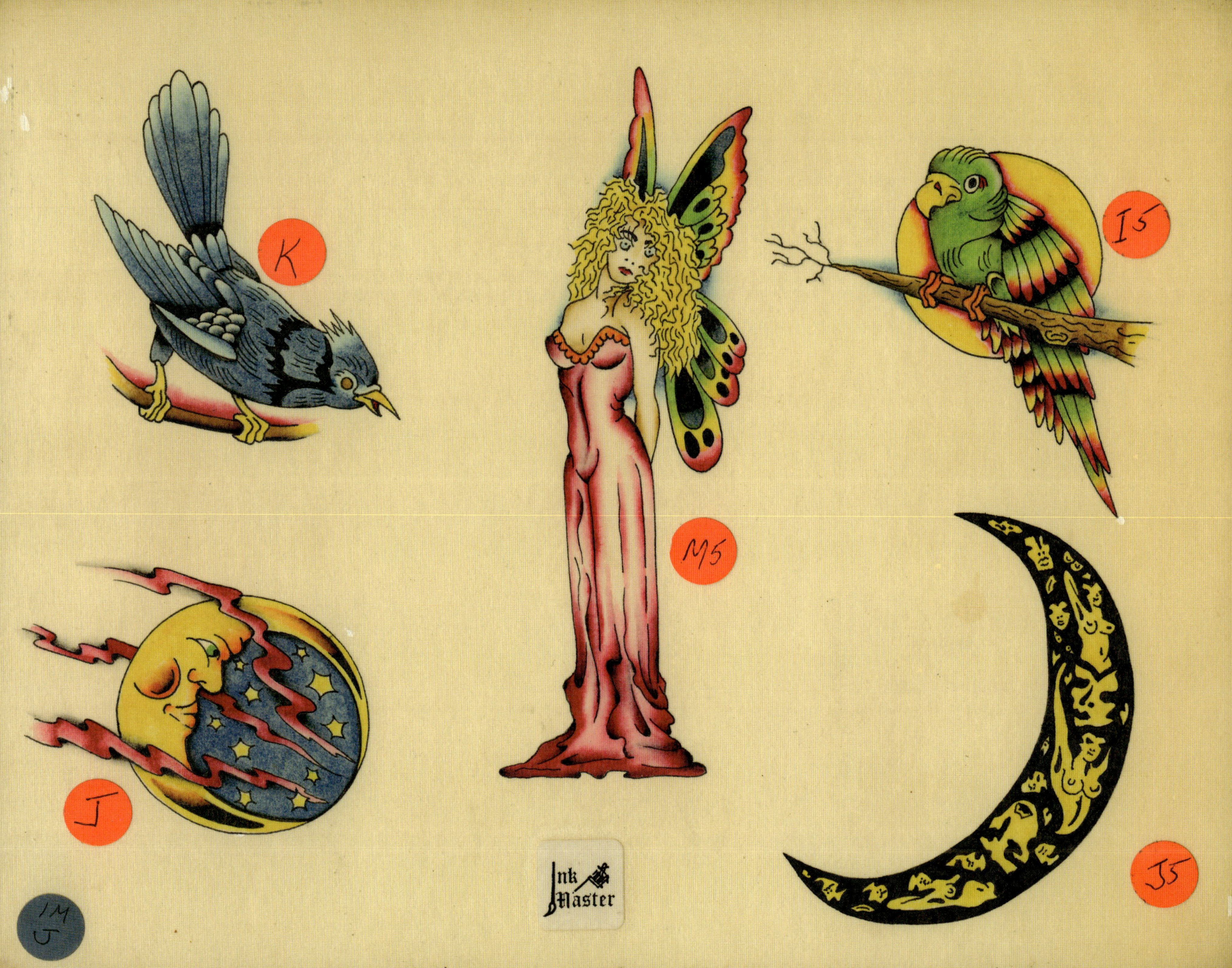

K

M5

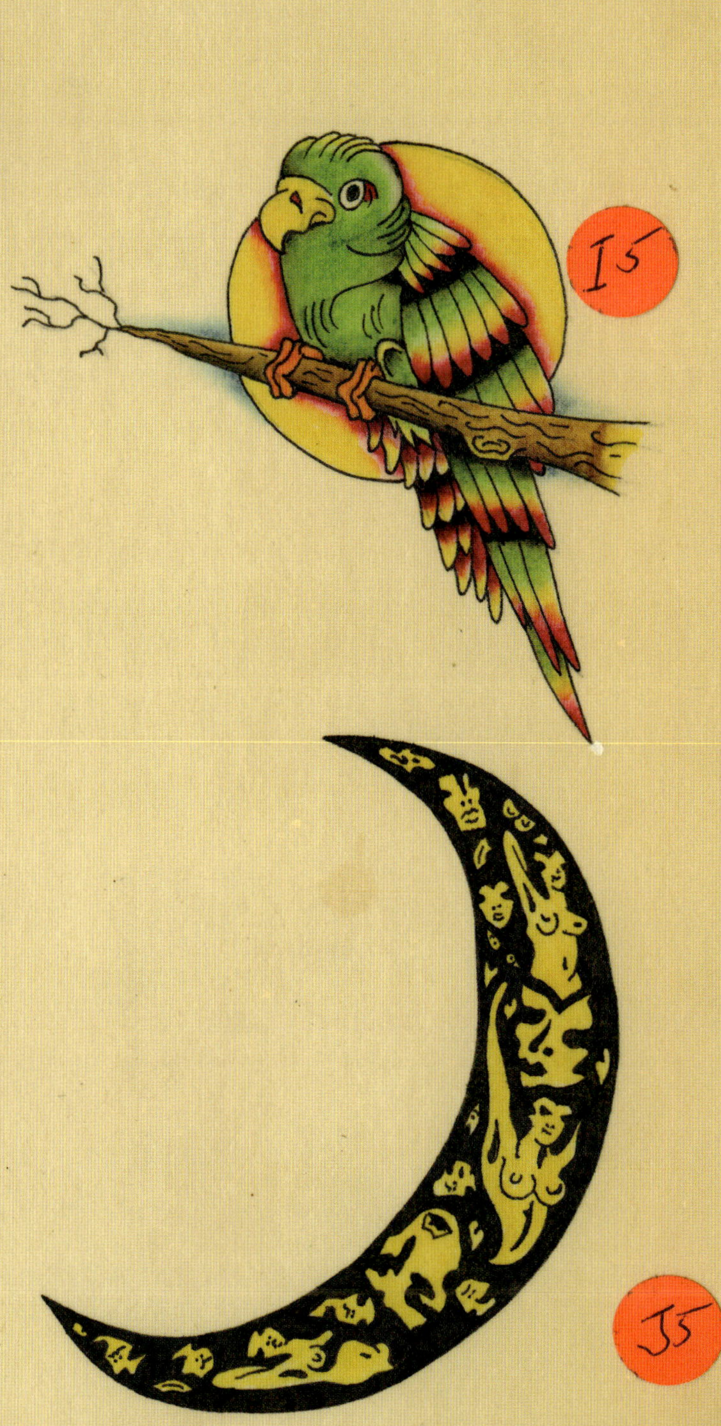

J

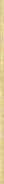

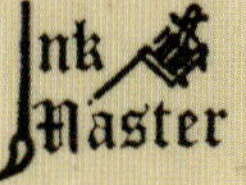

1M
J

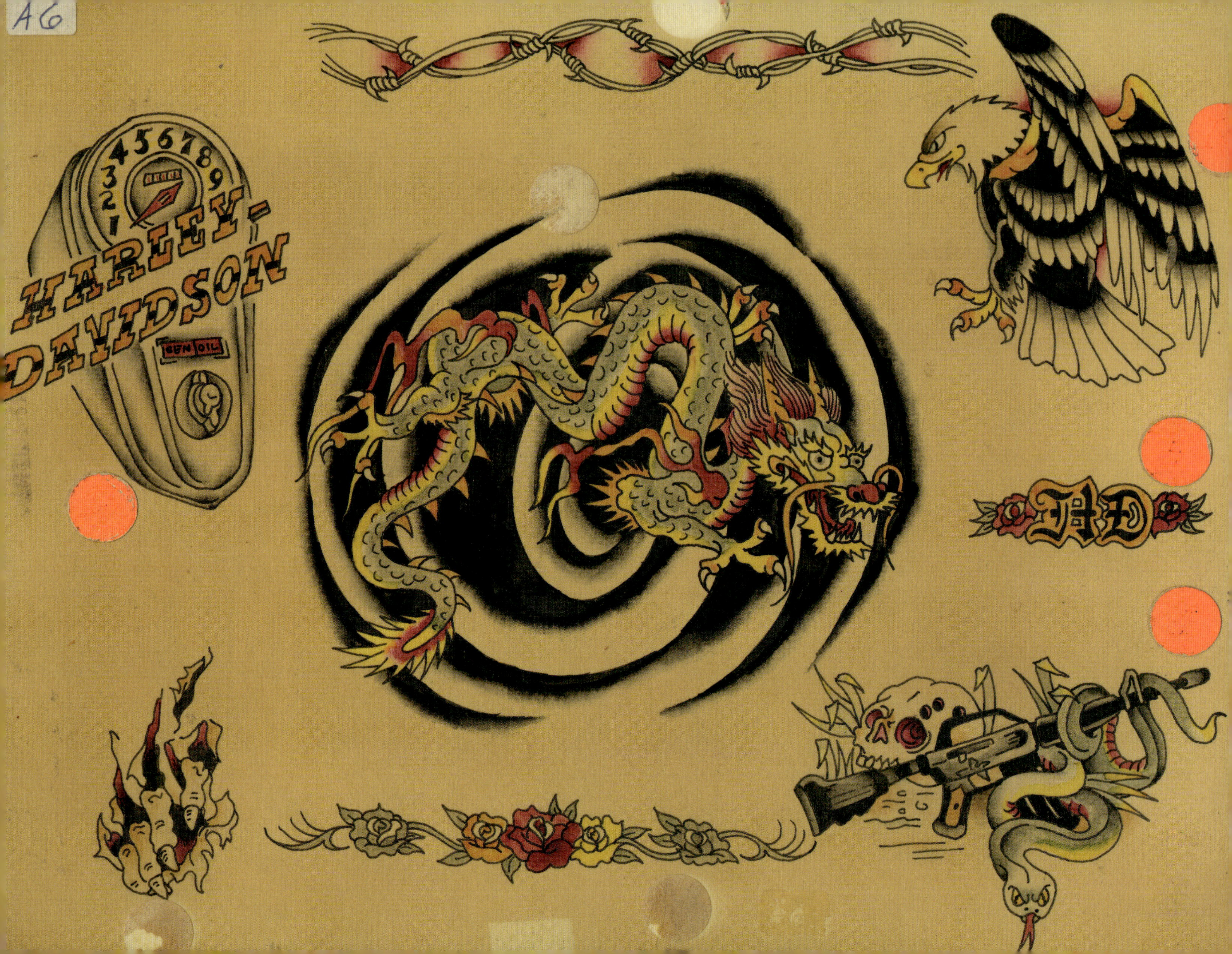
A6
1 2 3 4 5 6 7 8 9
HARLEY-
DAVIDSON
GEN OIL

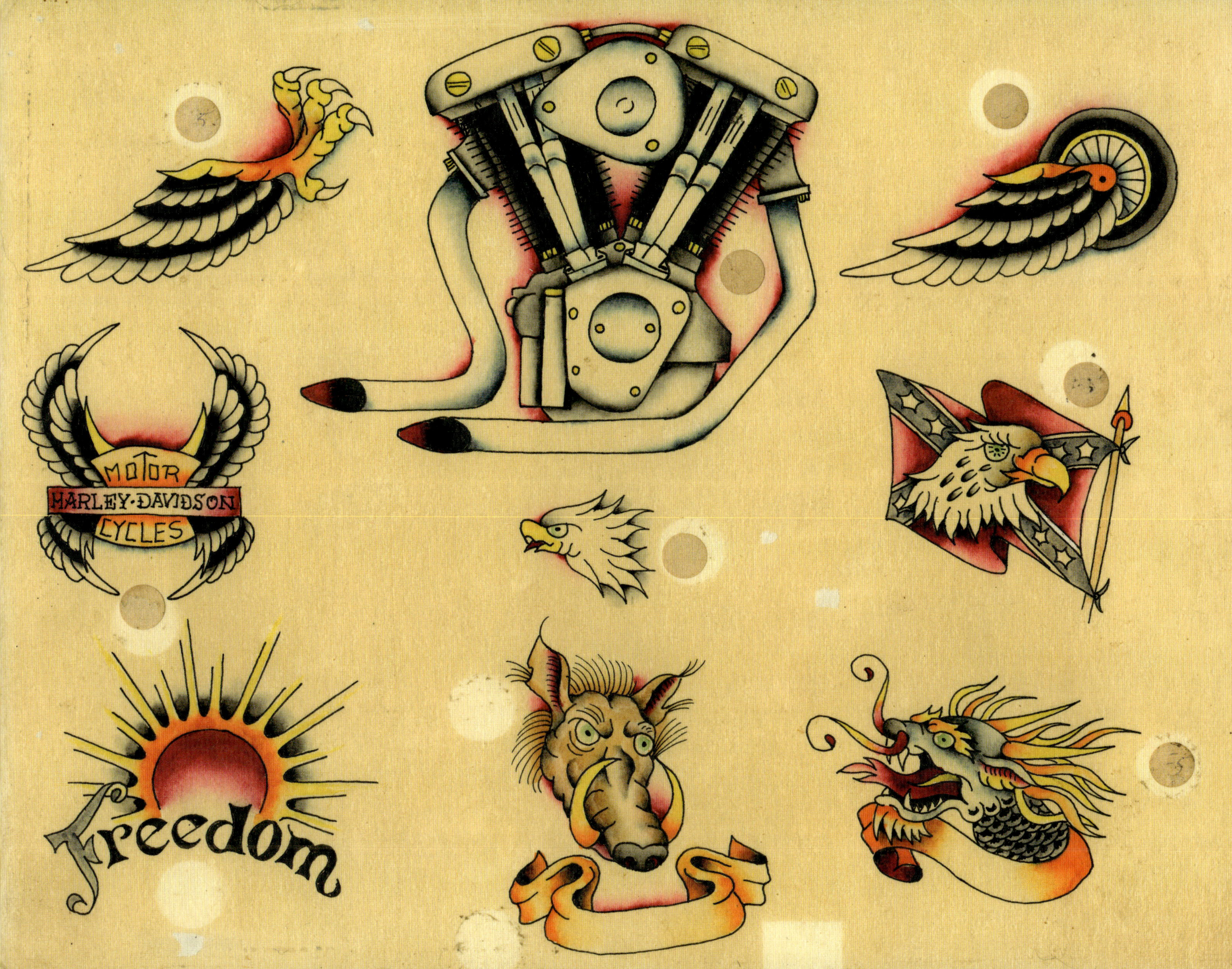
MOTOR
HARLEY-DAVIDSON
CYCLES
Freedom

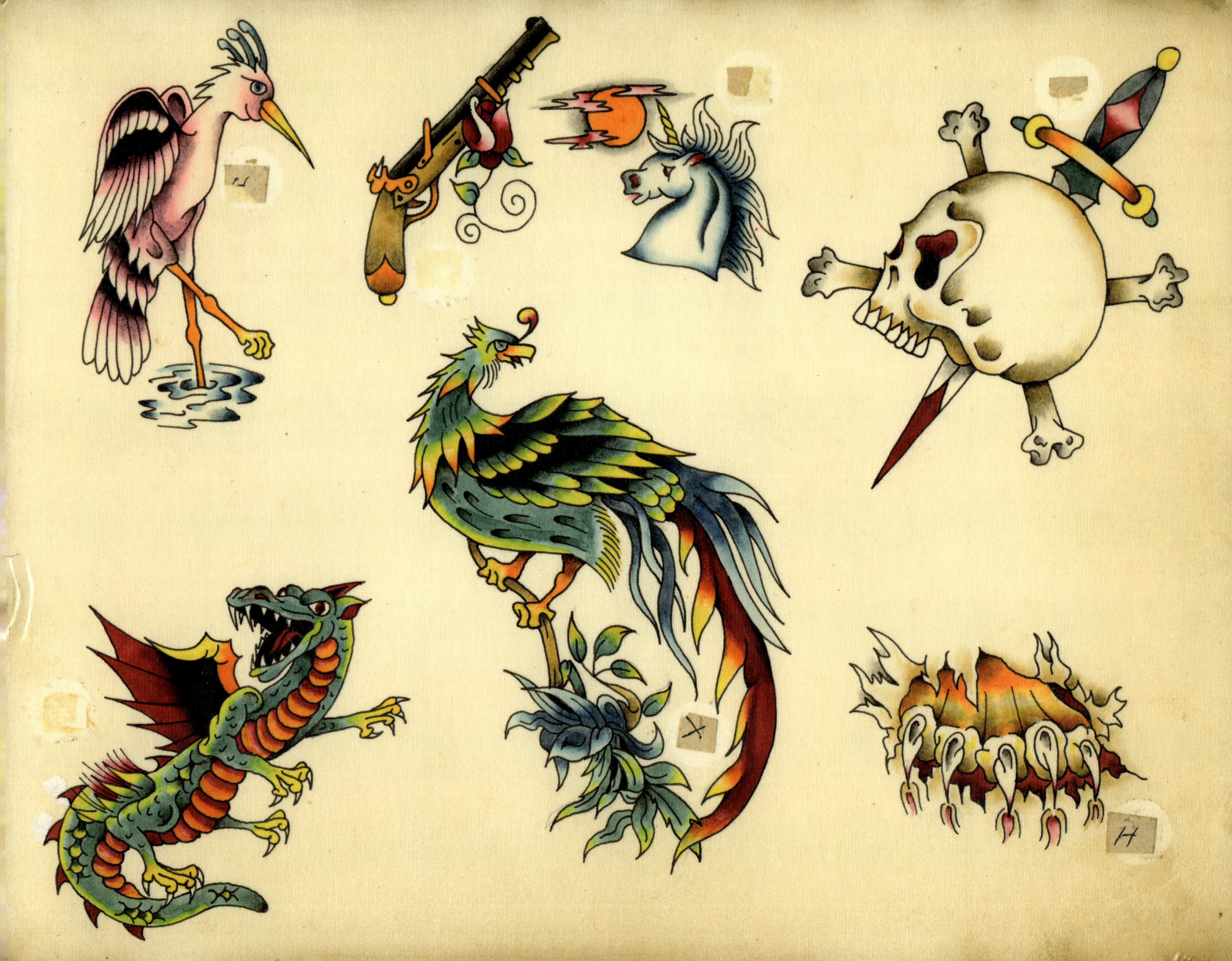

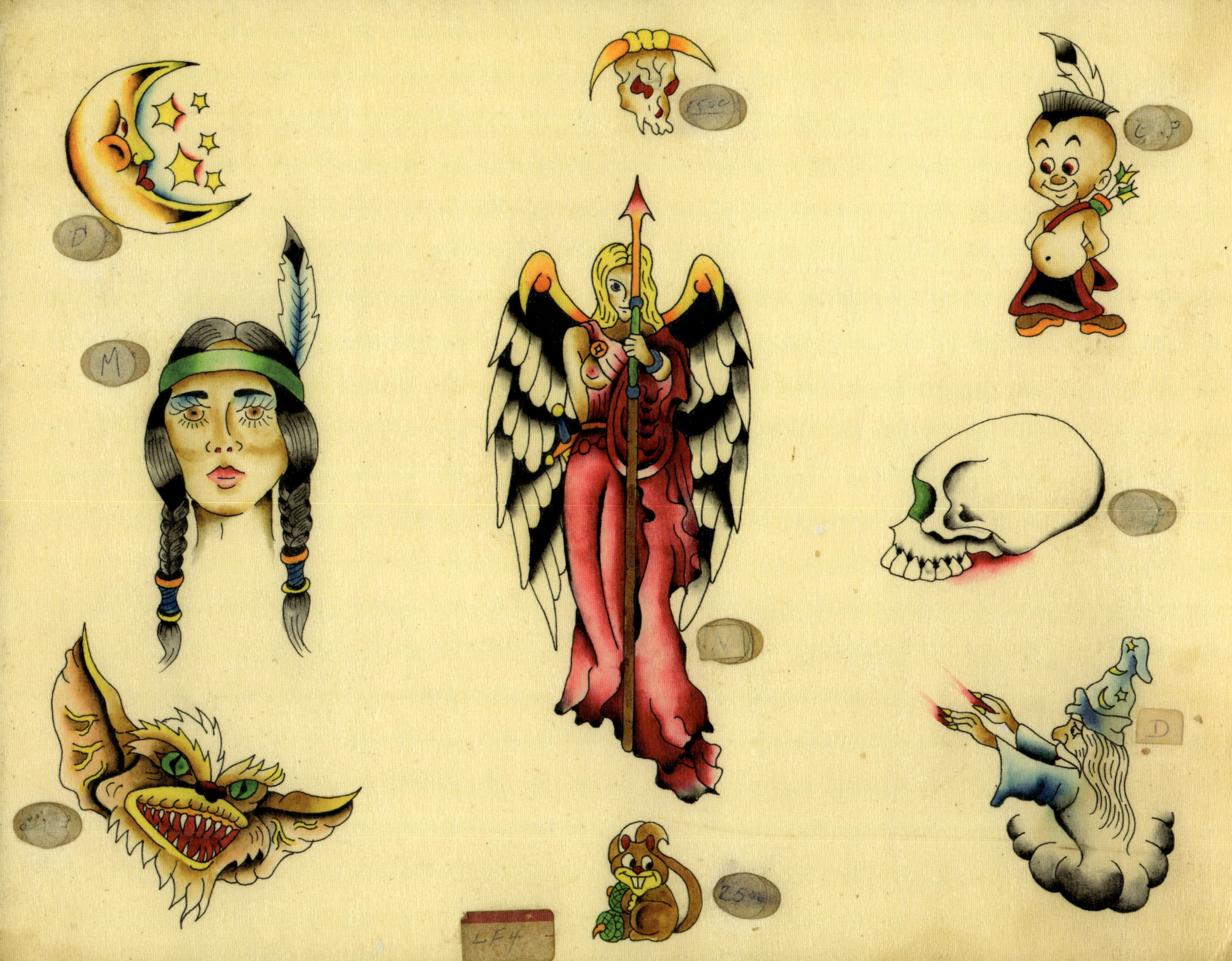
M
D
LF4

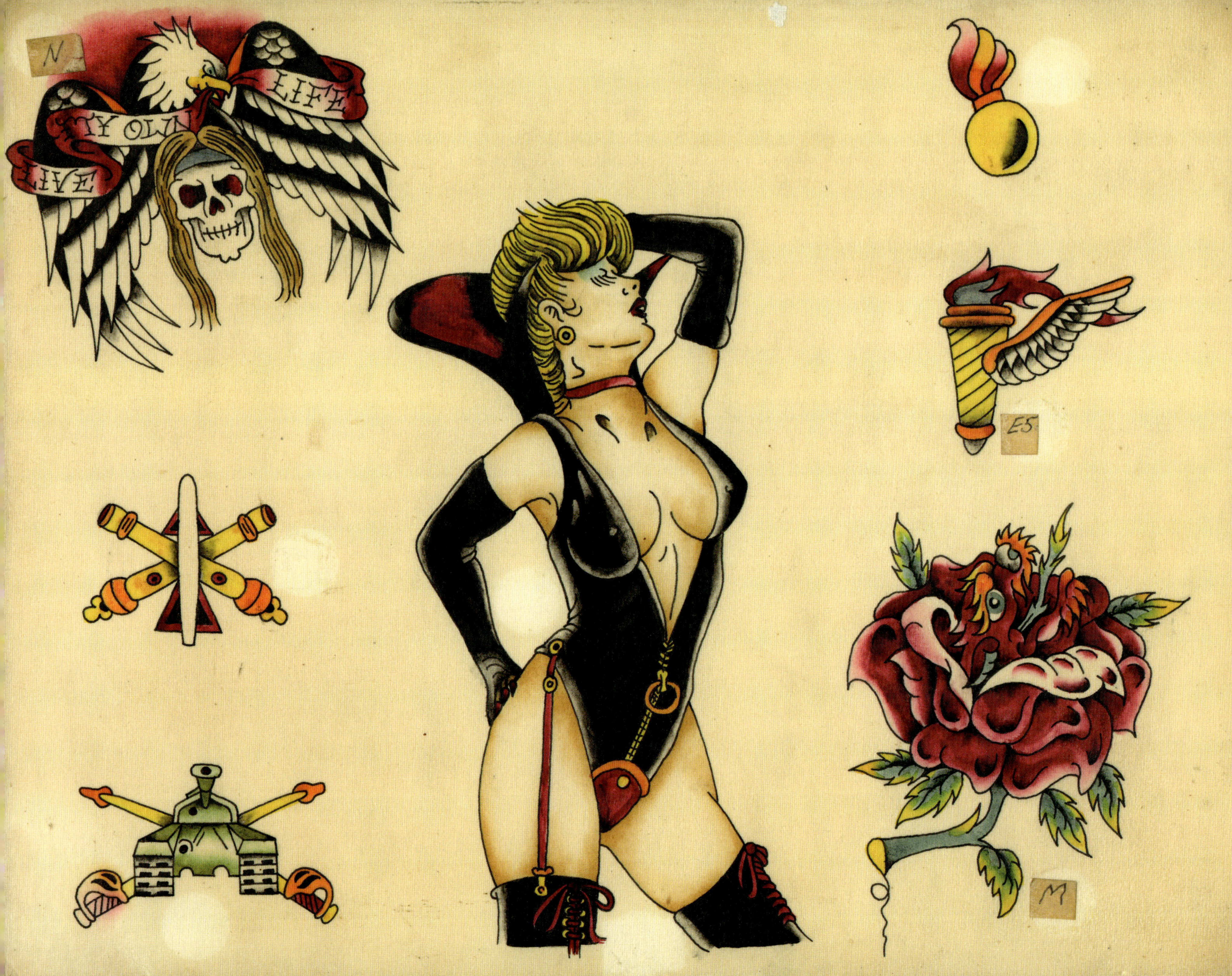
N
LIVE
MY OWN
LIFE
E5
M

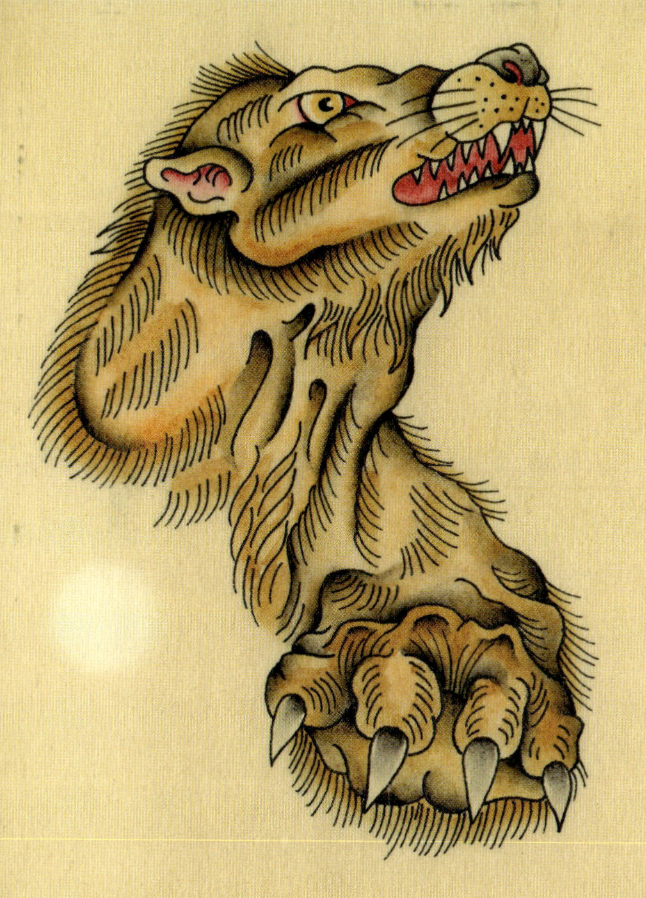
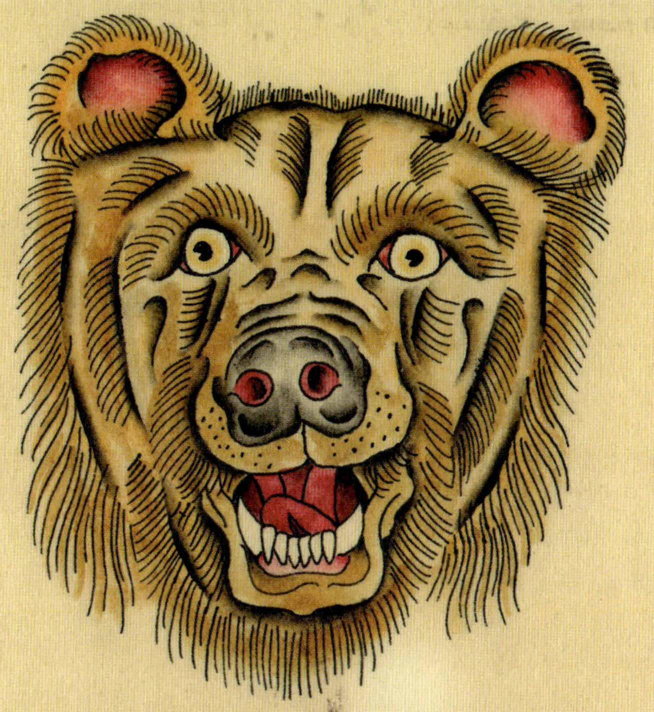
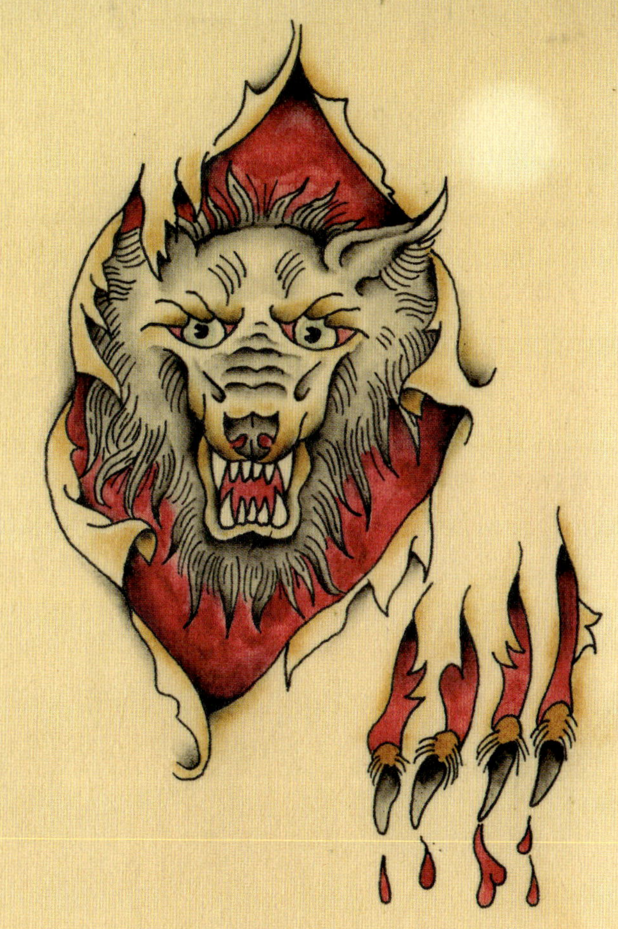
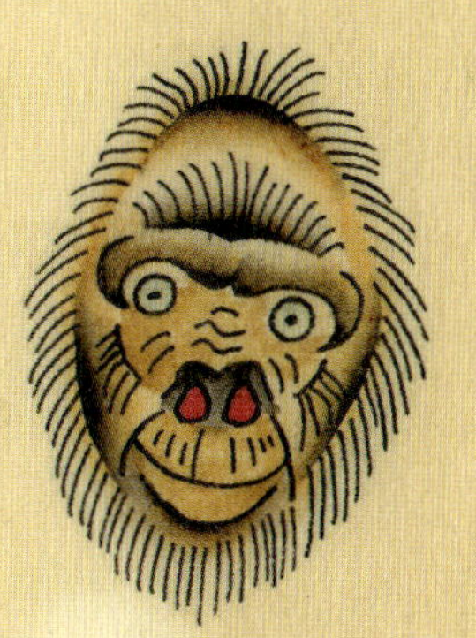
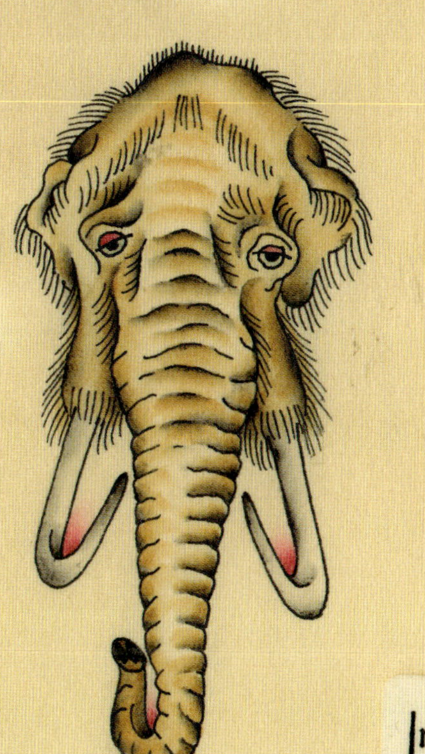
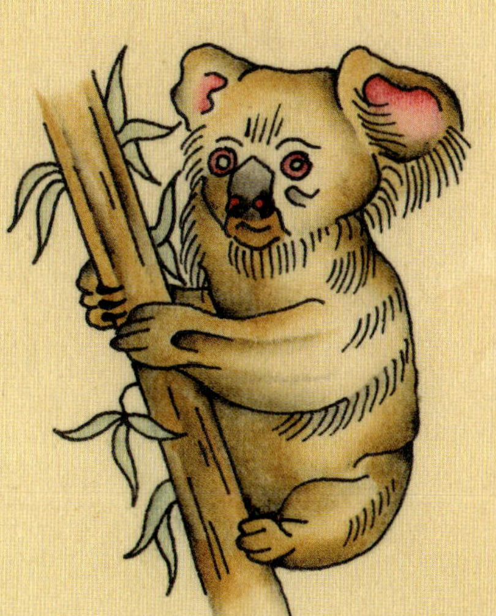
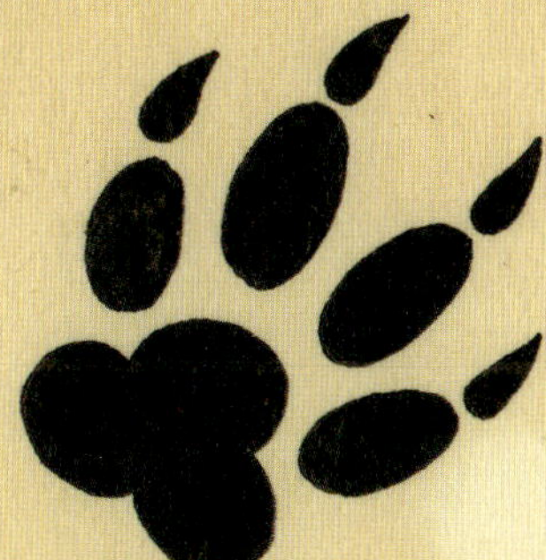
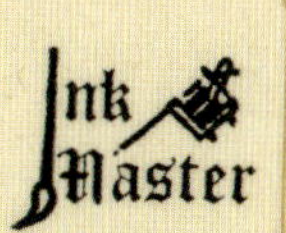
Ink
Master

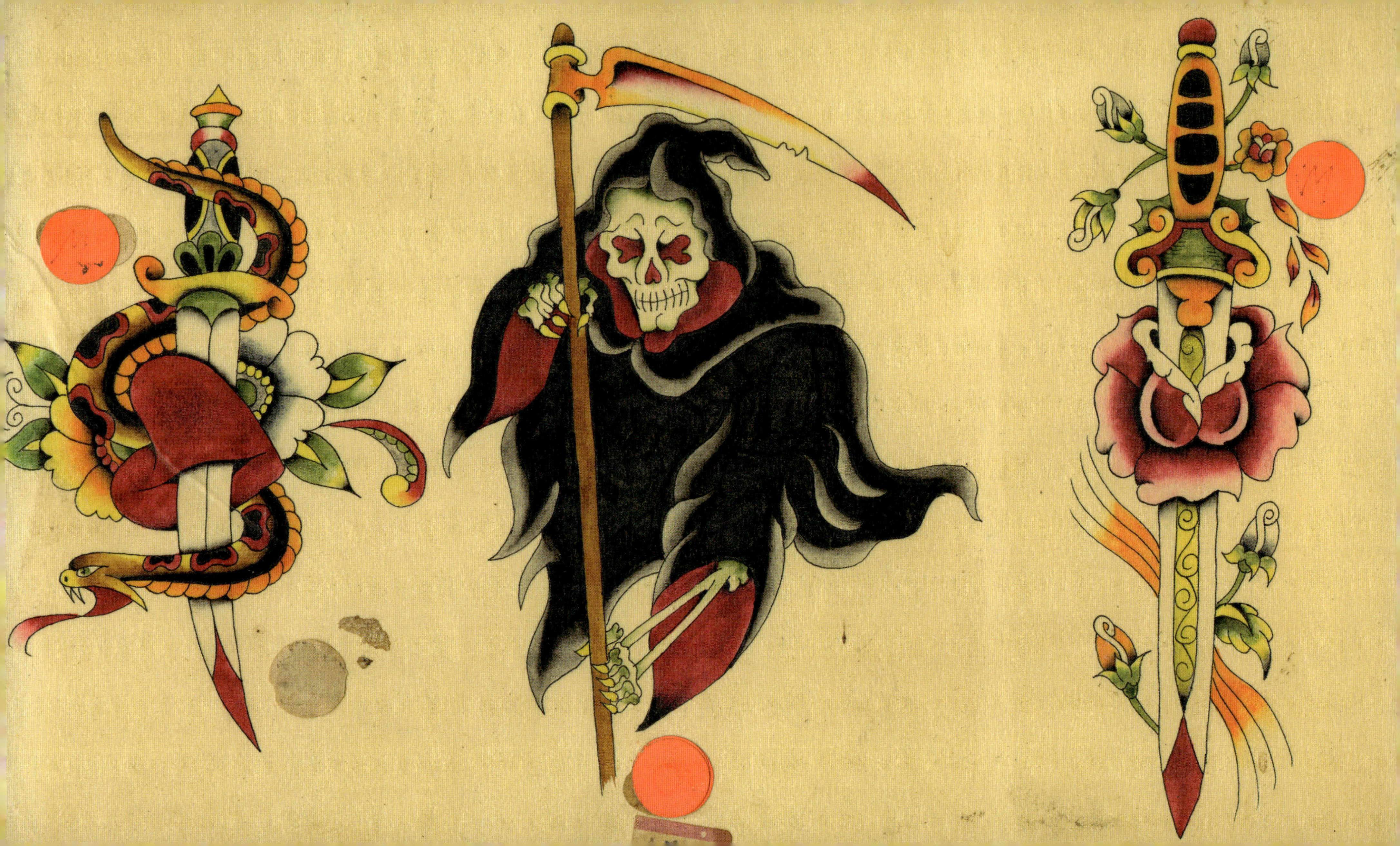

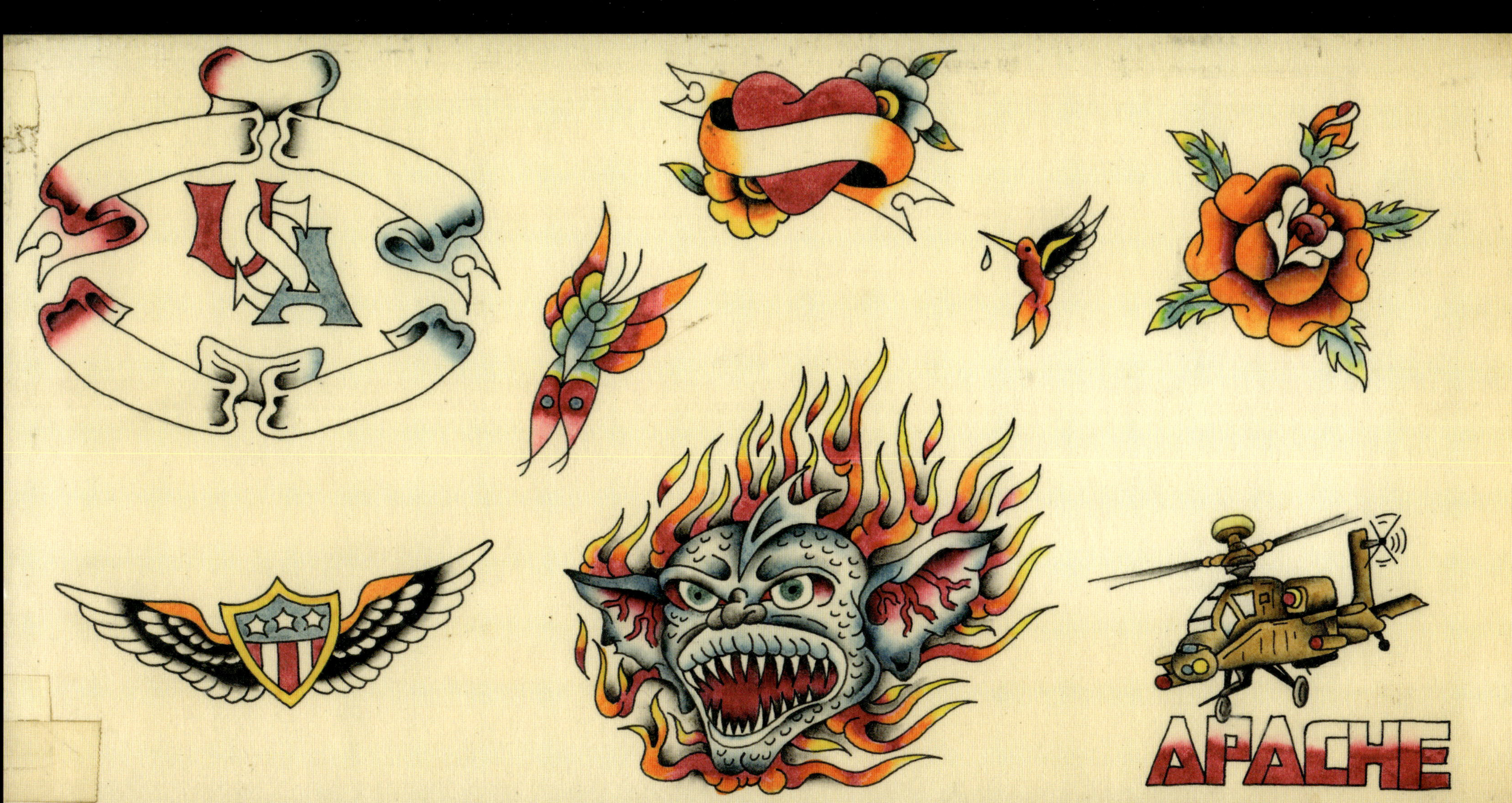
US
USA
APACHE

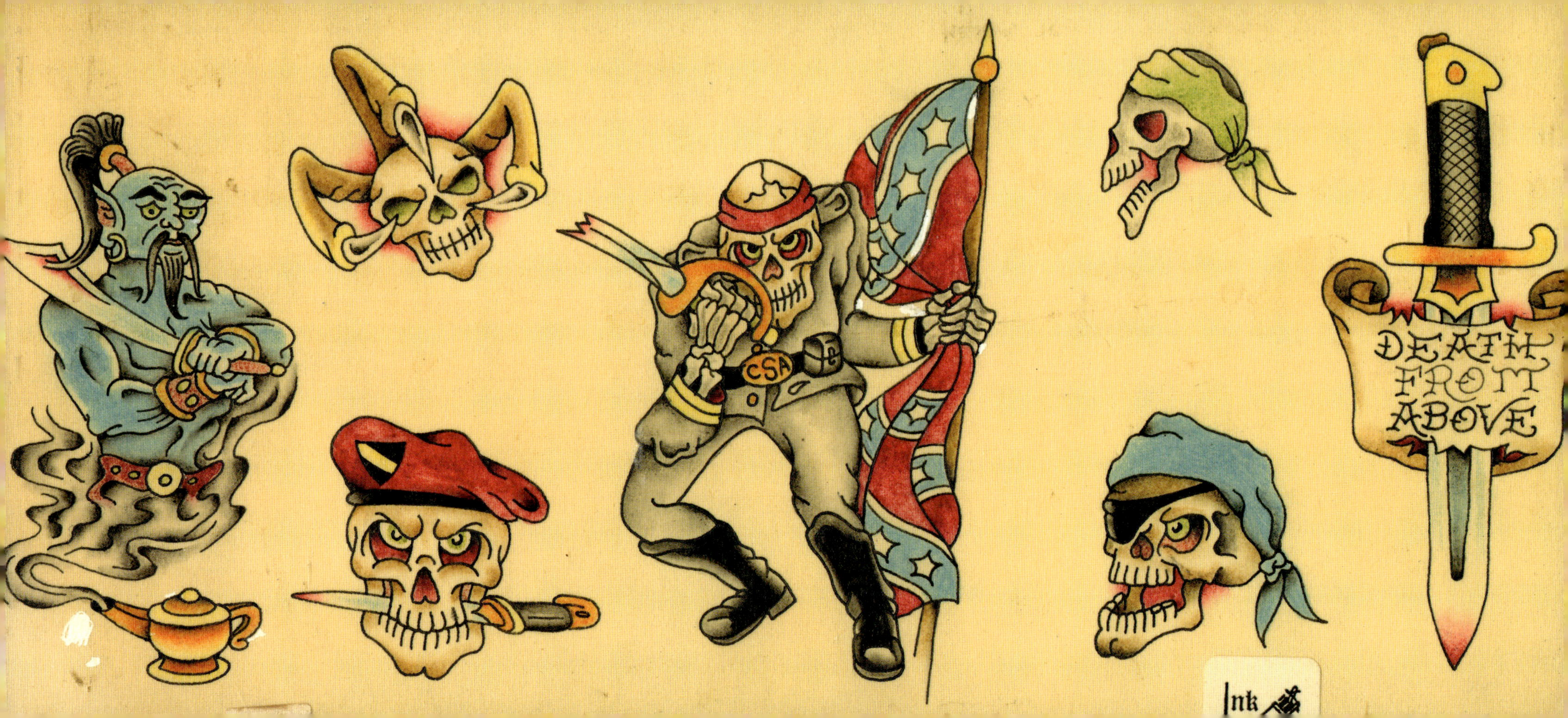
CSA
DEATH
FROM
ABOVE
Ink

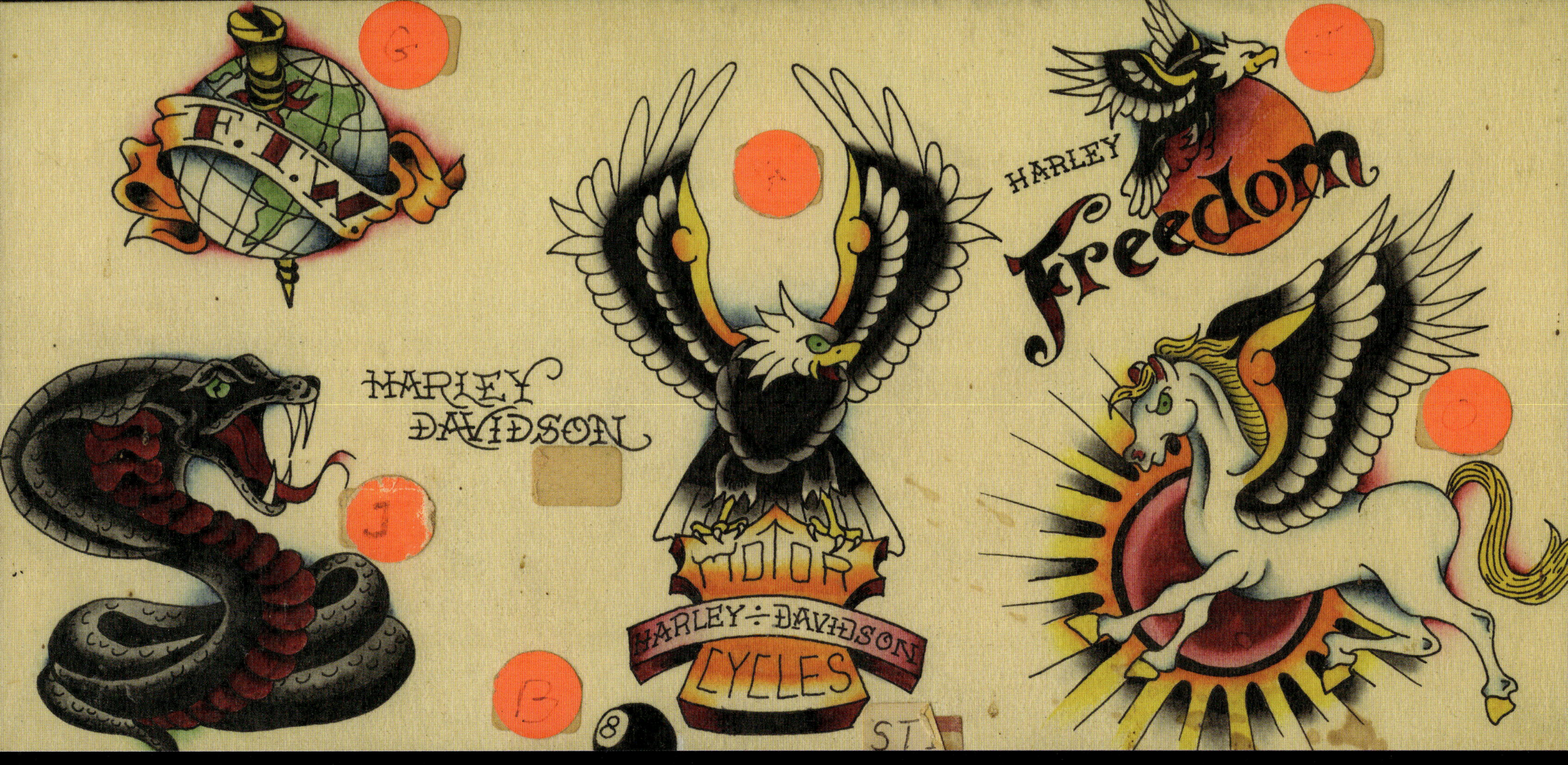
F.T.W.
HARLEY
DAVIDSON
MOTOR
HARLEY-DAVIDSON
CYCLES
HARLEY
Freedom

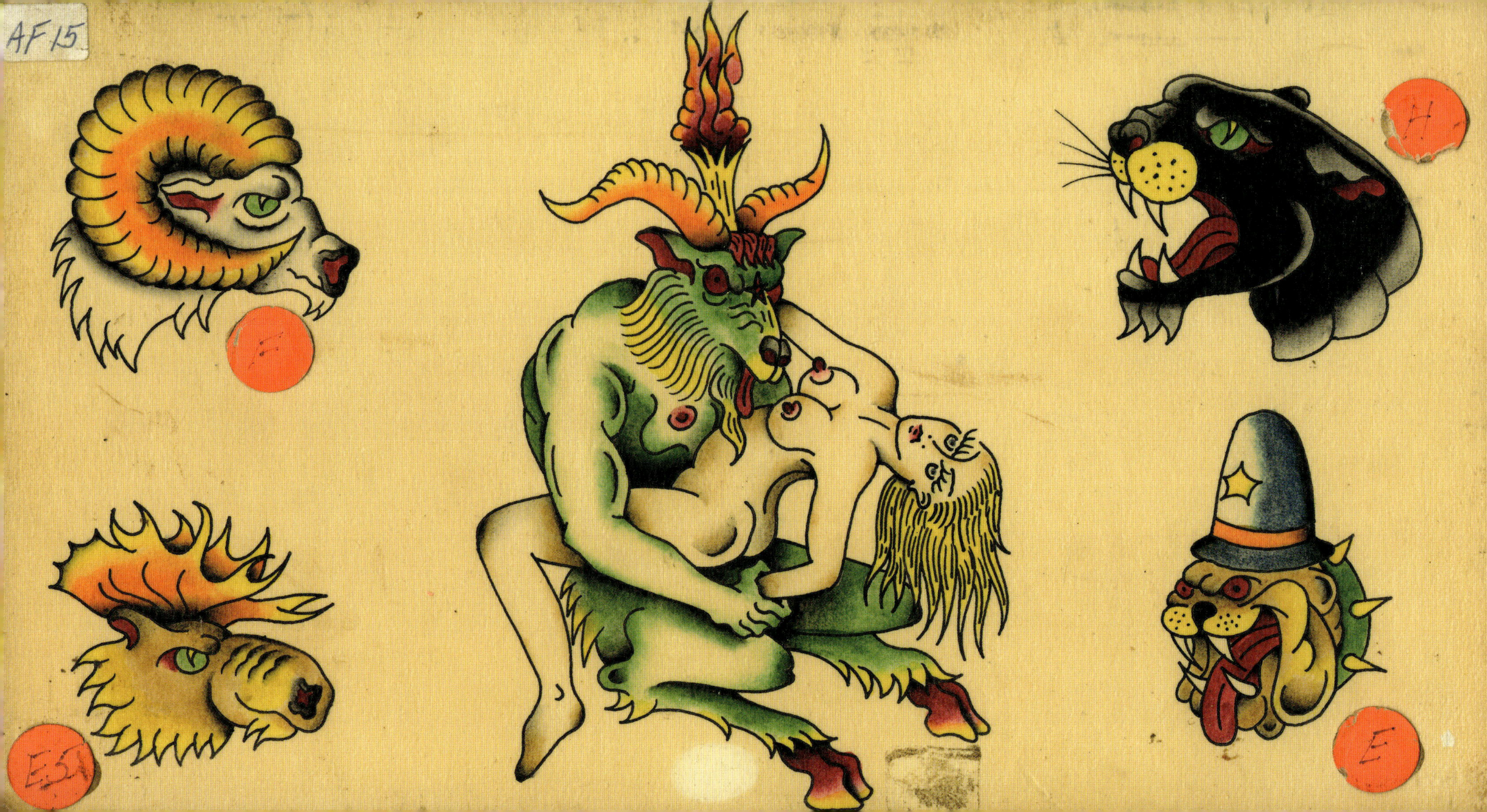
AF15

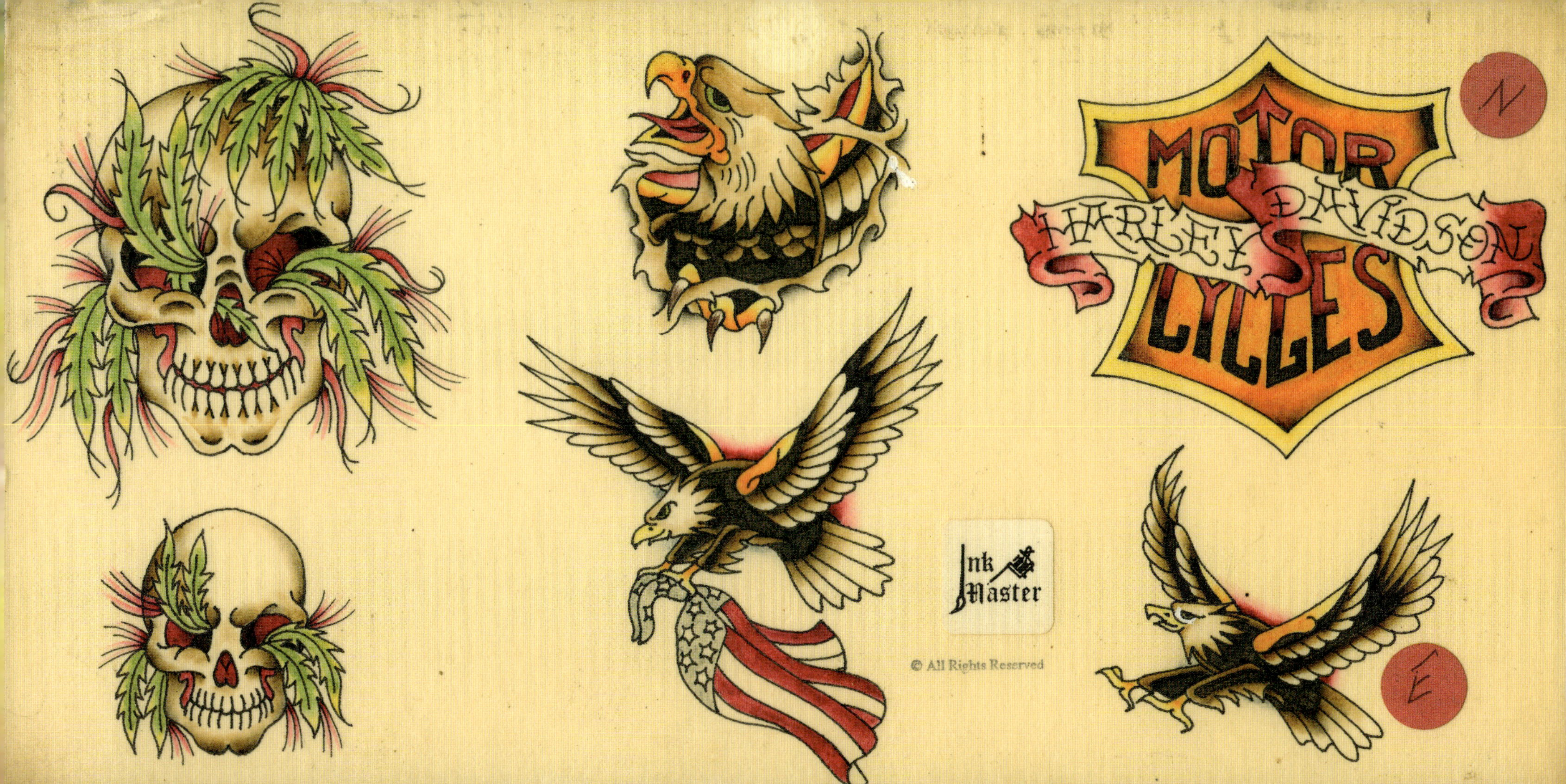
MOTOR
HARLEY DAVIDSON
CYCLES
Ink Master
© All Rights Reserved

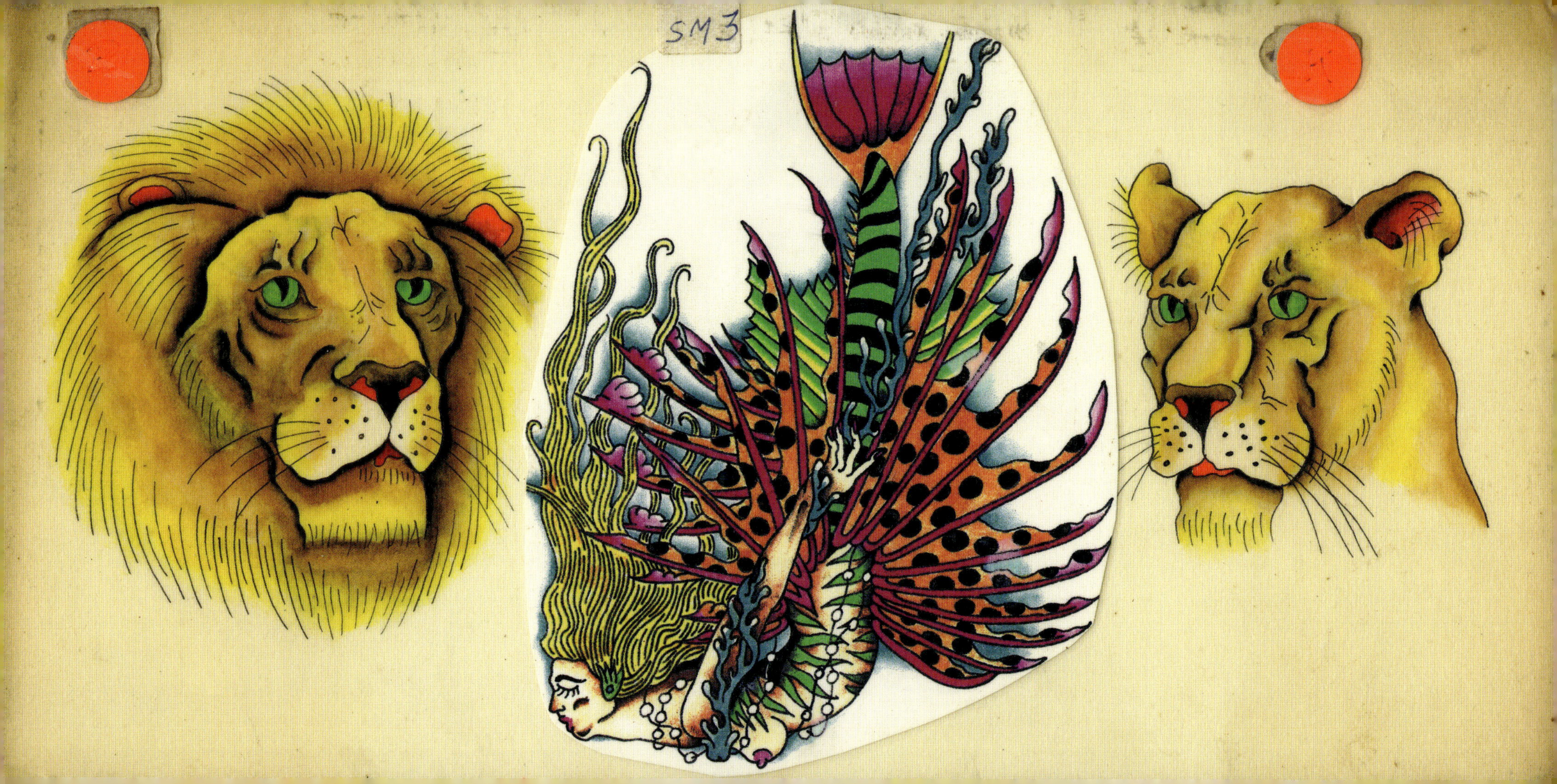
SM3

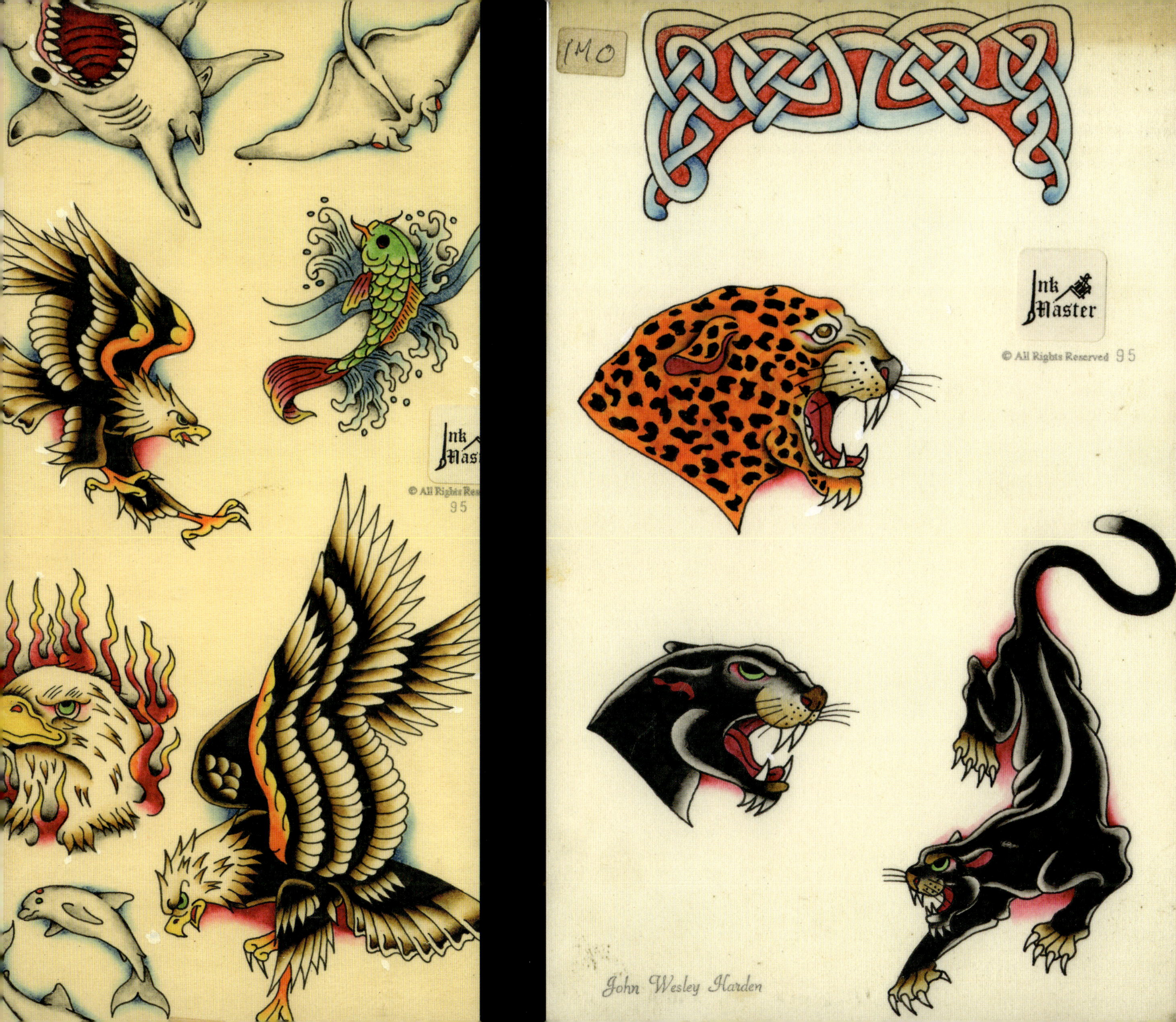
1MO
Ink Master
© All Rights Reserved 95
John Wesley Harden

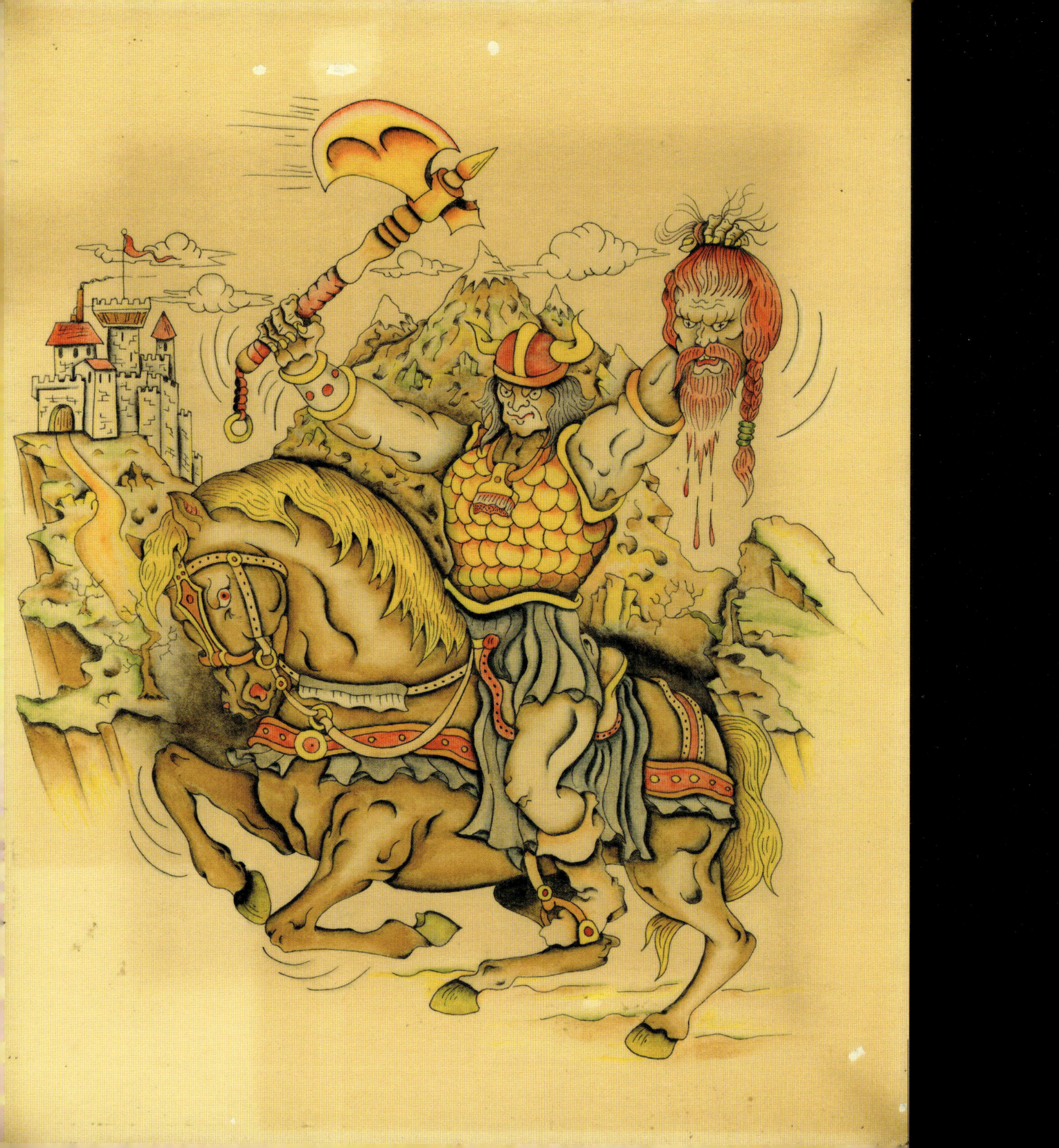

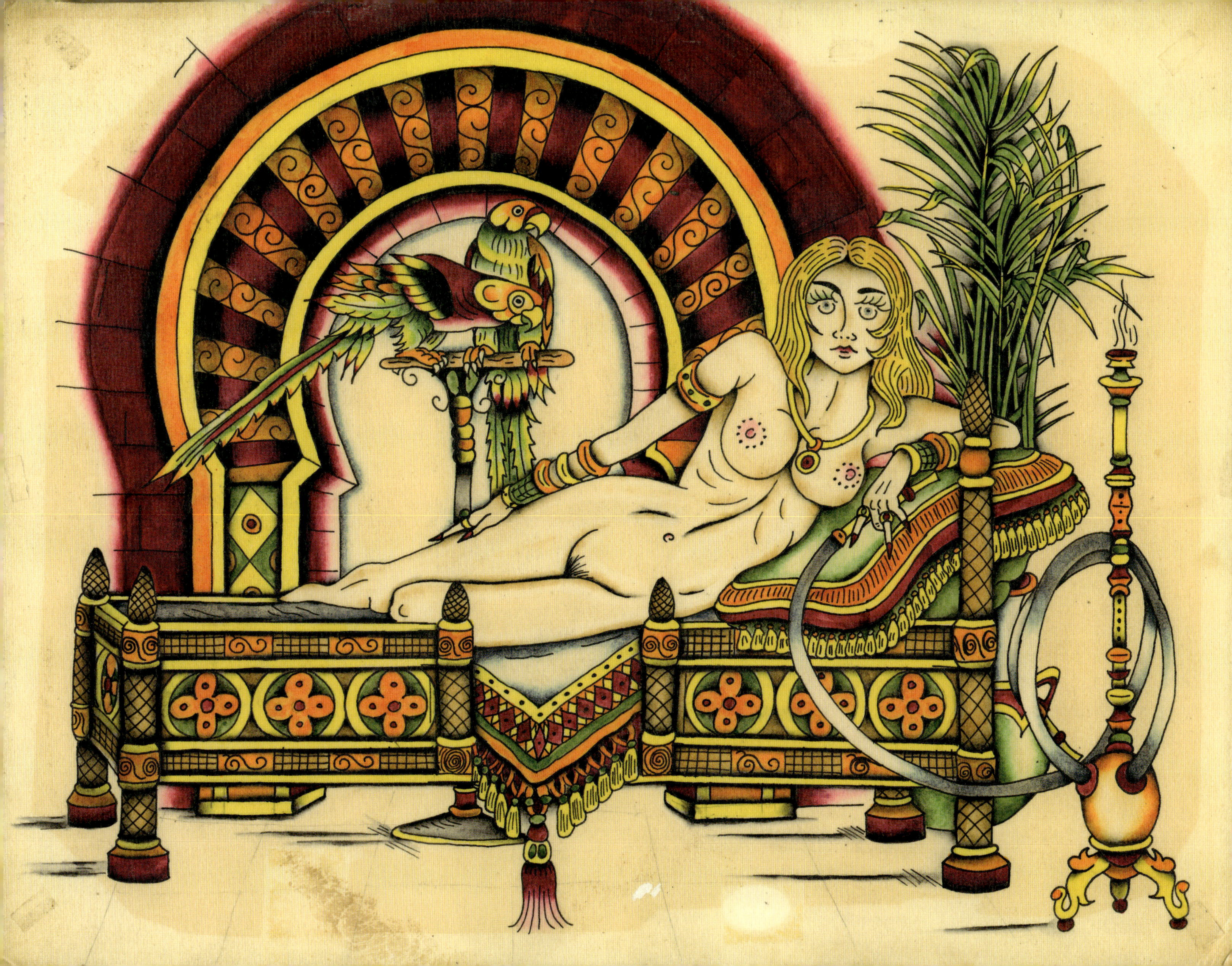

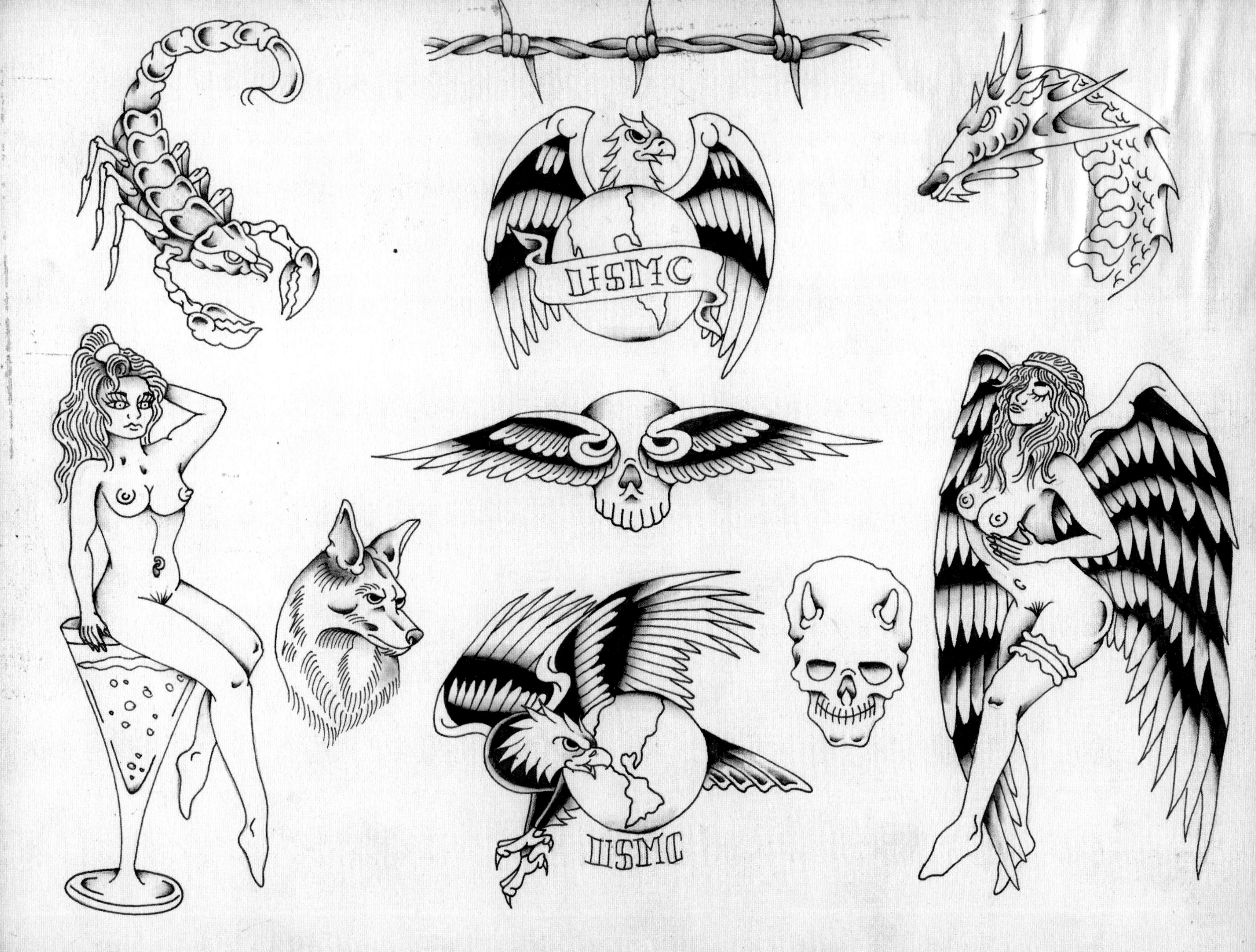
USMC
USMC

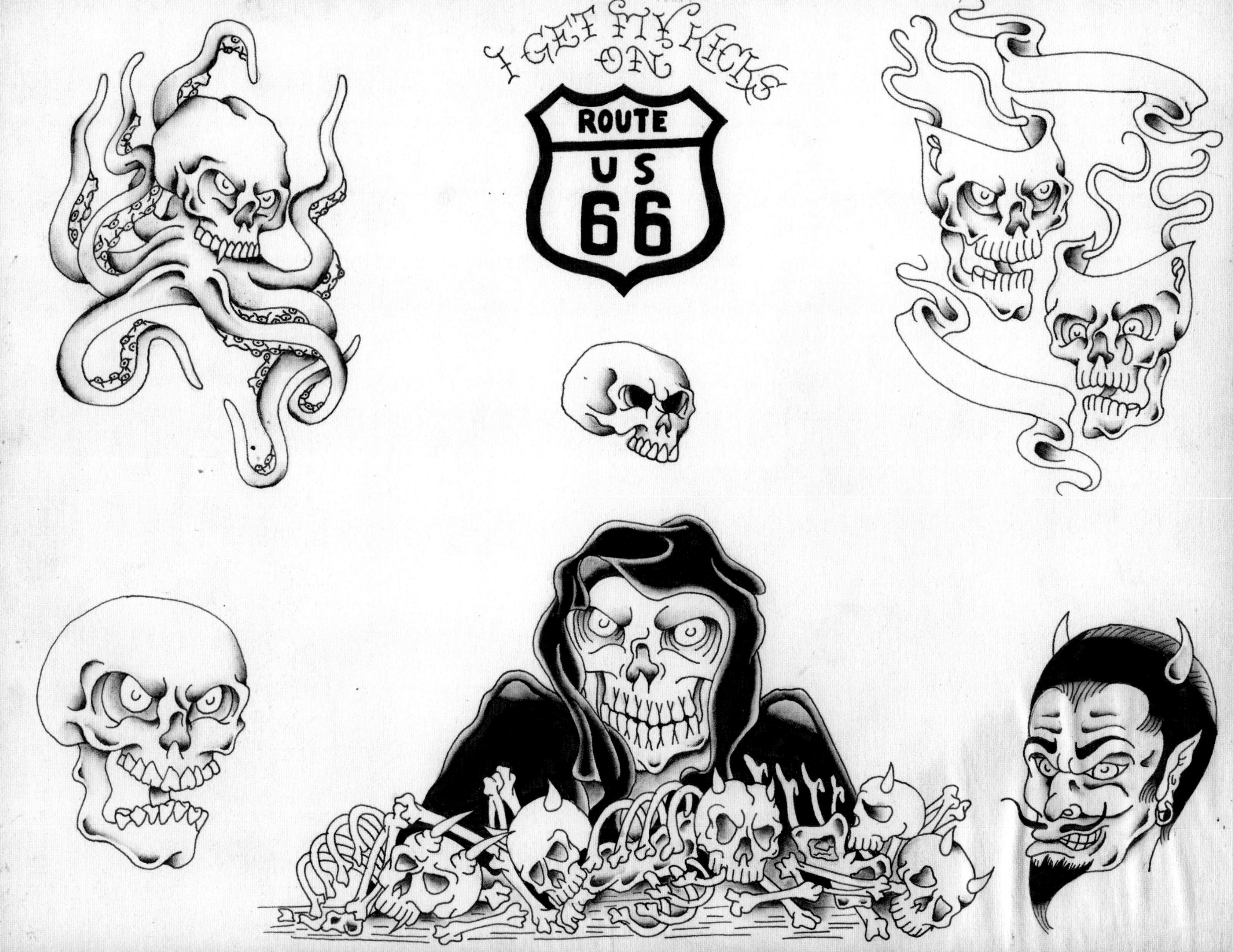
I GET MY KICKS
ON
ROUTE
US
66

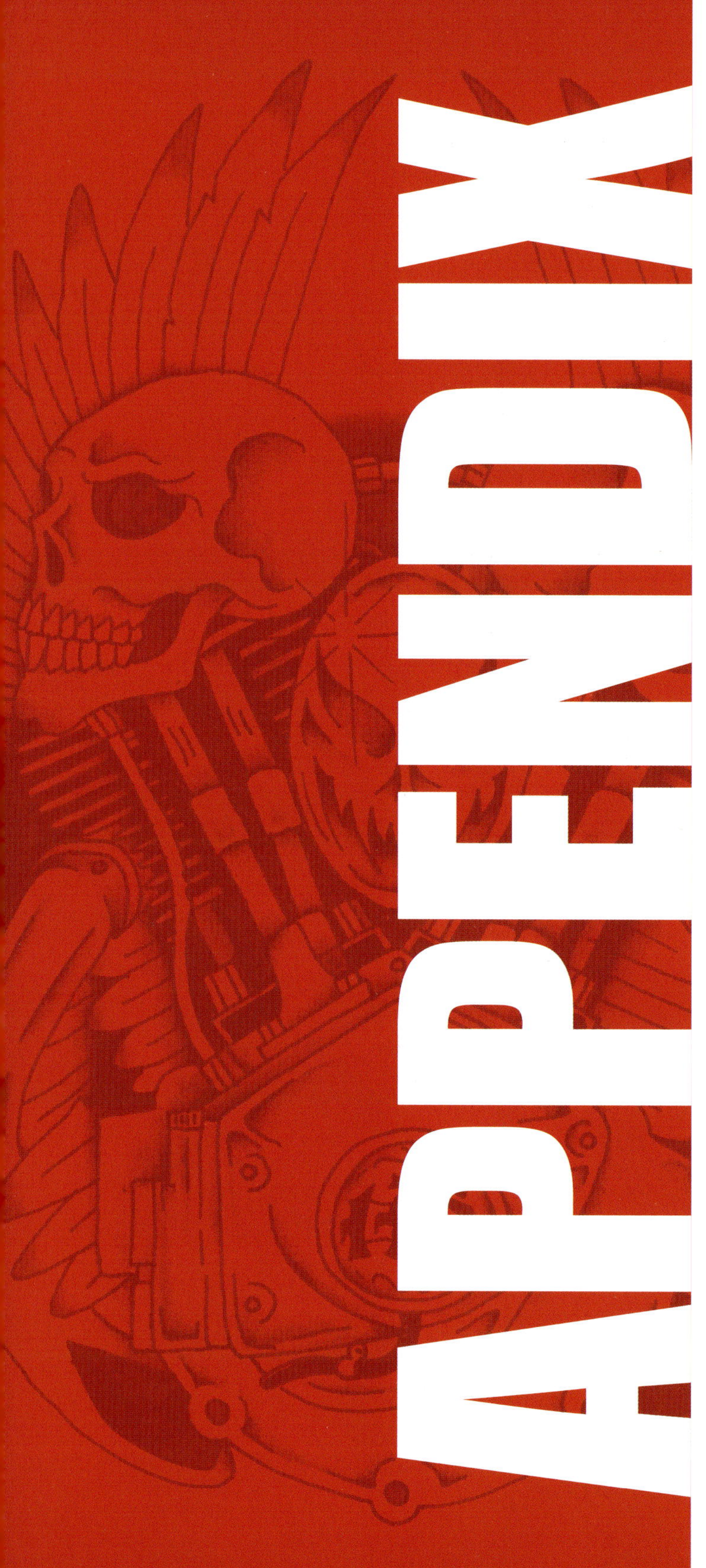

APPENDIX

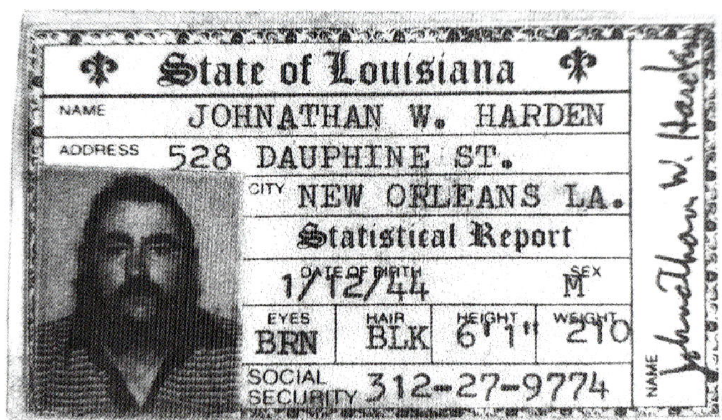

State of Louisiana
NAME JOHNATHAN W. HARDEN
ADDRESS 528 DAUPHINE ST.
CITY NEW ORLEANS LA.
Statistical Report
DATE OF BIRTH 1/12/44 SEX M
EYES BRN HAIR BLK HEIGHT 6'1" WEIGHT 210
SOCIAL SECURITY 312-27-9774
NAME Johnathan W. Harden

John Wesley Harden state of Louisiana fake ID

Robert Charles Kadel birth certificate

FORM 4 B—H. D. V. S. REV. 9-50

TO BE RETAINED BY PARENTS

HEALTH DEPARTMENT OF THE DISTRICT OF COLUMBIA

Certificate of Birth Registration

This is to Certify, *That in accordance with an Act to provide for the better registration of births in the District of Columbia and for other purposes, approved March 1, 1907, the birth of a* male *child to* Charles B. and Wilma M. Kadel *on* Dec. 4, 1945 *has been officially registered in the Health Office of the District of Columbia.*

Name of Child ROBERT CHARLES KADEL

Record No. 560081

Date of filing Dec. 10, 1945

Daniel L. Seckinger, M.D.
DANIEL L. SECKINGER, M. D., DR. P. H.,
Director of Public Health, D. C.

FA

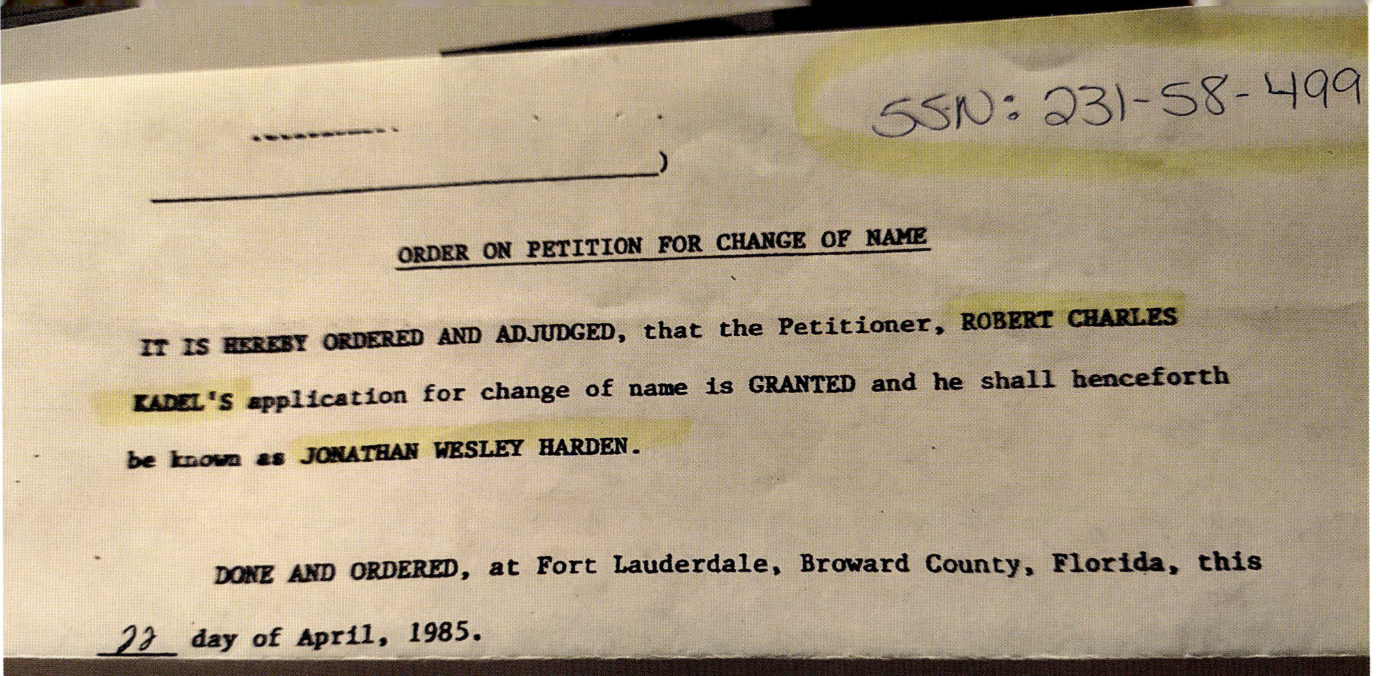
SSN: 231-58-499

ORDER ON PETITION FOR CHANGE OF NAME

IT IS HEREBY ORDERED AND ADJUDGED, that the Petitioner, ROBERT CHARLES KADEL'S application for change of name is GRANTED and he shall henceforth be known as JONATHAN WESLEY HARDEN.

DONE AND ORDERED, at Fort Lauderdale, Broward County, Florida, this 22 day of April, 1985.

Robert Kadel petition for a name change to John Wesley Harden

Upon further research, I decided to elaborate on some factual information I discovered, as well as some speculative information that I witnessed firsthand. Some of this information is backed by documented evidence, while other information comes from my personal memory and what I witnessed. John Harden's birth name was Robert C. Kadel. He was born in Washington, DC, on December 4, 1945, to parents Charles B. and Wilma M. Kadel. His official certificate of name change to John Wesley Harden was granted on April 22 1985, in Ft. Lauderdale, Broward County, Florida, by Judge Patricia Cocalis. John used a lawyer named Arnie Graskin, Esq., to assist him in this legal matter. Prior to 1985, I believe he was using the alias John Harden, because I have possession of a fake ID from the state of Louisiana that lists a different birth date and social security number. This name change did eventually cause him much difficulty later in life when he became medically disabled. John made many attempts to file and collect disability and social security while battling cancer. Because of his name and social security number not matching up due to the name change, he was denied time after time until he was assisted by a lawyer to resolve the matter.

Although I am not certain when John Harden started his tattooing career, I do know that he was active in Ft. Lauderdale, Florida, up until 1993 at his Platinum Needle shop location. Both of his parents are deceased and buried in Ft. Lauderdale as well. I assume it was after their deaths that he relocated to Daleville, Alabama, and opened his Platinum Dragon location in 1993. I am completely unaware of any family, siblings, or offspring he might have had. John Harden took on my high school friend Jason Lacrosse as a helper/apprentice for a brief time around spring 1998. Although I am unsure of the length of time Jason was with him, many years later we reconnected and reminisced on our time together with "Sleep" and some of the things he taught us. Jason's tattooing career never really took off, and he relocated to Birmingham, Alabama. Jason visited Philadelphia a few years ago, and I offered to help get him reestablished in tattooing. Unfortunately, weeks before he was to move to Philadelphia, he was brutally beaten and murdered in front of his own apartment in Birmingham, Alabama. Jason was the last person I knew who had any intimate connection to John Harden, a.k.a. "Sleep."

I also discovered that John Harden employed at least three other people at Platinum Dragon in 1999: Dave and Leia Lanier and Micheal Coleman, a.k.a. "Bubba." I was unable to find any information on them other than income records from tattoos done at the shop. Their employment correlates to the time period that Harden was suffering from stomach cancer. I can only assume he desperately needed their help to get by and keep his shop running.

Throughout his time in Alabama, Harden was running and maintaining his tattoo supply business called Ink Master Tattoo Supply. His catalogs listed all the supplies he had available for sale, and all were handmade by him. Harden was a decent machinist himself, but at times he did enlist the help of other local fabricators in the manufacture of some parts and supplies. He offered various machines, inks, needle-making jigs, needles, and power supplies. Most notable from his catalog was his manufacture of the original Coastal tattoo machines. His catalog states that the Coastal machines were made from the original molding plates of Coastal Tattoo Company, established in 1941. I personally have seen the paperwork of ownership of the company that was framed and displayed in his shop. I do believe its authenticity, because for other replica machines that John produced, he was sure to make reference to the fact that they were replicas, and he also gave credit to the frames' originators.

John Harden told me the following story. Keep in mind, I was very new to tattooing at the time and had never heard of the names and companies involved in these events. John stated that he had sold, over a period of time, Coastal tattoo machine frames to a guy named Mike Nicholson. He said Nicholson owned a supply company called Papillion. He told me that Nicholson had cleaned up his frames and even recast them, changing the way that Coastal appeared on the side of the frame, and even stamped a registered ®

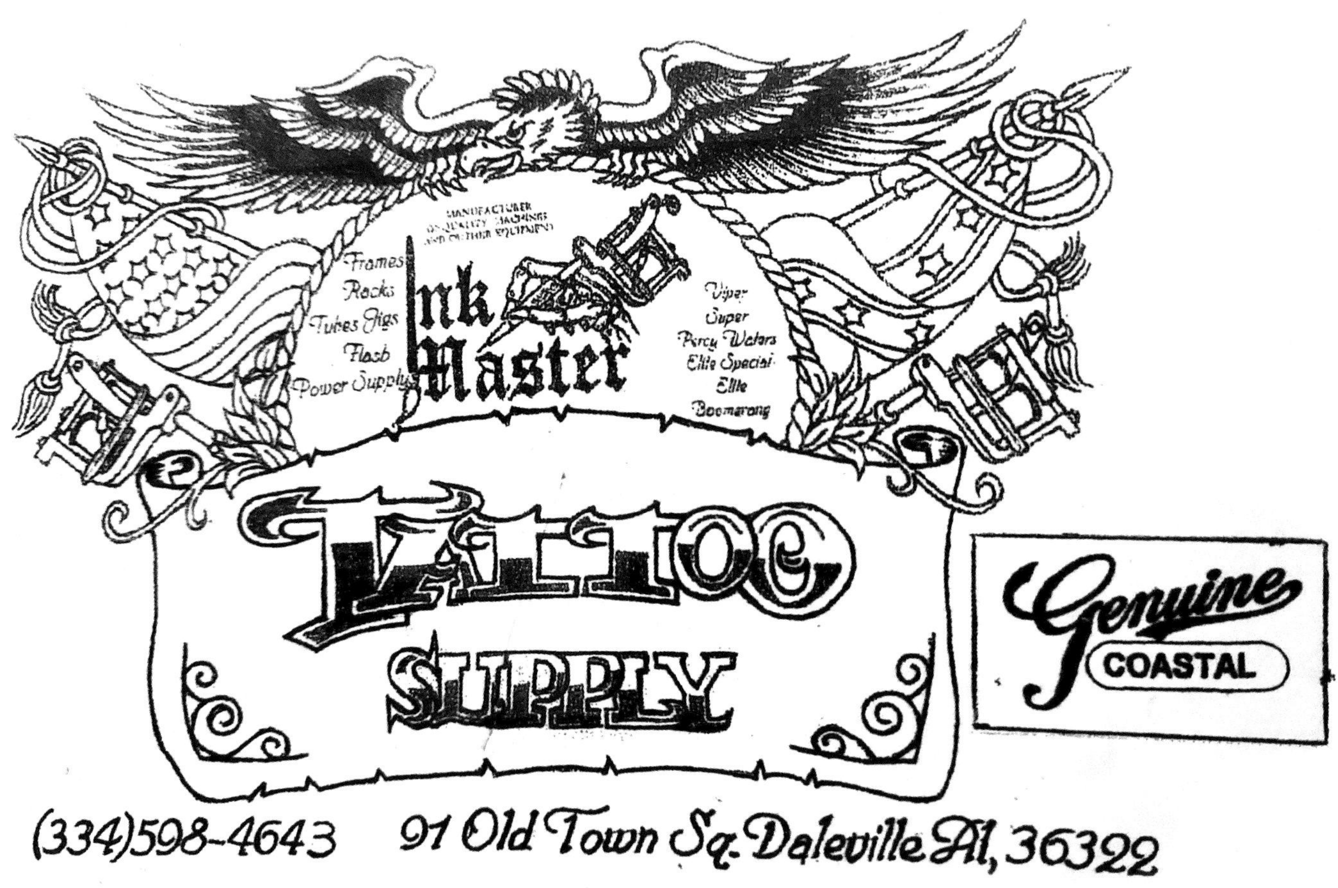

Front cover of an Ink Master tattoo supply catalog.

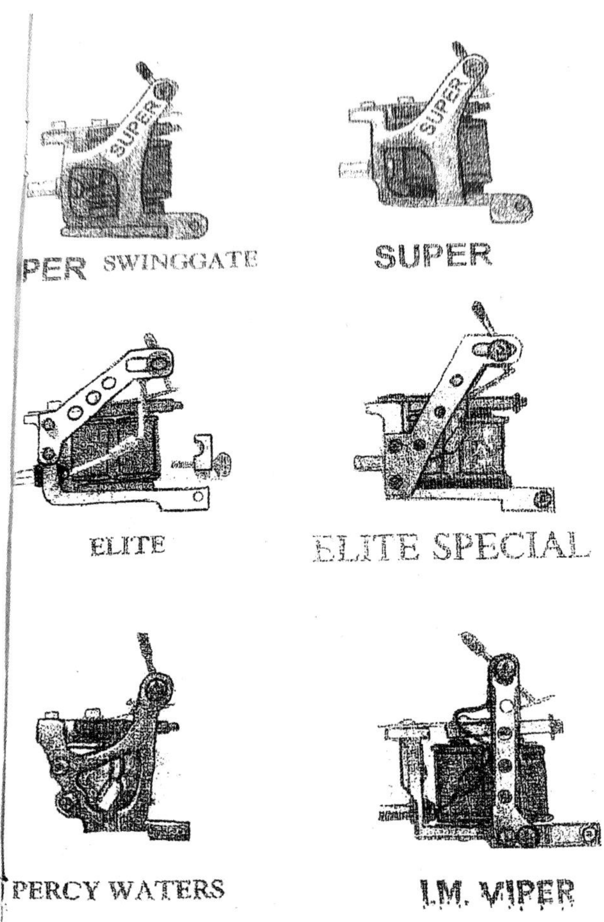

An Ink Master catalog page display of machines offered by John Harden

on the side as well. At the time I was in college, attending intellectual-property law classes. That is the reason John told me this story, in hopes I might be able to help him with his dispute. At that time there was really nothing I could have done. Over time I sort of let that story fade into my memory. Harden continued to manufacture his Coastal frames from the original molding plates. However, he eventually removed the Coastal name on the side plate and hand-stamped Super instead, which is the actual name of that Coastal frame from Sailor Barney.

Harden's Ink Master supply catalog listed sets of tattoo flash he had available for sale. His production sets consisted of eight sheets 11×14 inches and included sets A–Z. There were additions of sets, such as Tribal, later on. These production flash sets were sometimes mash-ups from the original painted sheets. He would often color-photocopy and cut and paste images from other pages together to create a new sheet for a set. I have seen many original hand-painted sheets that were never offered in the production sets.

In hindsight, what seems most impressive to me is the immense workload that Harden put on himself, manufacturing and supplying equipment, hand-painting tattoo designs, and tattooing to keep his ship afloat. I can honestly say that rarely any tattooer today takes on a workload anywhere near what Harden was doing up until his death. I feel like a lesser person would likely crumble under the kind of pressure Harden placed upon himself to keep on creating.

FULL COLOR TATTOO FLASH

Dear Prospective Buyer

All INK MASTERS FLASHis painted by a tattoo artist for tattoo artist.All our sets are full of popular designs that make it easy to make your money back, almost as fast as you can hang them on the wall.All FLASH are quality copies of Tradional hand painted Water Color Flash.

There are currently 18 sets of flash availible, and more being added all the time.

All sets consist of EIGHT 11 X 14 sheets with stencil copies of same. Each set cost $80.00 U.S. Funds. If you buy four sets you get the fifth set FREE.

All Art work is painted by JOHN W. HARDEN.

THE FOLLOWING SETS ARE AVAILAIBLE

Set A - Dragons,Skulls,Cats,Rebel, and more.
Set B - Animals,Dragons,Flowers,Skulls and more.
Set C - Women,Cats,Rebel States,Dragons and more.
Set D- All assorted Dragons.
Set E - Colored Tribel,Snakes,Fantasy,Skulls and more.
Set F - Birds,Reapers,Eagles,Mermaids,Harts & more
Set G- Wild Women,Unicorns,Eagels,Panthers & more
Set H- Assorted Harley
Set I - Eagles,Indian Tribal,Fantasy & more.
Set J - Wizards,Reapers,Unicorns,Fantasy & more
Set K- Eagles,BigCats,Cross,Bear,Hearts&Bann. & more
Set L1- LIMITED EDITION SET 5 Sheets
Back Pc. Mermaids,Bad Girls,Winged Harley Skull
Set L2- LIMITED EDITION SET 5 Sheets
Rebel,Eagels,BigCats,TheSea,Skulls
Set M- MILITARY Army,Navy,Marinens
Set N- Tigers,FantasyDragons,Tribal,Skulls & more
Set O- IndianGirls,Taz,Taz,Taz,Fantasy,Small stuff &more
Set S - Assorted Skeletons,Skulls,Skulls,Skulls
Set T - All Assorted Tribal,Tribal,Tribal

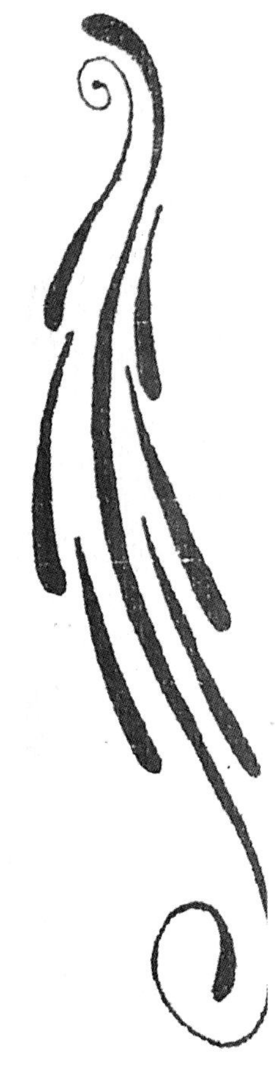

A list of production style flash offered by Ink Master tattoo supply.

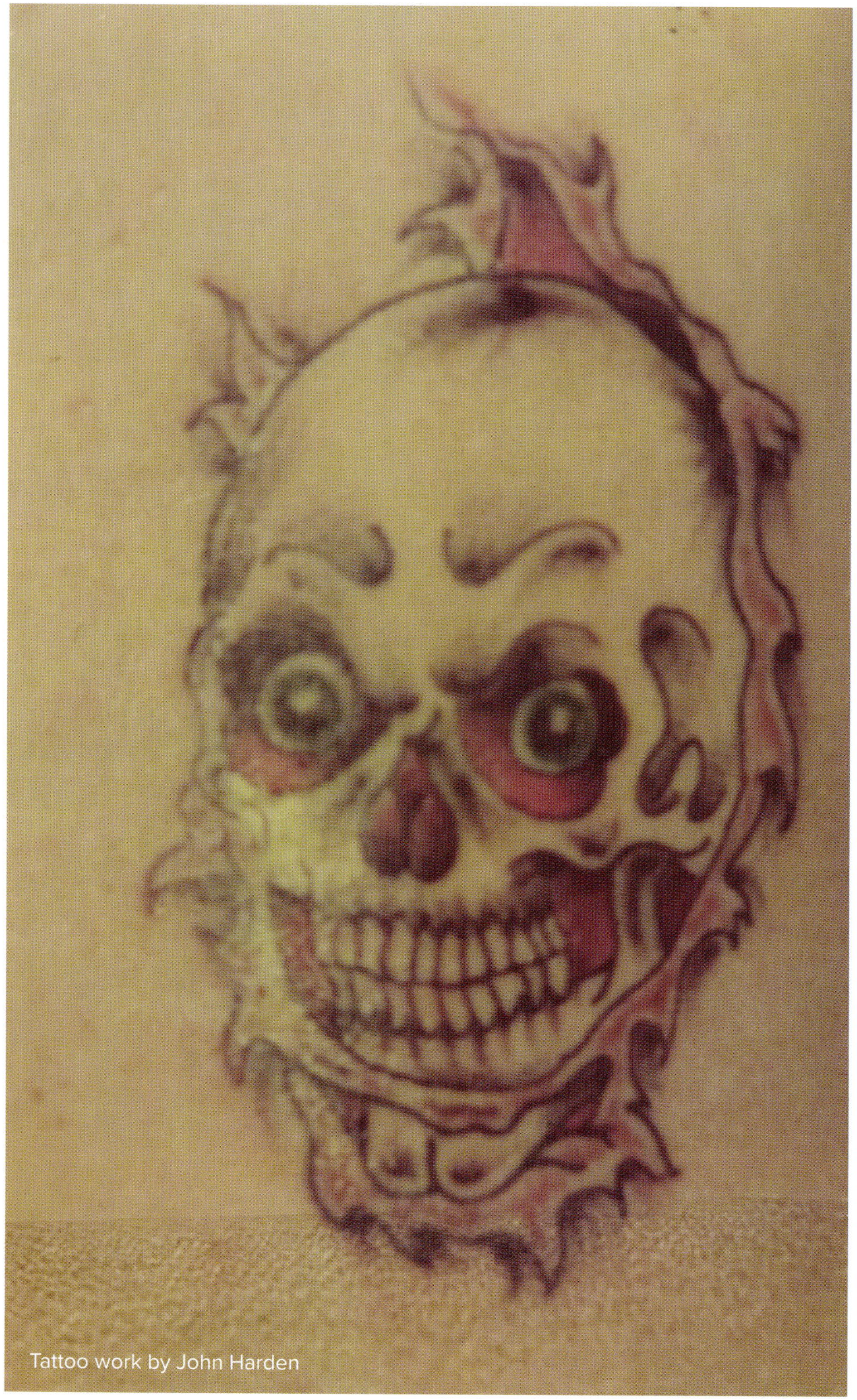

Tattoo work by John Harden

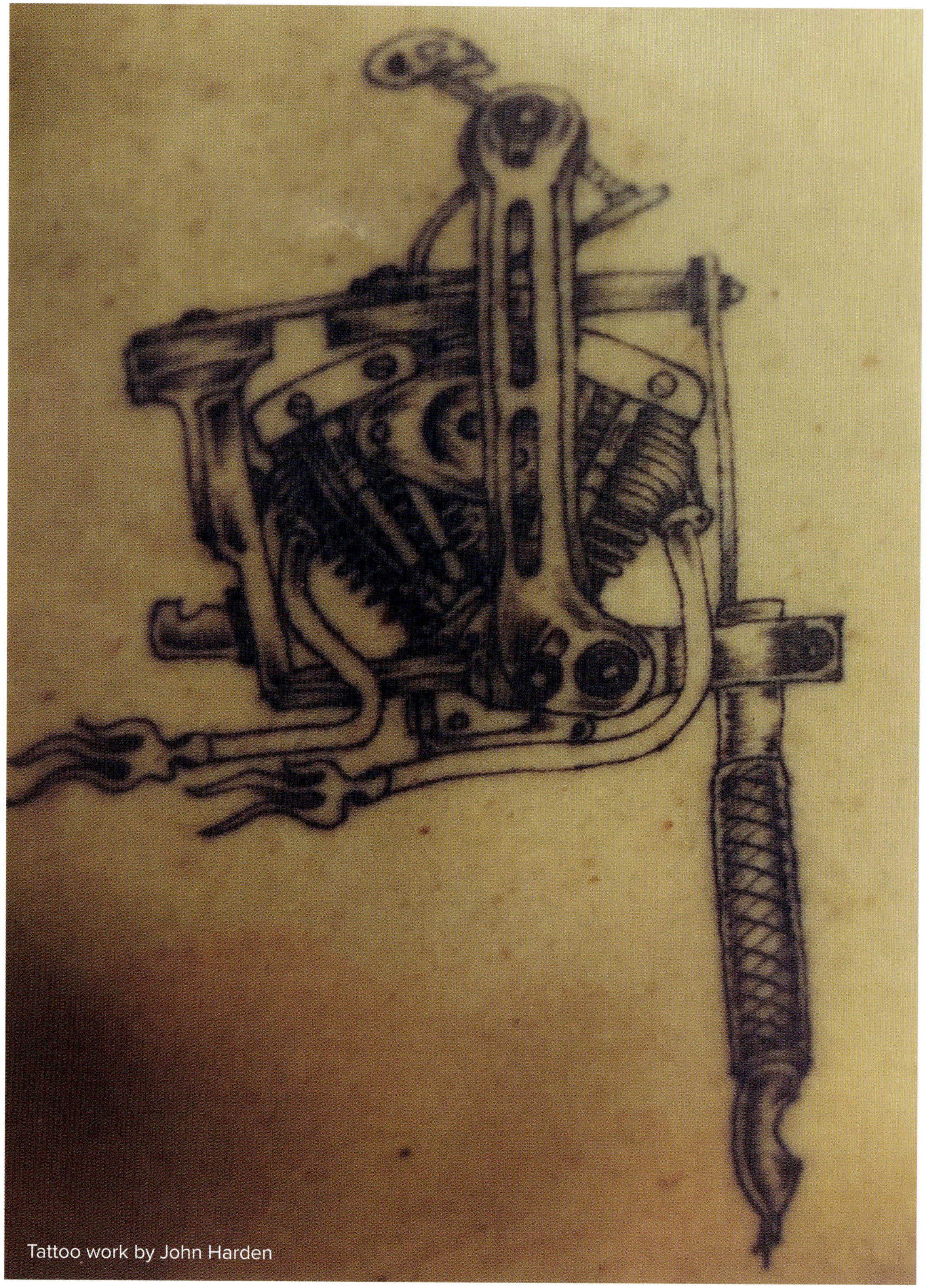

Tattoo work by John Harden

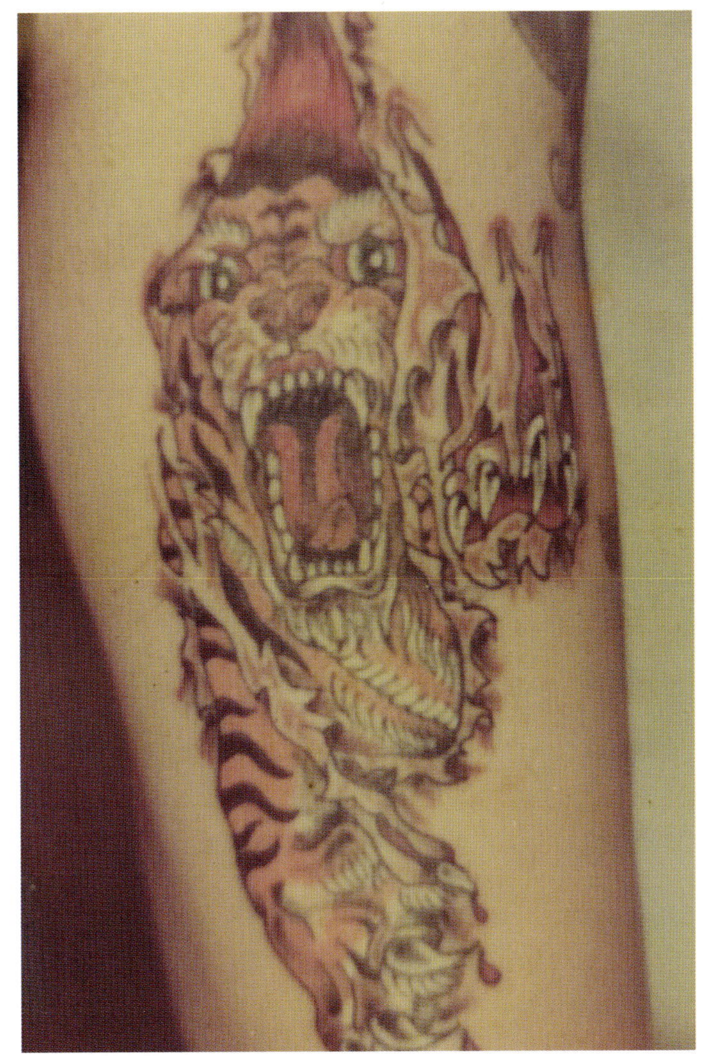

Tattoo work by John Harden

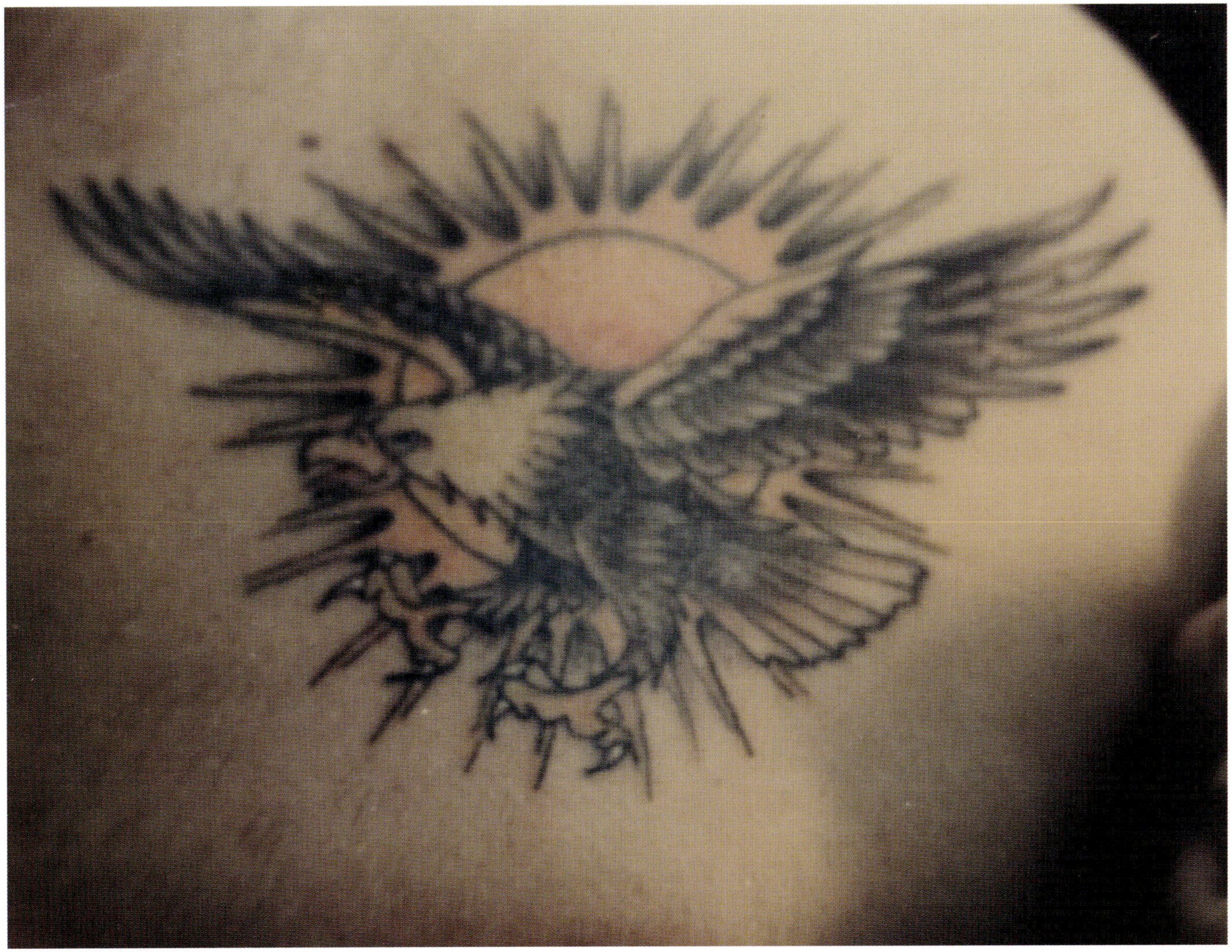

Tattoo work by John Harden

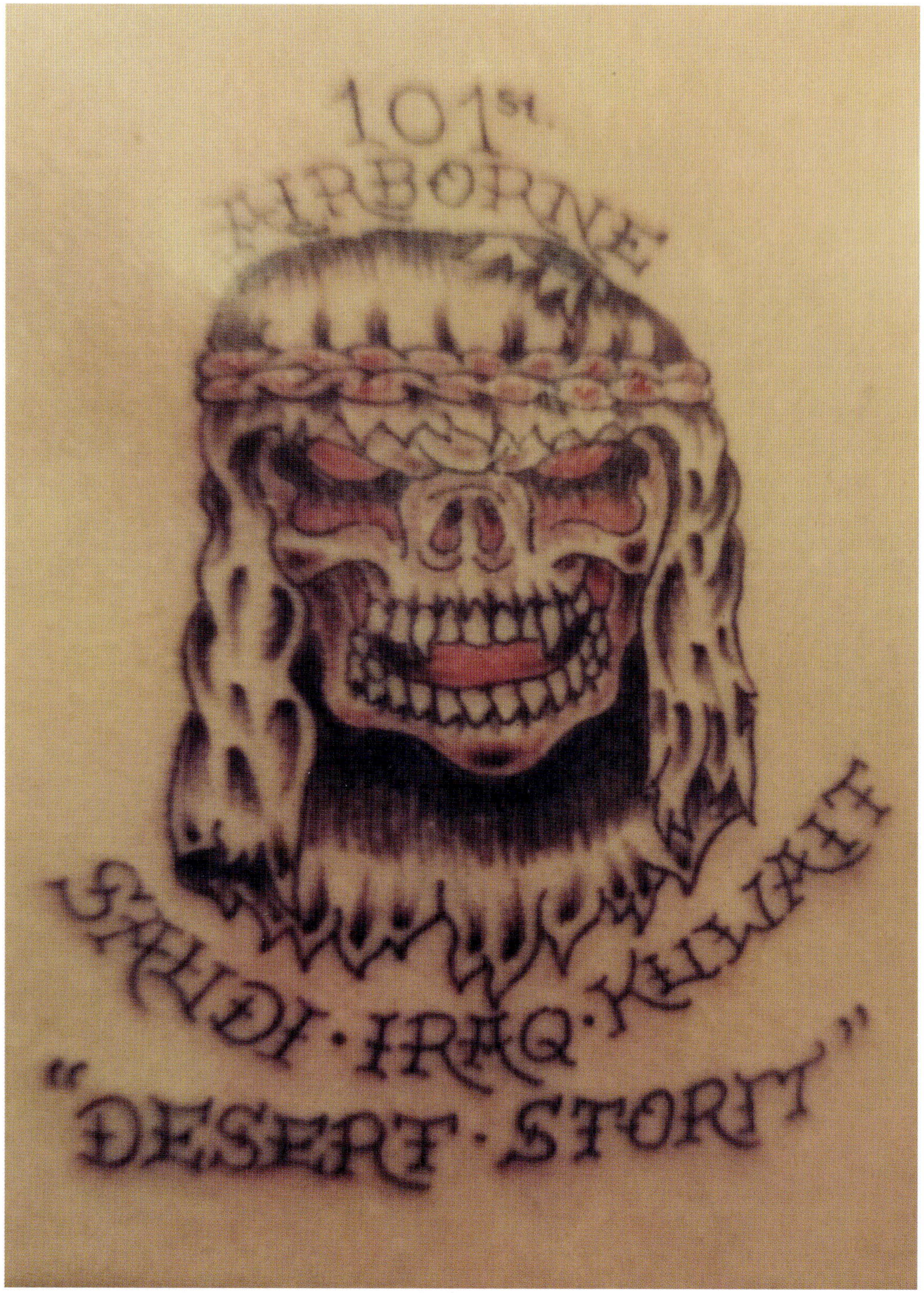

Tattoo work by John Harden

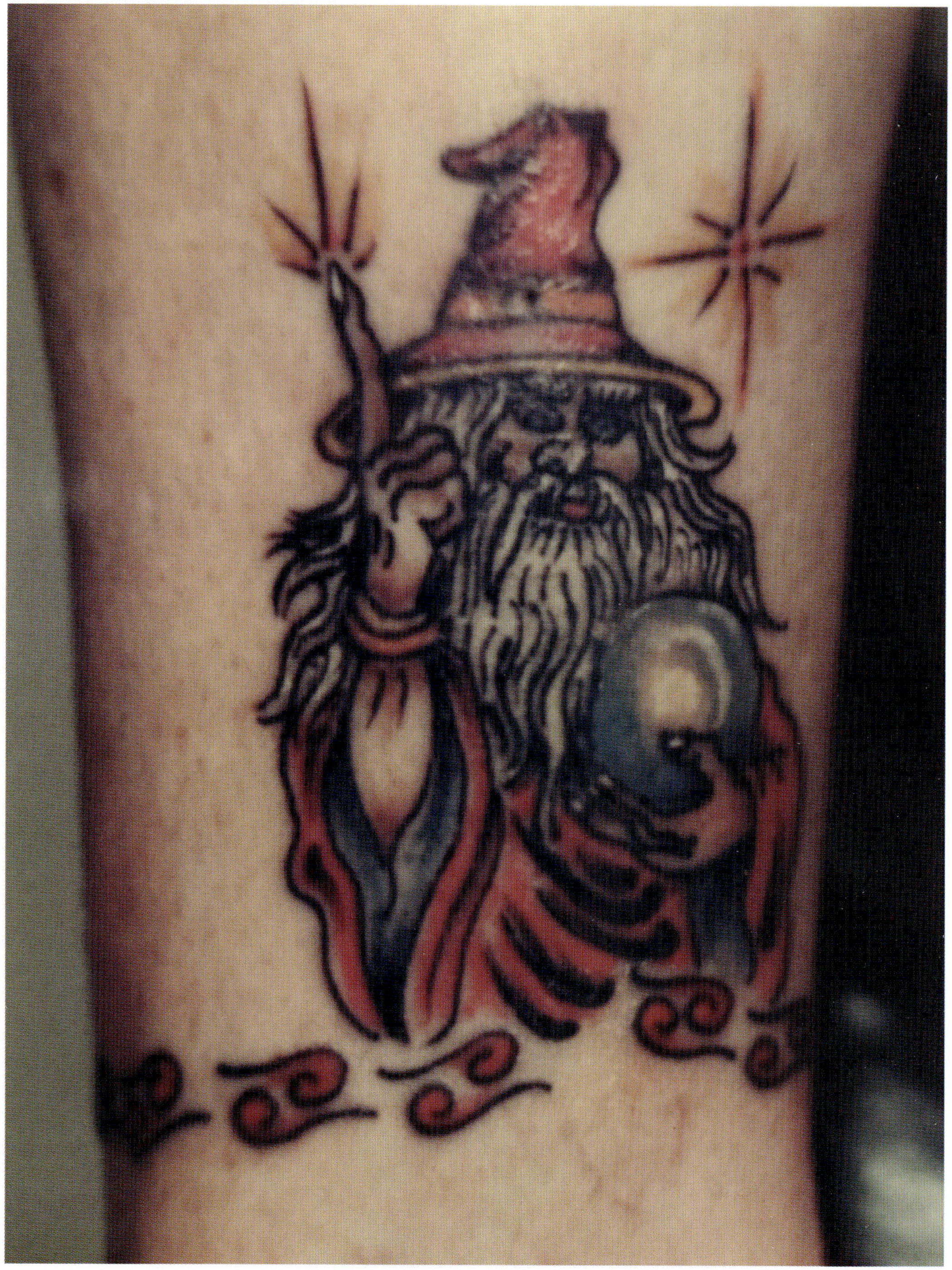

Tattoo work by John Harden

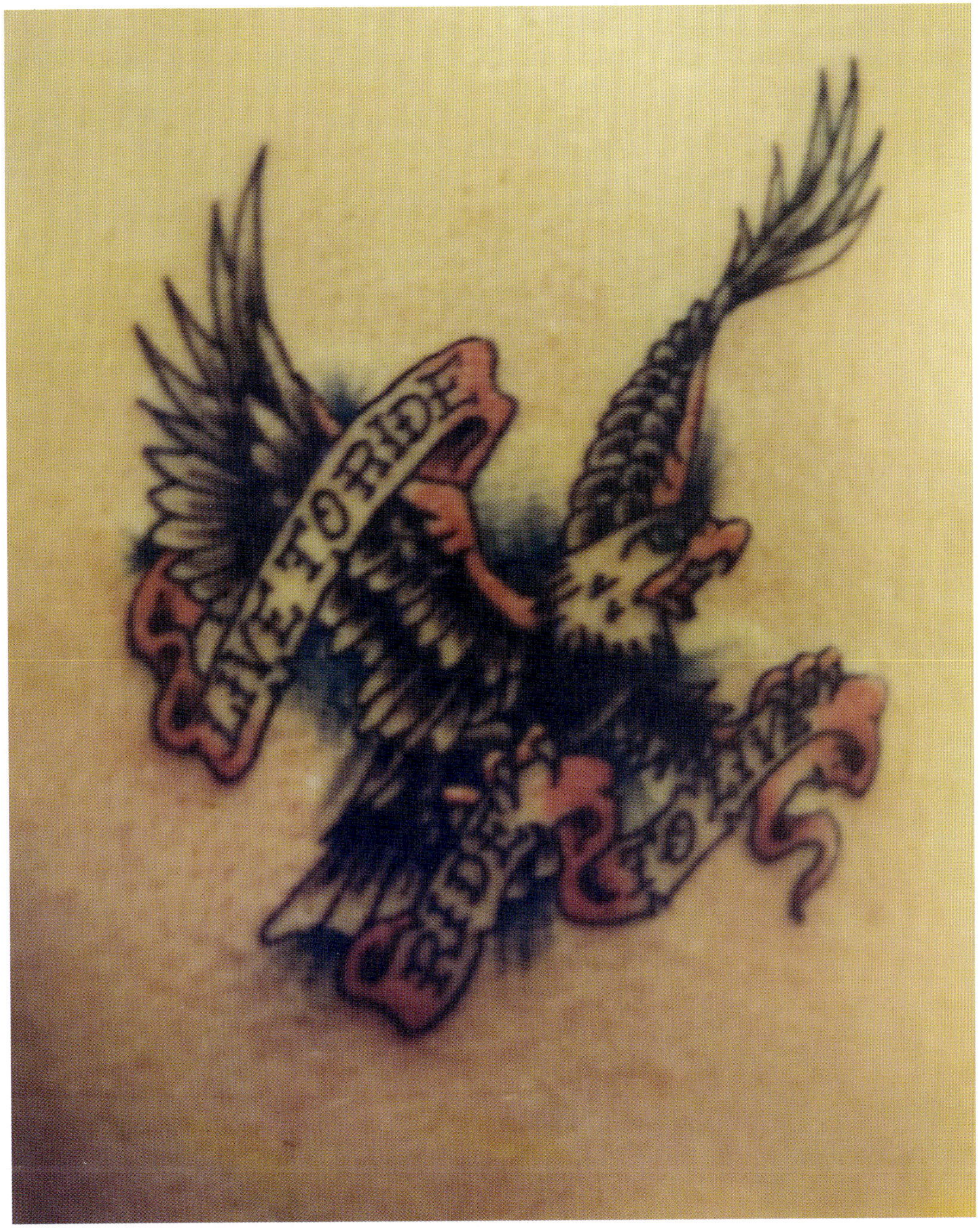

Tattoo work by John Harden

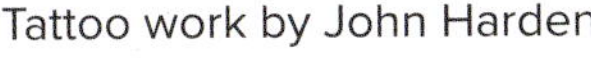

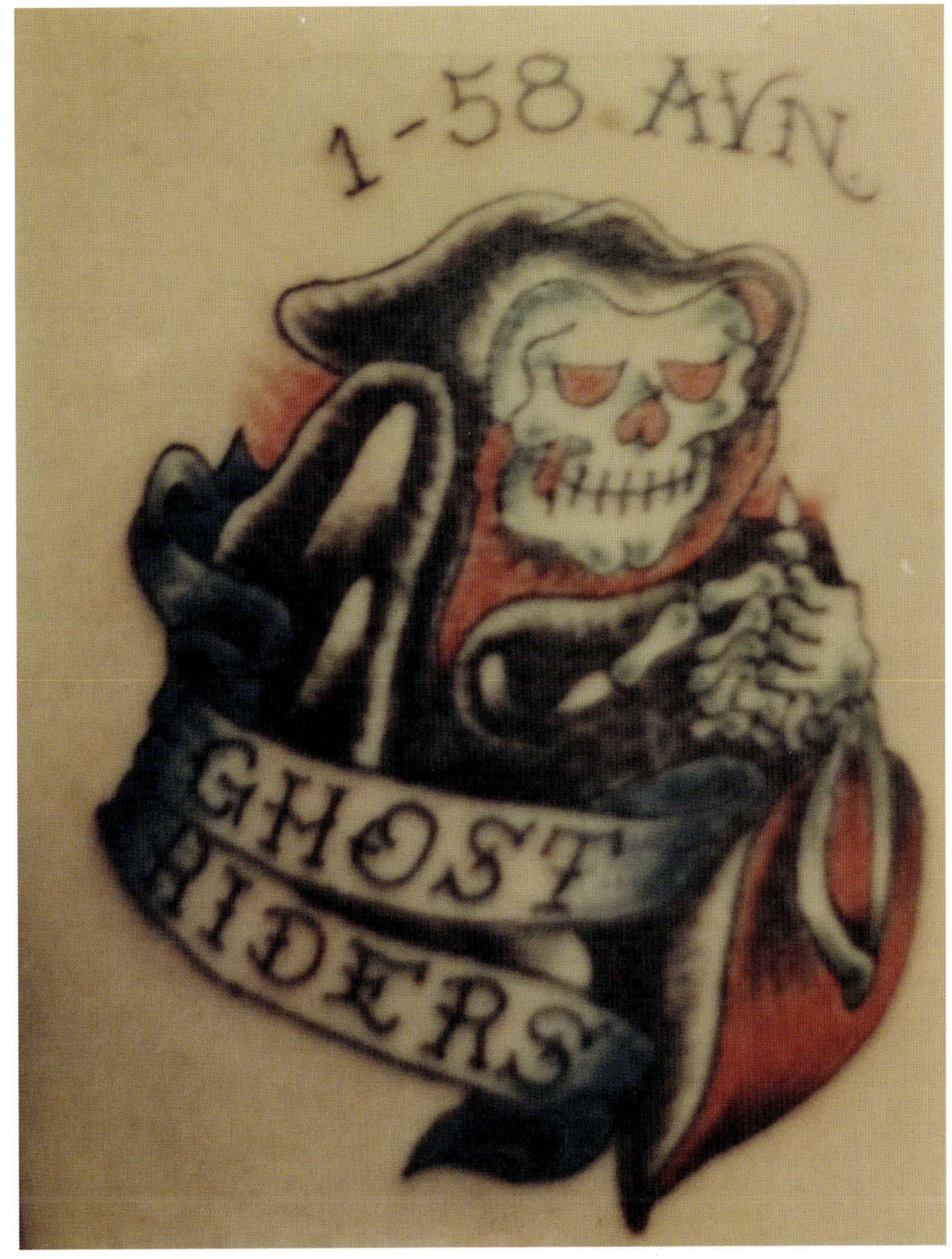

Tattoo work by John Harden

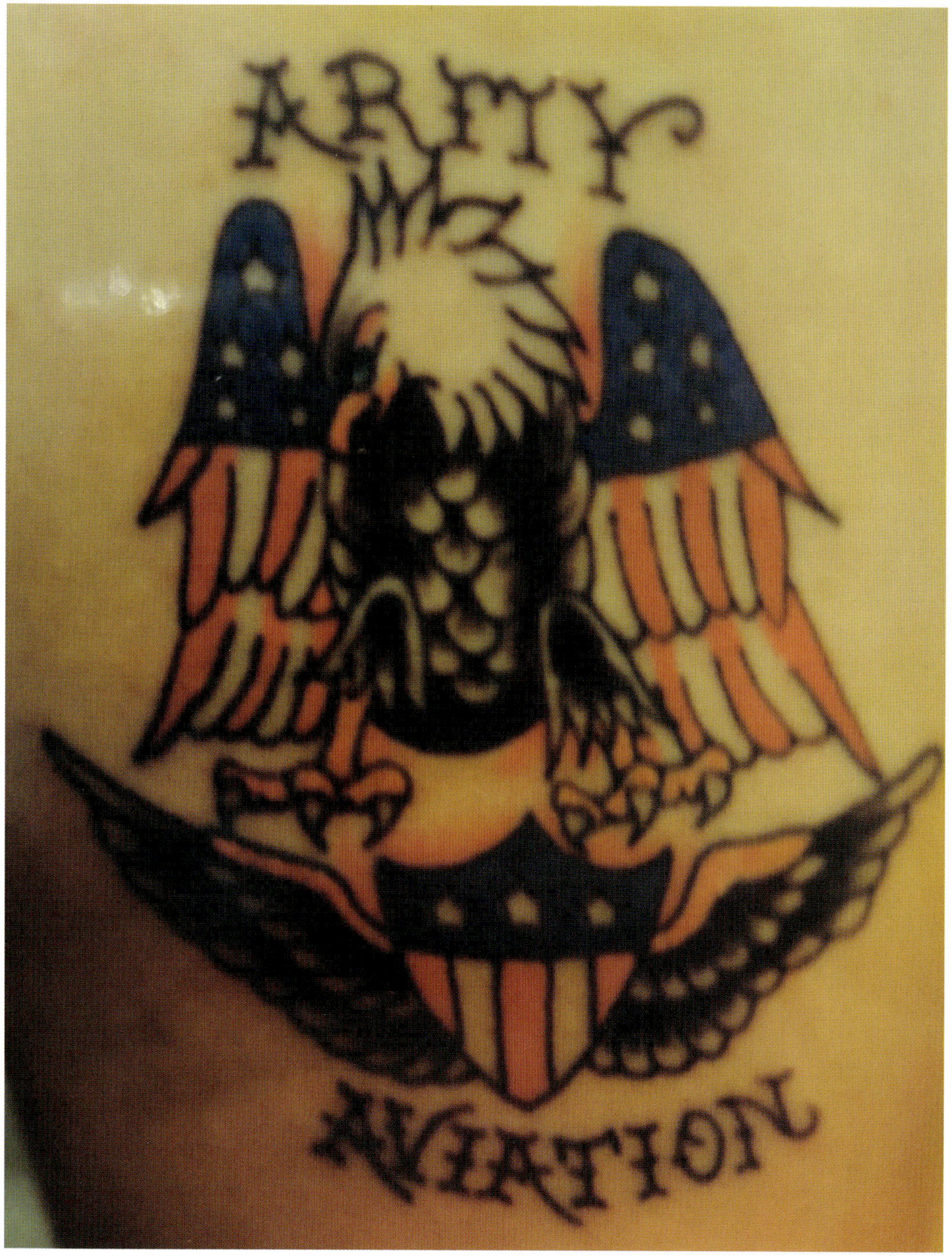

Tattoo work by John Harden

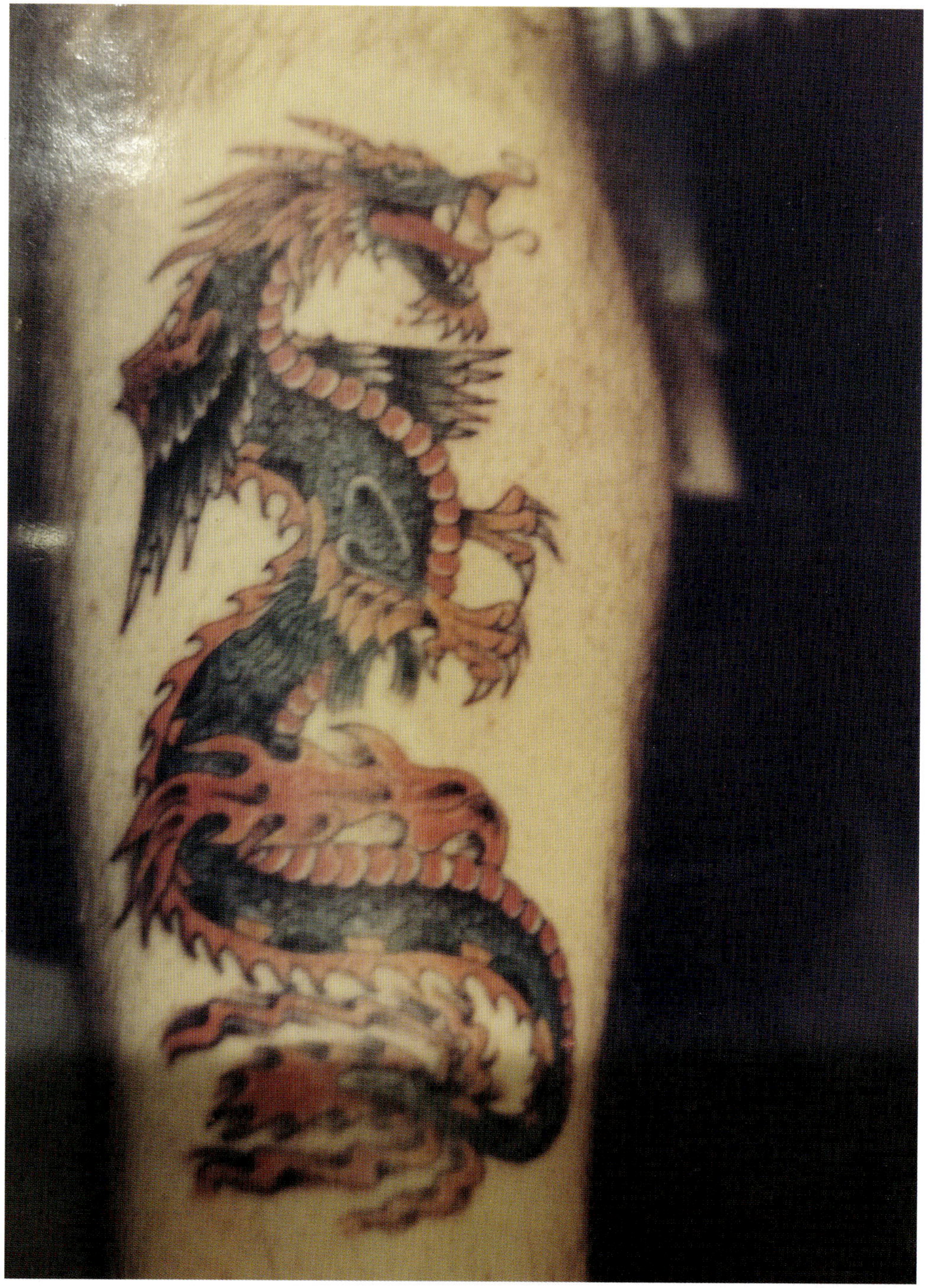

Tattoo work by John Harden

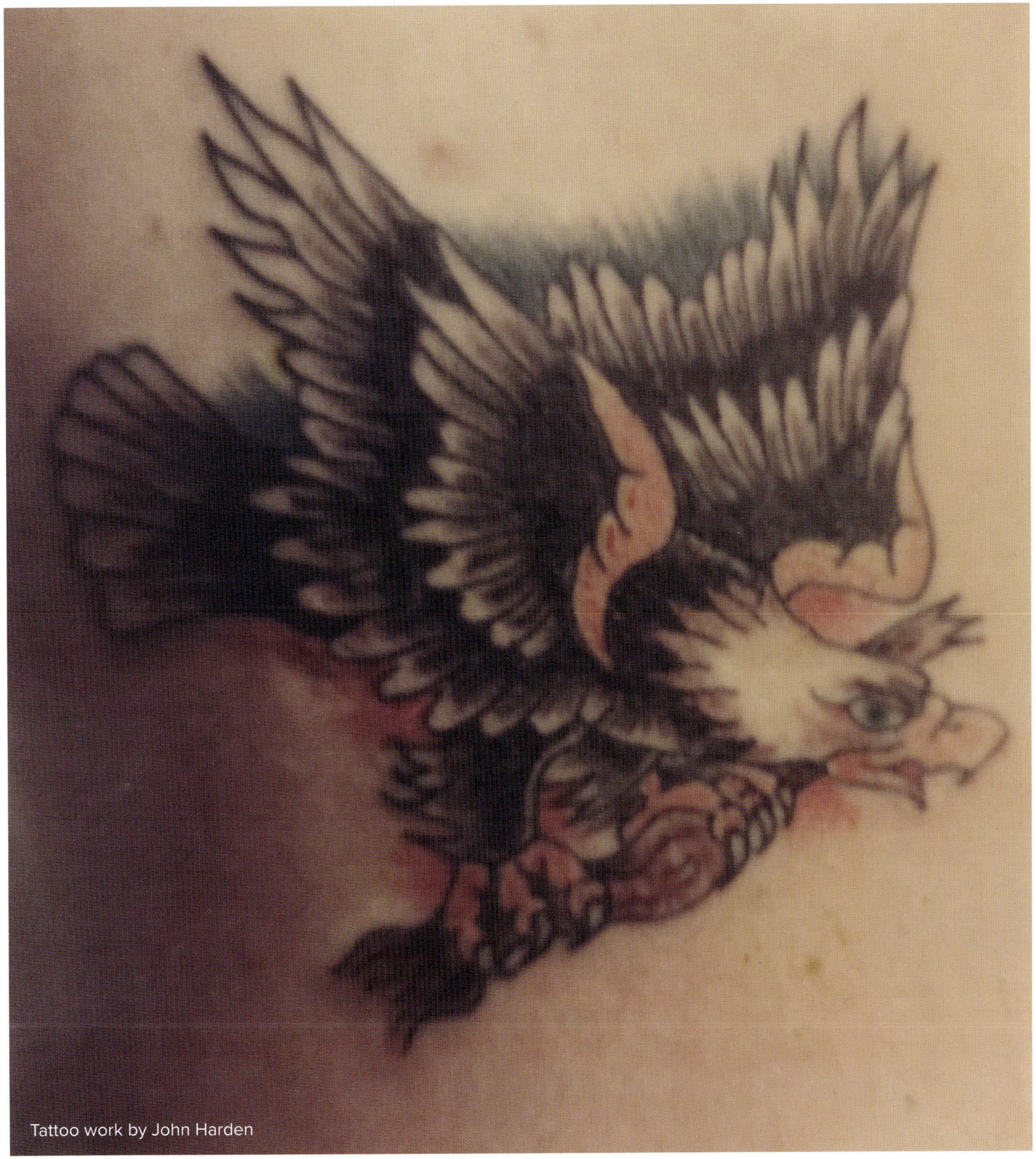

Tattoo work by John Harden

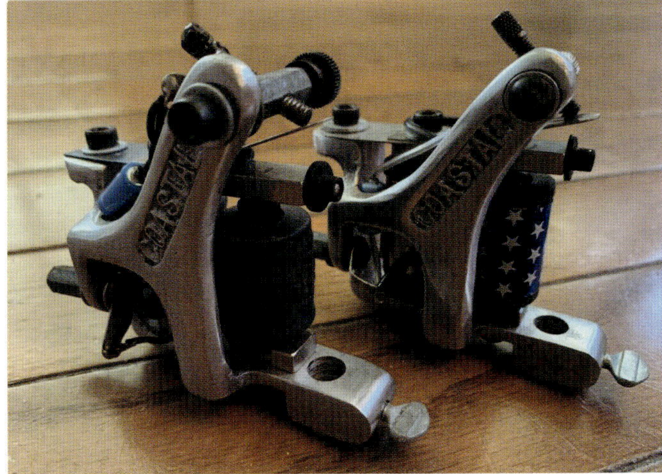

Coastal tattoo machines made by John Harden

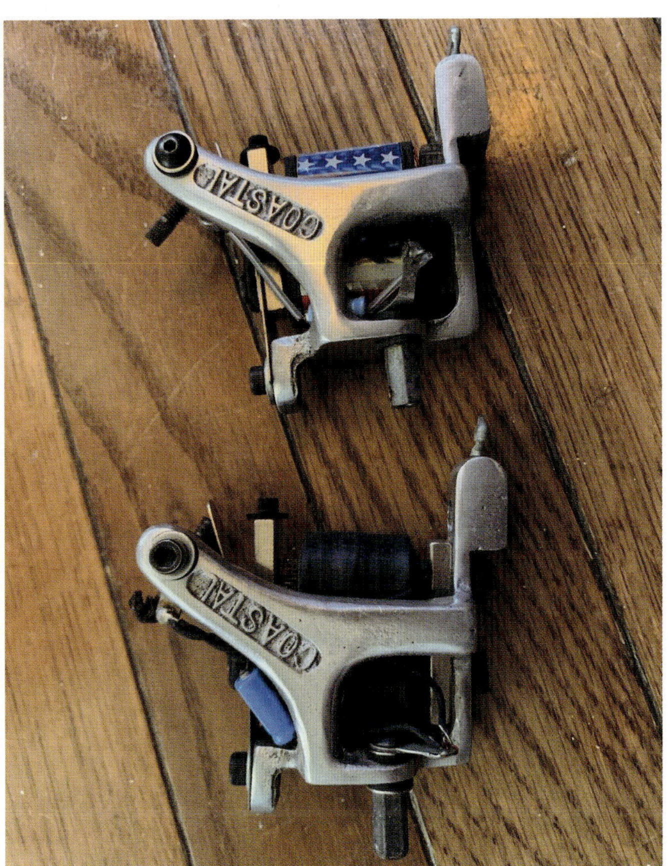

Coastal tattoo machines made by John Harden.

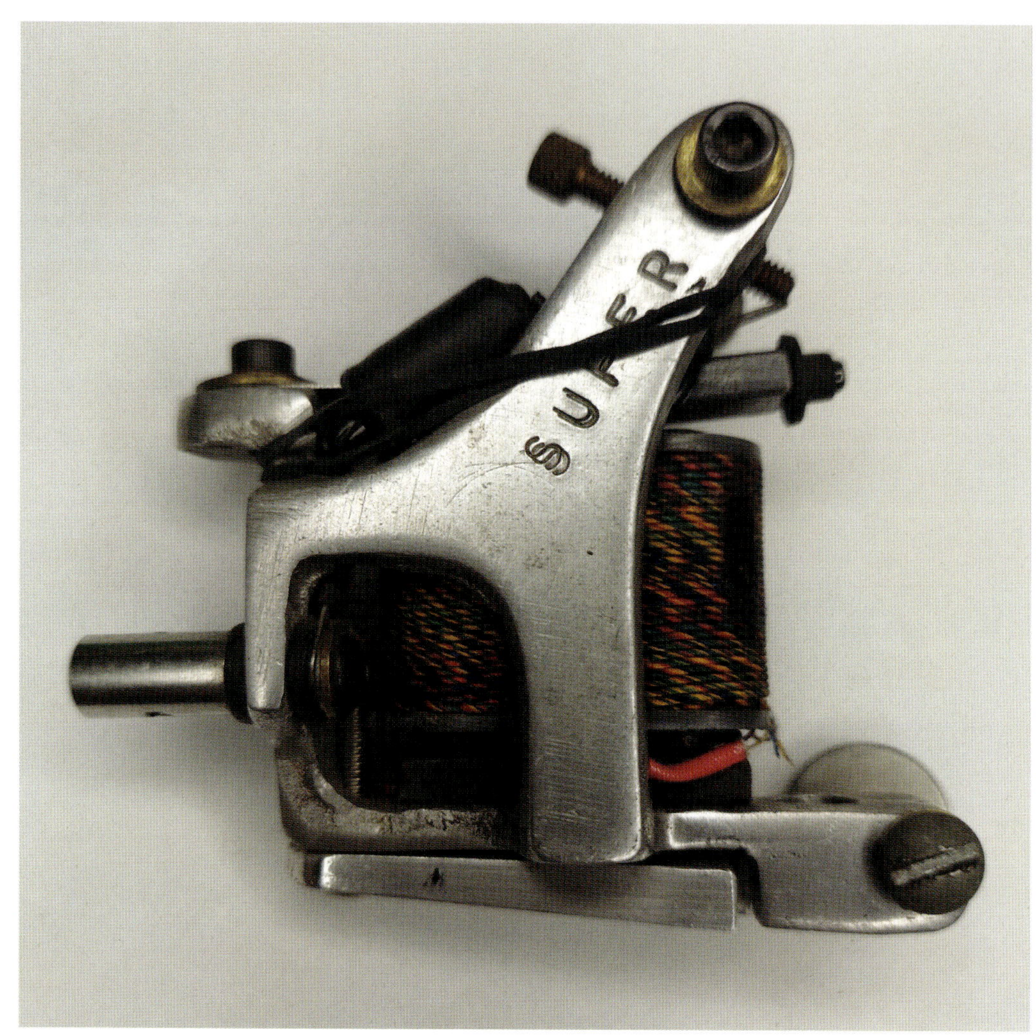

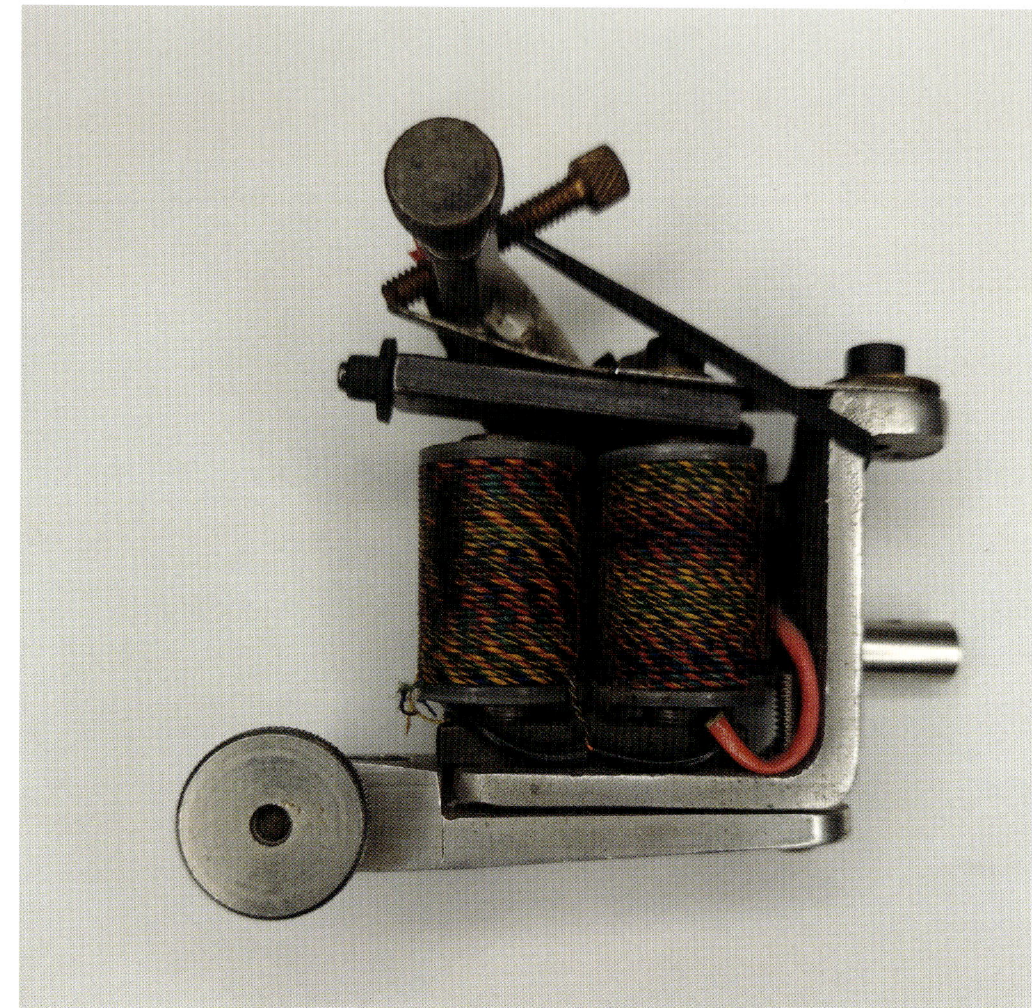

Late-model Coastal tattoo machine stamped as Super

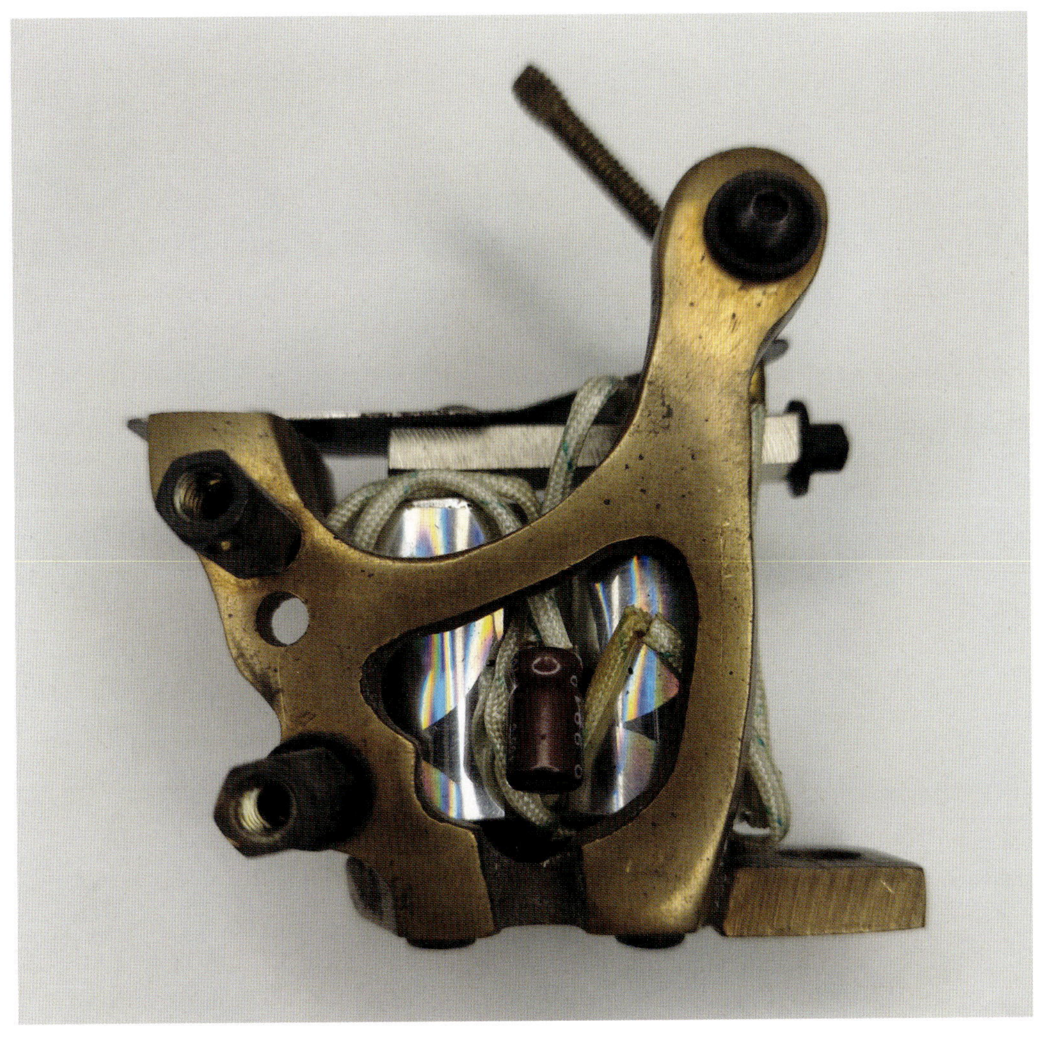

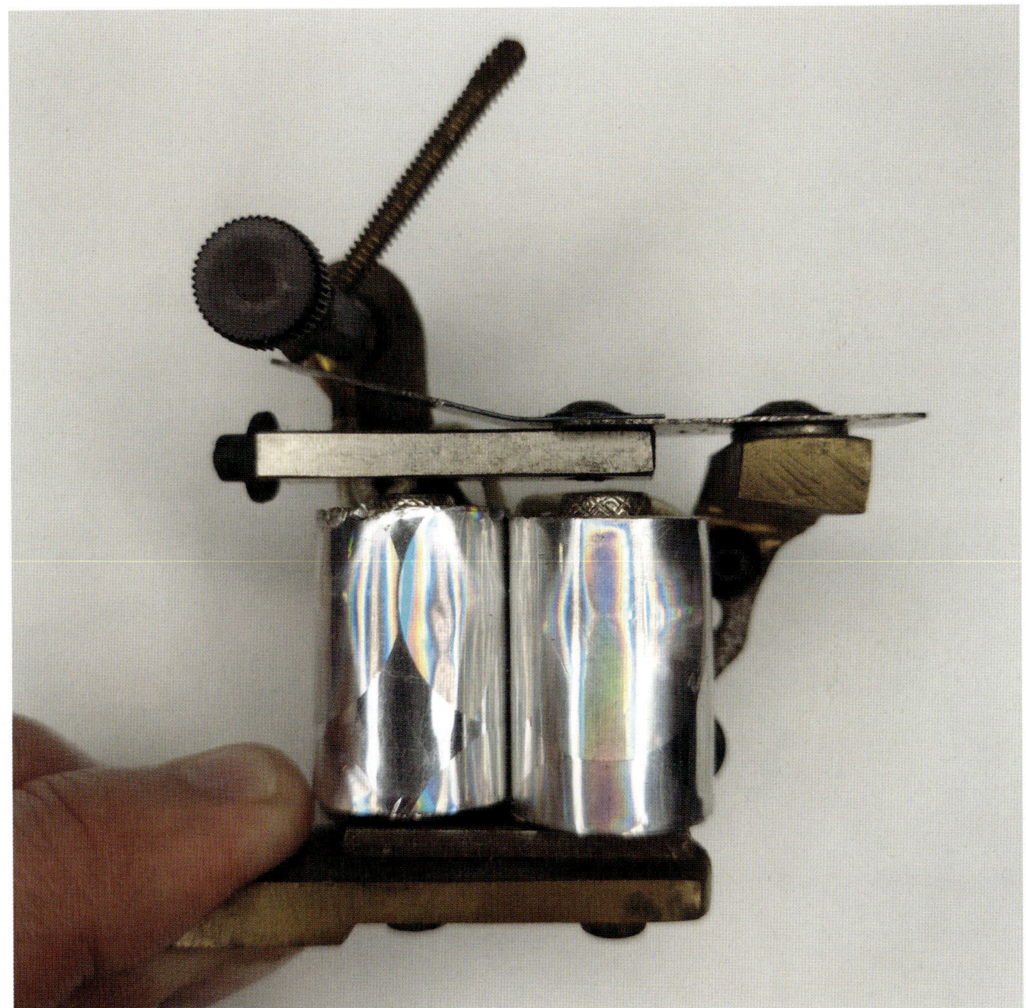

John Harden Sidewheeler Percy Waters replica machine

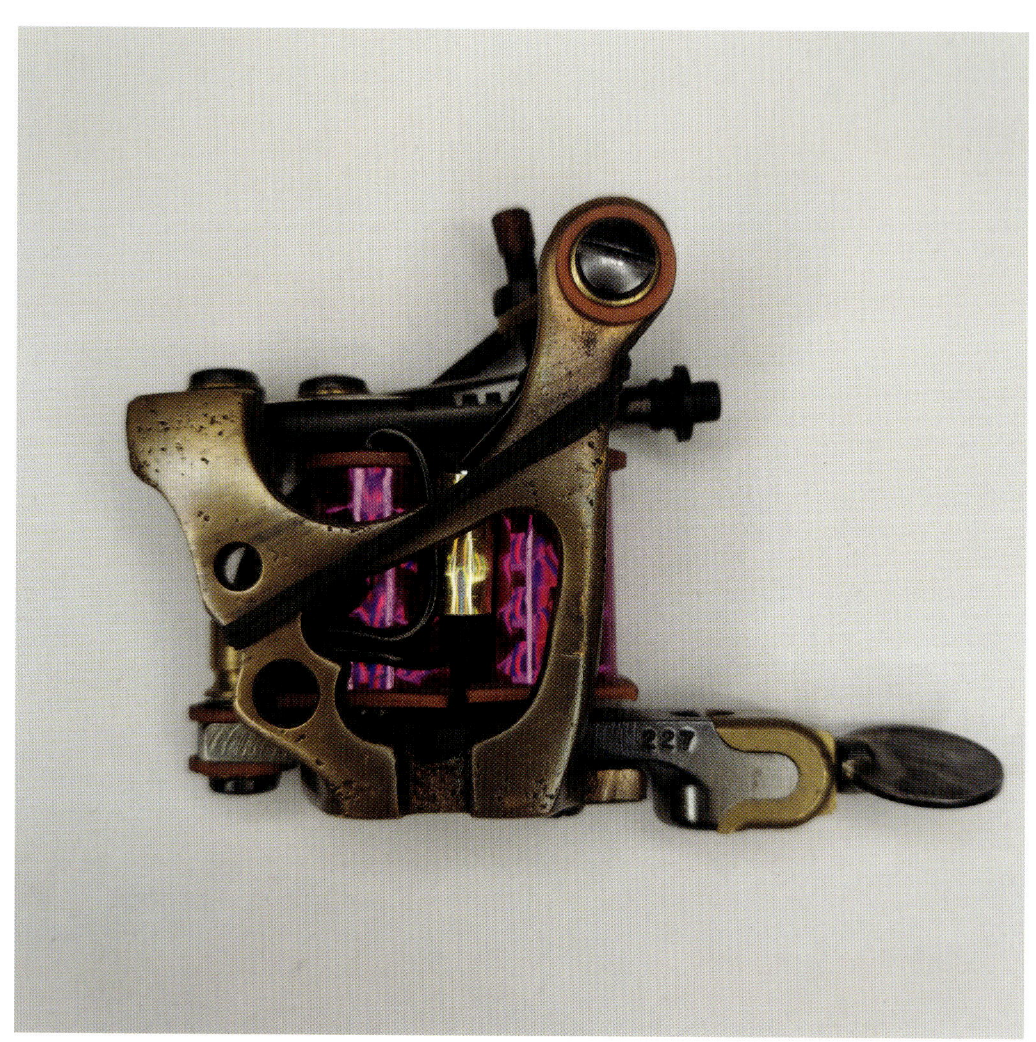

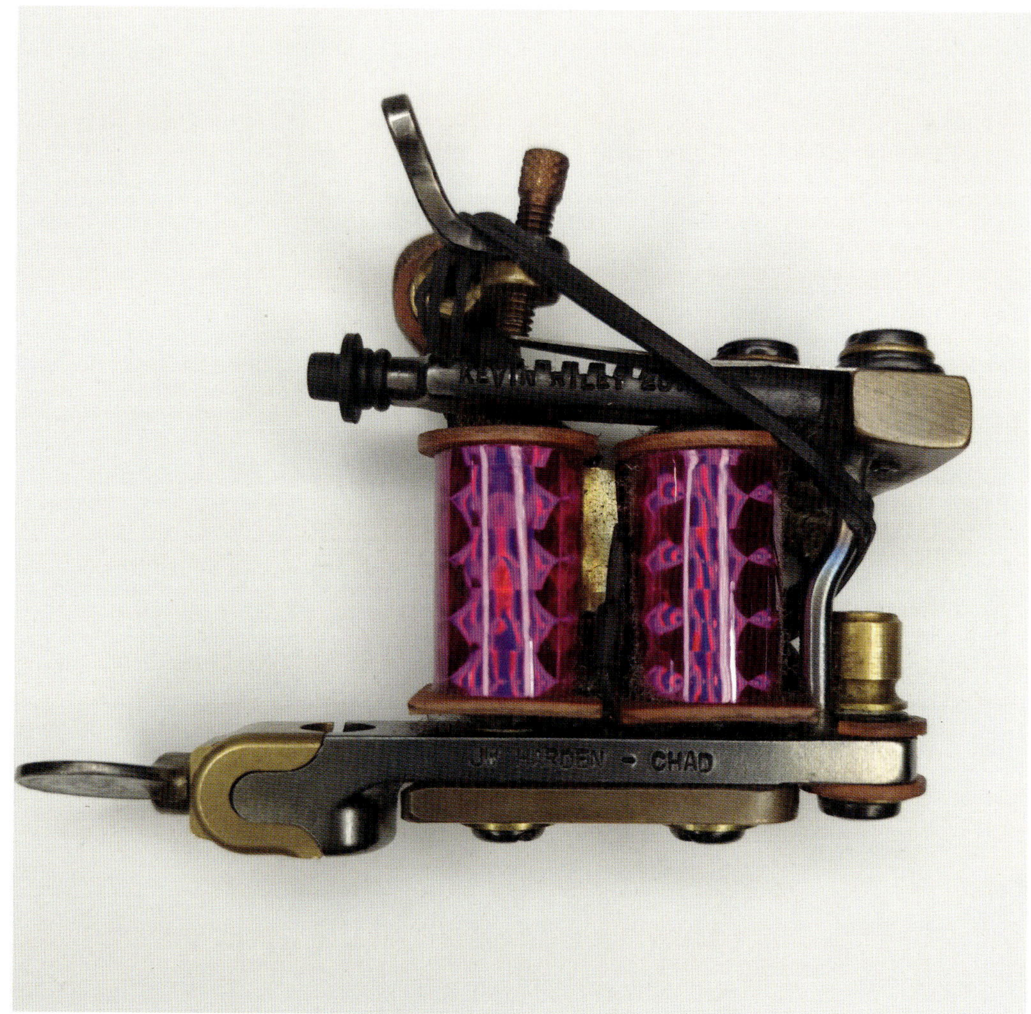

Kevin Riley rebuild of a Harden Sidewheeler machine

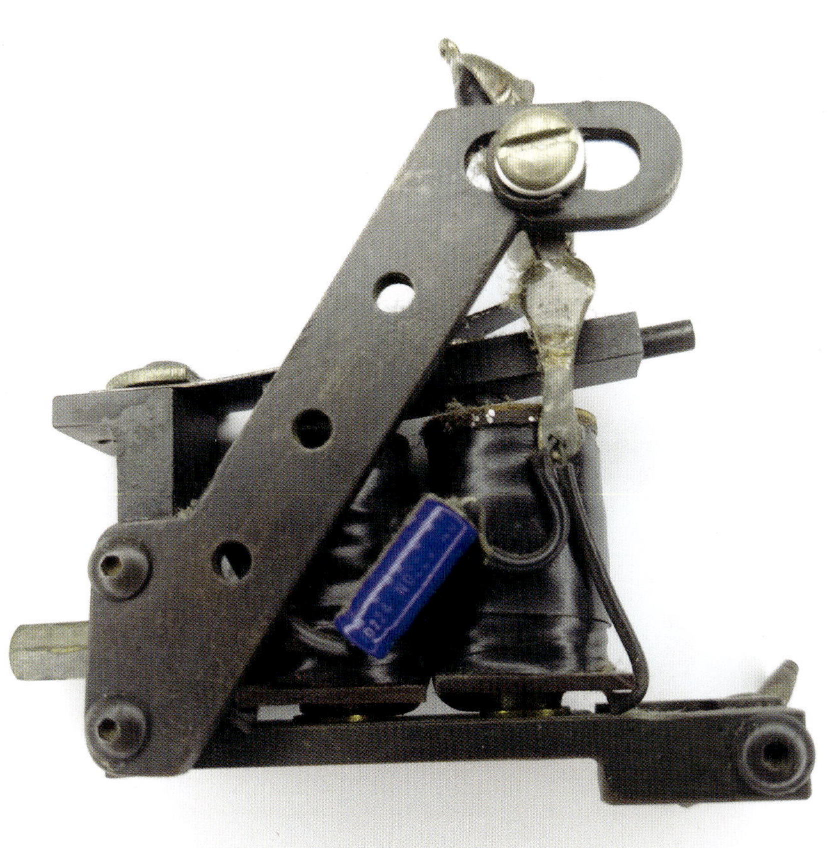

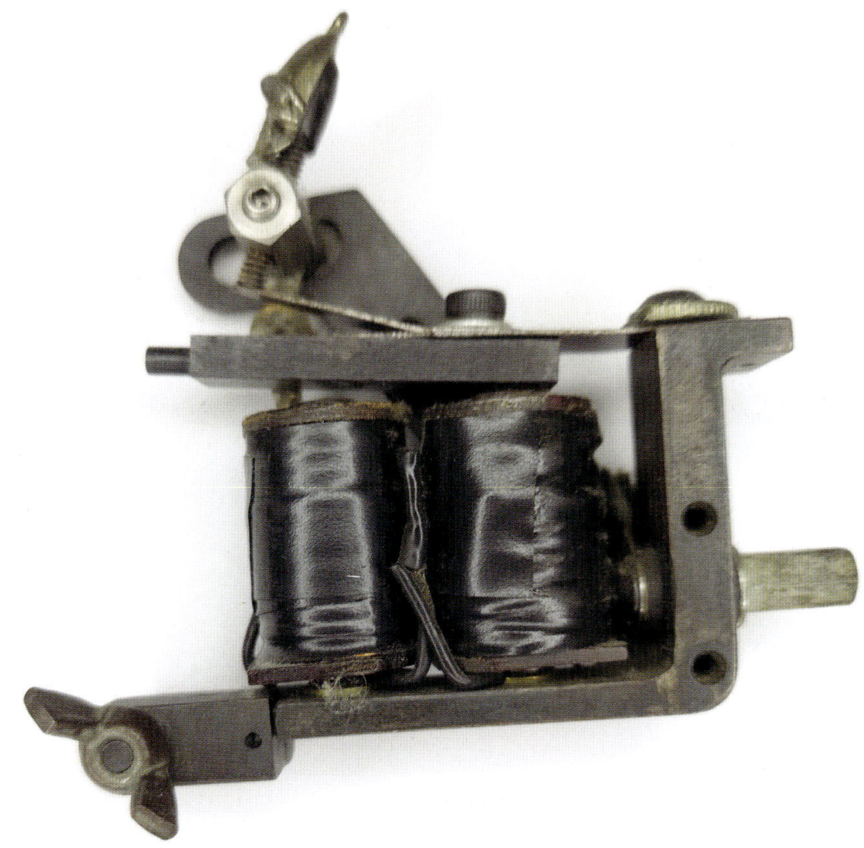

John Harden Elite special machine

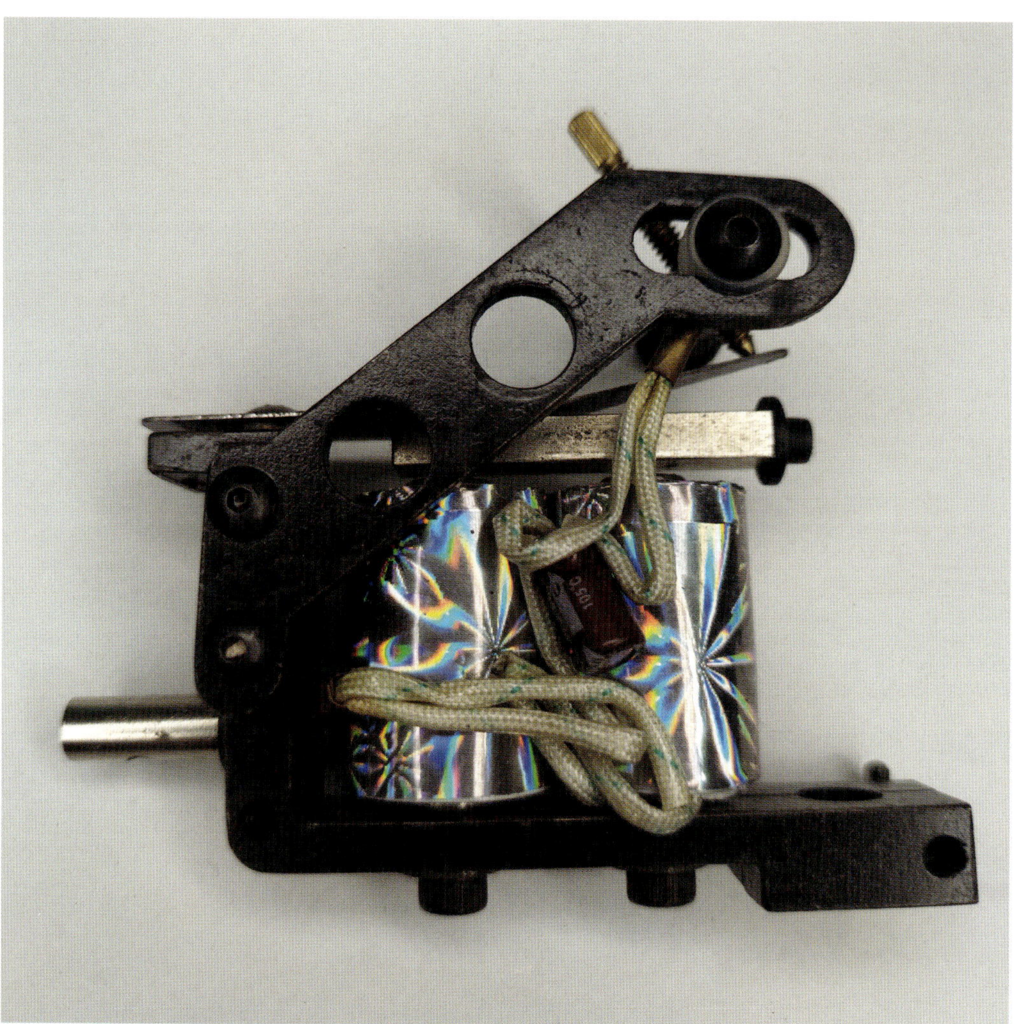

John Harden Elite machine

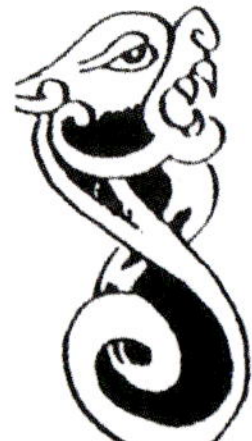

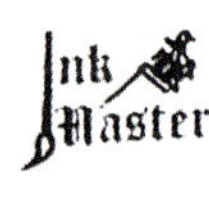

Ink Master TATTOO SUPPLY

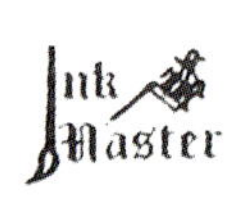

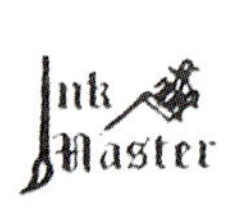

MACHINES & FRAMES

I.M.VIPER — QUICKFIX
MINI MIGHT — A QUICKCHANGE
ELITE — REPAIR ADAPTER
ELITE SPECIAL — FOR FRAMES
PERCY WATERS (REP.)
COLEMAN BOOMERANG
COASTAL SUPER
ALL COASTAL FRAMES ARE FROM THE (ORIGINAL) MOLDING PLATES OF THE (COASTAL TATTOO SUPPLY CO.) ESTABLISHED IN 1941.

~~~~~~~~~~~~~~~~~~~~~~~~~~~~

MISALLIANCE PARTS

COILS — NEEDLEBAR JIG
ARMATURES BARS — GROUPING JIGS
YOKES — TIGHTENING JIG
RACKS — MACHINE HOLDE
EYE LOUPES — TUBES:TIPS:GRIPS
FLASH BY *John Harden*

~~~~~~~~~~~~~~~~~~~~~~~~~~~~

POWER SUPPLYS

TRIP LITE PRECISION REGULATED 13.8 V D.C.
INK MASTER 0-24 V D.C. POWER~ PACK.

~~~~~~~~~~~~~~~~~~~~~~~~~~~~

(334) 598-4643
91 Old Town Square
Daleville, AL 36322

STERILIZERS

ALL AMERICAN (CANISTER CHAMBER) 11 1/8"D X 5 3/4"L TOP LOAD.

ULTRASONICS

MINI ULTRA~KLEEN S S TANK
SONIX 1V 1/2 QT. (MEDICAL GRADE)

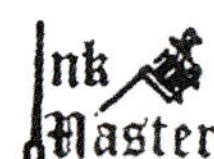

Ink Master tattoo supply catalog page, listing machines and specifying authenticity of the Coastal tattoo machine
~~~~~~~~~~~~~~~~~~~~~~~~~~~~

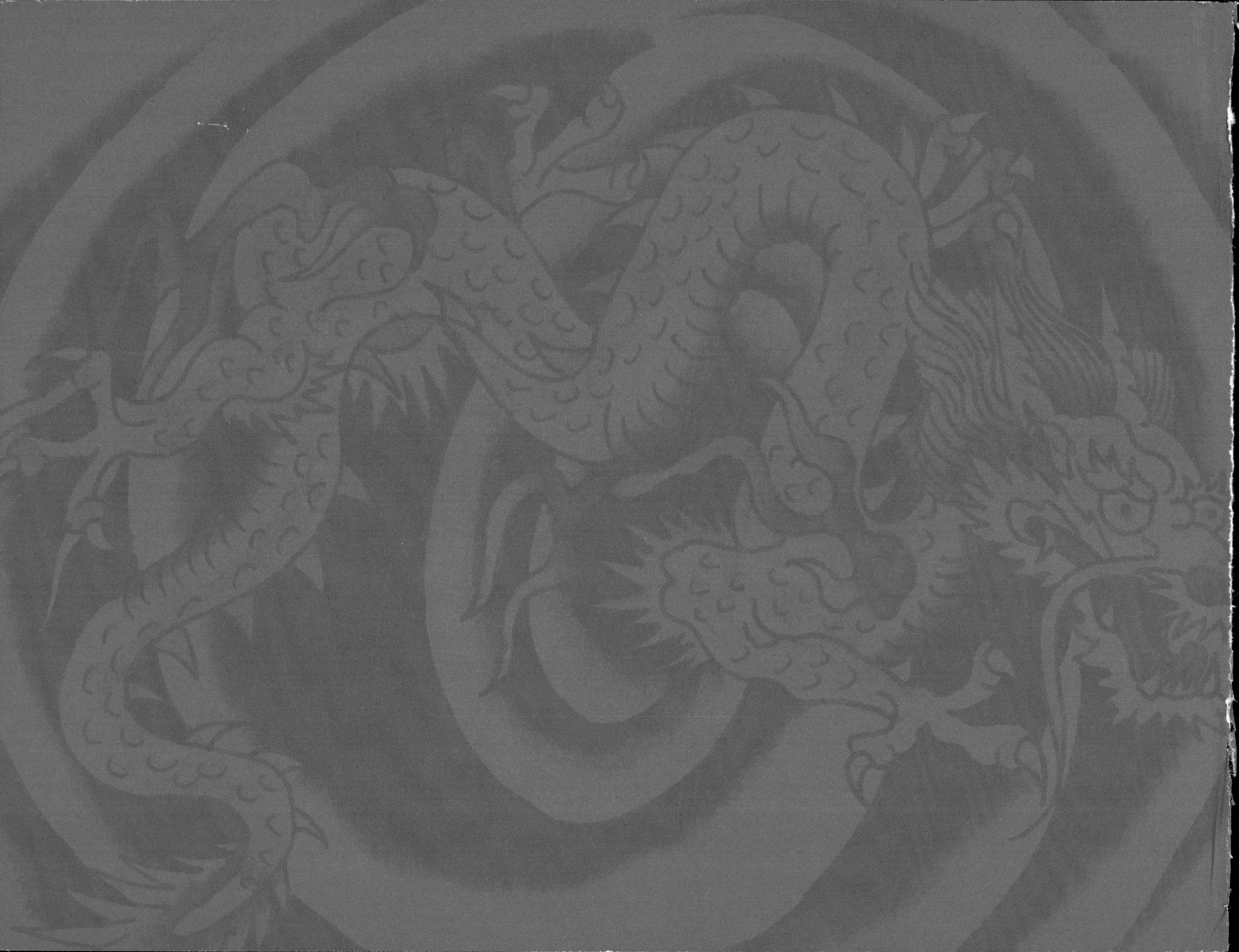